6/30/2022

Sexual Assault and Harassment in America

Recent Titles in Contemporary Debates

SEXUAL ASSAULT AND HARASSMENT IN AMERICA

Examining the Facts

Sarah Koon-Magnin

Contemporary Debates

An Imprint of ABC-CLIO, LLC

Santa Barbara, California • Denver, Colorado

Library of Congress Cataloging-in-Publication Data

Names: Koon-Magnin, Sarah, 1984– author.
Title: Sexual assault and harassment in America : examining the facts / Sarah Koon-Magnin.
Description: Santa Barbara, California : ABC-CLIO, [2022] | Includes bibliographical references and index.
Identifiers: LCCN 2021055621 (print) | LCCN 2021055622 (ebook) | ISBN 9781440876554 (cloth) | ISBN 9781440876561 (ebook)
Subjects: LCSH: Rape—United States. | Sexual harassment—United States.
Classification: LCC HV6561 .K655 2022 (print) | LCC HV6561 (ebook) | DDC 362.883—dc23/eng/20220113
LC record available at https://lccn.loc.gov/2021055621
LC ebook record available at https://lccn.loc.gov/2021055622

ISBN: 978-1-4408-7655-4 (print)
       978-1-4408-7656-1 (ebook)

26 25 24 23 22   1 2 3 4 5

This book is also available as an eBook.

ABC-CLIO
An Imprint of ABC-CLIO, LLC

ABC-CLIO, LLC
147 Castilian Drive
Santa Barbara, California 93117
www.abc-clio.com

This book is printed on acid-free paper ∞

Manufactured in the United States of America

Contents

How to Use This Book

Sexual Assault and Harassment in America: Examining the Facts is part of ABC-CLIO's Contemporary Debates reference series. Each title in this series, which is intended for use by high school and undergraduate students as well as members of the general public, examines the veracity of controversial claims or beliefs surrounding a major political/cultural issue in the United States. The purpose of this series is to give readers a clear and unbiased understanding of current issues by informing them about falsehoods, half-truths, and misconceptions—and confirming the factual validity of other assertions—that have gained traction in America's political and cultural discourse. Ultimately, this series has been crafted to give readers the tools for a fuller understanding of controversial issues, policies, and laws that occupy center stage in American life and politics.

Each volume in this series identifies 30 to 40 questions swirling about the larger topic under discussion. These questions are examined in individualized entries, which are in turn arranged in broad subject chapters that cover certain aspects of the issue being examined, for example, history of concern about the issue, potential economic or social impact, or findings of latest scholarly research.

Each chapter features 4 to 10 individual entries. Each entry begins by stating an important and/or well-known **Question** about the issue being studied—for example, "Are all people at equal risk of being sexually assaulted?" or "Are false reports of sexual assault a common problem in the United States?"

The entry then provides a concise and objective one- or two-paragraph **Answer** to the featured question, followed by a more comprehensive, detailed explanation of **The Facts**. This latter portion of each entry uses quantifiable, evidence-based information from respected sources to fully address each question and provide readers with the information they need to be informed citizens. Importantly, entries will also acknowledge instances in which conflicting data exists or data is incomplete. Finally, each entry concludes with a **Further Reading** section, providing users with information on other important and/or influential resources.

The ultimate purpose of every book in the Contemporary Debates series is to reject "false equivalence," in which demonstrably false beliefs or statements are given the same exposure and credence as the facts; to puncture myths that diminish our understanding of important policies and positions; to provide needed context for misleading statements and claims; and to confirm the factual accuracy of other assertions. In other words, volumes in this series are being crafted to clear the air surrounding some of the most contentious and misunderstood issues of our time—not just add another layer of obfuscation and uncertainty to the debate.

Introduction

Sexual assault is perhaps the most misunderstood violent crime in the United States. High profile cases like those involving celebrities or well-known institutions attract media attention and generate intense public discourse. However, these conversations are often based on unrepresentative cases, incorrect information, or faulty assumptions about sexual assault, its victims, and its perpetrators. Some of the most hotly contested areas focus on what constitutes sexual assault, beliefs about who is likely to be sexually assaulted (and implicitly, who is not), how sexual assault victims should react following the assault, and how both victims and offenders are treated by society and the criminal justice system. Each of these topics will be explored in the coming chapters, with suggestions for further reading on each subject.

This book will serve as an introduction to the major issues surrounding sexual assault in the United States and give readers a data-driven background from which to discuss these issues more knowledgeably and fully. The questions posed and answered throughout this book attempt to address some of the most common sources of confusion and controversy in discussing sexual assault. Assertions are supported with empirical citations so that readers may go to the original study or report and read the data for themselves if they so choose. By the end of this text, a reader should be familiar with the major sources of data for assessing sexual assault occurrences and impacts as well as the most influential scholars currently contributing to this literature. In short, controversial topics will be presented in a straightforward and data-driven manner.

Even a data-driven approach, when covering a topic as difficult and traumatic as sexual assault, can be emotionally challenging. Much of the content of this text is potentially triggering, particularly to survivors of sexual assault. Many communities throughout the United States have their own locally run rape crisis centers, child advocacy centers, or other services that may be helpful to individuals who find the material contained here upsetting or who want more resources on preventing and responding to sexual assault.

The website RAINN.org hosts an abundance of information relating to sexual assault, including resources about the immediate aftermath of the trauma, tips to help identify or prevent abuse, how to support a loved one who discloses a sexual assault, sexual assault laws in all 50 states, and much more. The Rape, Abuse & Incest National Network (RAINN) also houses the National Sexual Assault Telephone Hotline, which can be reached at 800-656-HOPE (800-656-4673). If an individual calls this hotline, they will be routed to a rape crisis center or other victim advocacy center in their own area where they can receive confidential information and support from someone who is trained to respond to sexual assault survivors and able to connect them to additional resources in the community (e.g., medical, legal, counseling). The text also includes three detailed profiles (in Q8, Q12, and Q31) that discuss specific resources that may be useful to criminal justice practitioners and the general public.

As a final note, I want to acknowledge the terminology used throughout the text. There is active debate regarding the terms "survivor" or "victim" to describe someone who has experienced a sexual assault. Because my background is in criminal justice, I tend to use the term "victim" more frequently than "survivor." Some people do not prefer the term "victim" because they view it as limiting toward the person who has been sexually assaulted. When I use this term, it is in no way intended to be judgmental or degrading of an individual who has experienced a sexual assault. I also sometimes use the term "survivor" in this book. Many people prefer the term "survivor" because they believe that it focuses on the individual's strength in making it through a traumatic and potentially life-threatening event. However, not all people who have experienced a sexual assault are in a stage of recovery that feels to them like a victory, which may be implied by the term "survivor," and thus do not identify with the term. My use of the term "survivor" is not intended to imply that an individual who has experienced a sexual assault should be at a specific stage of recovery. It is also worth noting that "victim" and "survivor" are not the only two terms—rape crisis advocates often call individuals who seek their services "clients" and sexual assault nurse examiners generally use the term "patients"—but within the literature on sexual assault, "victim" and "survivor" are the two most common descriptors. Finally, a few topics covered here relate to legislation and thus there are excerpts of statutes included to illustrate. It was common that laws were written using male pronouns intended to be read as gender-neutral and many of these laws have not been updated to reflect current language. Therefore, if an excerpt refers to "he," it does not necessarily imply a gender unless otherwise noted in the text.

In closing, this book is intended to be an introduction to the major points of confusion or debate or misunderstanding regarding sexual assault. The answers provided here summarize the major findings of the most up-to-date academic literature. However, each of these topics is complex, and the articles and reports suggested as "further reading" at the end of each featured question will give readers even more detail.

1

❖❖❖

Sexual Assault in the United States: What We Know and How We Know It

Before digging into problems surrounding sexual assault in the United States, it is critical that readers understand what is meant by the term "sexual assault," how it is measured, how it is legally defined, how frequently it occurs, and how the criminal justice system responds to it. The first question covered in this section (Q1: Is there a single definition of sexual assault?) will discuss the varying definitions of sexual assault that are present in laws across the nation and the different definitions used by researchers who study the phenomenon. This variation will inform the second question (Q2: Is there an agreed-upon measure of sexual assault in the United States?).

In addition to defining sexual assault in different ways, scholars also measure its occurrence using different sampling strategies. The major methods for studying sexual assault will be discussed in the second question. A key aspect of the crime of sexual assault is the fact that the victim did not consent to the sexual act(s). As discussed in the third question included in this section (Q3: Do all states define consent in the same way?), variations also exist in how state laws address the phenomenon of "consent."

The last two questions in this section provide an overview of what research demonstrates about the frequency and impact of sexual assault and responses to these events within the criminal justice system. As will be shown in the fourth question (Q4: Is sexual assault a big problem in the United States?), millions of lives in the United States have been impacted by sexual assault. And as will be discussed in the final question included in this section (Q5: Are all forms of sexual assault treated equally seriously by the criminal justice system?), certain sexual offenses are regarded as more serious than others. This includes the potential punishment associated with the crime under the law as well as the likelihood that the case will progress through the criminal justice system. Taken together, the information addressed in answering these questions will provide helpful background for future sections of the book that go into greater detail on the problem of sexual assault in the United States, outcomes for victims, outcomes for perpetrators, and the current state of prevention and response services.

Q1. IS THERE A SINGLE DEFINITION OF SEXUAL ASSAULT?

Answer: No. Researchers, the written law, and the general public may all use this term and may all be referring to different things. Although there is consensus around the idea that rape is a form of sexual assault, the term "sexual assault" can include a variety of acts and be used or interpreted differently by different people. Researchers who study sexual assault may employ different definitions across studies. In addition, not all states have laws that specifically refer to "sexual assault" but instead use other terminology to refer to these acts (e.g., sexual battery, criminal sexual contact). Regarding use of the term in the general population, data indicates that factors such as the amount of force used and the relationship between the victim and the perpetrator impact how likely an individual is to apply the label of rape or sexual assault to a situation.

The Facts: There are certain acts, such as rape, that are broadly agreed upon by researchers, criminal justice practitioners, and the general public to constitute "sexual assault." Penetrative acts are particularly likely to be categorized as rape when physical force is used and the victim physically fights back or says, "no" (Cleere & Lynn, 2013; Estrich, 1987; Newins, Wilson, & Kanefsky, 2021). Most any penetrative act (e.g., the insertion of a penis, finger, or object into a vagina or anus; genital contact with mouth) would be included in measurements of sexual assault by researchers, and all such acts are recognized as a serious criminal violation across all states. When people use the term "rape" and "sexual assault" interchangeably, they may be referring specifically to penetrative sexual assaults.

However, the term "sexual assault" is often perceived to be a broader term and may be used to reference some acts that are not penetrative.

For example, forcible fondling is an act that not all people may immediately recognize as a form of sexual assault but that many researchers and technical reports would include in estimates. For example, all institutions of higher education are required to produce annual reports revealing the number and frequency of a variety of crimes that took place on their campuses, including sexual assault. For compliance with the provisions of the Clery Act, a consumer protection law passed in 1990 to provide the public with more information about campus crime, colleges and universities are instructed that "'sexual assault' includes rape, fondling, incest, or statutory rape" (Department of Education, 2014). Some measures (e.g., the Centers for Disease Control's National Intimate Partner and Sexual Violence Survey) also include noncontact violations, such as indecent exposure or masturbating in front of the victim, as sexual assault (see Q2). However, not all researchers who study sexual assault include these acts when measuring the occurrence of sexual assault.

There is also some difference within the criminal justice system as to what precisely constitutes "sexual assault," because few jurisdictions use this specific terminology. Penal codes defining sexual offenses generally prohibit the same types of acts, but label these offenses a variety of different names. In South Carolina's criminal code, the term used is "sexual battery," which is defined as "sexual intercourse, cunnilingus, fellatio, anal intercourse, or any intrusion, however slight, of any part of a person's body or of any object into the genital or anal openings of another person's body . . ." (SC Stat § 16-3-651). A person who engages in sexual battery in violation of the state's criminal code is charged with "criminal sexual conduct." Regardless of the legal terminology, when members of the public in South Carolina discuss one of these crimes or when a news story reports on such an offense, the residents or journalists may frequently use the term "sexual assault" or "rape" rather than either "sexual battery" or "criminal sexual conduct," because these are more common terms.

The state of New Mexico's criminal code defines a crime that is essentially the same as South Carolina's "criminal sexual conduct," but uses alternative terminology, calling the act "criminal sexual penetration" (NM Stat § 30-9-11). Another sexual crime in New Mexico is "criminal sexual contact," which refers to "the unlawful and intentional touching of or application of force, without consent, to the unclothed intimate parts of another who has reached his eighteenth birthday, or intentionally causing another who has reached his eighteenth birthday to touch one's intimate parts" (NM Stat § 30-9-12). This definition describes what other jurisdictions may call forcible fondling, and what some researchers would include in their measures of sexual assault but other researchers would not.

South Carolina's criminal sexual conduct (SC Stat § 16-3-651) and New Mexico's criminal sexual penetration (NM Stat § 30-9-11) are just two examples of state penal codes in which the crimes defined are not specifically labeled "sexual assault," but the acts that are covered by these statutes would certainly be included in any measure of sexual assault and most people would refer to these acts as a form of "sexual assault."

Legal definitions have changed substantially over time and continue to change to reflect cultural changes in the understanding of sexual assault. Major changes have included creating laws that are gender-neutral (i.e., recognizing both males and females as potential perpetrators and victims of sexual assault), removing requirements that the victim prove they provided physical resistance to the assault, introducing rape shield laws to protect victim confidentiality, and expanding the number of sexual acts committed without the victim's consent that are classified—and can be prosecuted—as crimes (i.e., not just penile-vaginal penetration). These changes and other ongoing debates regarding sexual assault legislation further demonstrate the lack of consensus on precisely what the term "sexual assault" means.

Perhaps the best-known national organization providing resources for sexual assault survivors (including a National Sexual Assault Hotline, a 24-hour emergency number) is the Rape, Abuse & Incest National Network (RAINN). RAINN's website indicates the wide variety of acts that may be included in a definition of sexual assault:

> The term sexual assault refers to sexual contact or behavior that occurs without explicit consent of the victim. Some forms of sexual assault include: attempted rape; fondling or unwanted sexual touching; forcing a victim to perform sexual acts, such as oral sex or penetrating the perpetrator's body; penetration of the victim's body, also known as rape.

The organization further clarifies that, "Rape is a form of sexual assault, but not all sexual assault is rape" (RAINN, 2020).

For academic purposes, the broadest definitions of sexual assault are those that include any form of unwanted sexual interaction, whether penetrative or nonpenetrative, contact or noncontact, regardless of whether force or coercion was used, and regardless of whether the victim was able to consent (see Q3). However, criminal statutes are far narrower; they typically do not recognize unwanted sexual acts obtained through the use of psychological coercion or manipulation (e.g., attempting to persuade the victim with arguments such as, "If you really love me you will want to do this . . ."). Furthermore, a variety of other factors come into play when people are asked whether they would label hypothetical acts as "sexual assault."

In a study in which participants were given a scenario describing a sexual assault and then asked what label they would apply, participants were most likely to select the label, "rape" if they held attitudes that were more supportive of the victim, less supportive of the perpetrator, and did not accept inaccurate beliefs—broadly known as "rape myths"—about rape and sexual assault (see Q20; Sasson & Paul, 2014). A similar study that used a hypothetical scenario and then asked respondents whether the described act constituted a sexual assault found that participants were more likely to apply such a label if the perpetrator was an athlete compared to other occupations depicted (e.g., reporter, college student; Henry et al., 2019). Both of these studies found that participants were more likely to label the sexual assault as such if they did not believe in rape myths (Q20).

Some published work has focused specifically on whether victims of sexual assaults identify themselves in this way by answering "yes" when asked, "Have you ever been raped/sexually assaulted?" Many people who answer "no" to this question, however, do in fact report experiences that meet the legal standard of rape. These individuals are known as "unacknowledged rape victims" (Koss, 2011). One study of unacknowledged victims revealed that women were more likely to label their experiences as "rape" if the assailant was a not a loved one, physical force was used, the victim was asleep when the attack began, she was a child at the time of the assault, or the assault involved vaginal penetration (Kahn et al., 2003). Participants in this study were less likely to label their experiences as "rape" if they were intoxicated at the time of the assault.

Moreover, the term "sexual assault" can refer to different acts and can be interpreted differently by different people. Nearly any penetrative sexual encounter obtained without the victim's consent (regardless of whether physical force was used) would be classified as a sexual assault by academic researchers, criminal statutes (though perhaps under a different name), and the general public. In short, acts of "rape" are largely considered "sexual assaults." However, there are acts other than rape that some researchers also include in measures of sexual assault, even if others do not (see Q2).

FURTHER READING

Cleere, Colleen, and Steven J. Lynn. "Acknowledged versus unacknowledged sexual assault among college women." *Journal of Interpersonal Violence* 28, no. 12 (2013): 2593–2611.

Department of Education; Violence Against Women Act. 79 Fed. Reg. 62,752 (October 20, 2014).

Estrich, Susan. *Real Rape.* Harvard University Press, 1987.

Henry, Dayna S., Laura K. Merrell, Sarah R. Blackstone, Erika Collazo-Vargas, Christina Mohl, Michael Tolerico, Lauren Singley, and Sarah Moody. "Does perpetrator occupation affect classification of sexual assault?" *Journal of Interpersonal Violence* (2019). https://doi.org/10.1177%2F0886260519873331

Jeanne Clery Disclosure of Campus Security Policy and Campus Crime Statistics Act of 1990, 20 U.S.C. §1092(f) (2018).

Kahn, Arnold S., Jennifer Jackson, Christine Kully, Kelly Badger, and Jessica Halvorsen. "Calling it rape: Differences in experiences of women who do or do not label their sexual assault as rape." *Psychology of Women Quarterly* 27, no. 3 (2003): 233–242.

Koss, Mary P. "Hidden, unacknowledged, acquaintance, and date rape: Looking back, looking forward." *Psychology of Women Quarterly* 35, no. 2 (2011): 348–354.

Newins, Amie R., Laura C. Wilson, and Rebekah Z. Kanefsky. "What's in a label? The impact of media and sexual assault characteristics on survivor rape acknowledgment." *Journal of Traumatic Stress* 34, no. 2 (2021): 405–415.

RAINN. "Sexual assault." Rape, Abuse & Incest National Network, 2020. https://www.rainn.org/articles/sexual-assault

Sasson, Sapir, and Lisa A. Paul. "Labeling acts of sexual violence: What roles do assault characteristics, attitudes, and life experiences play?" *Behavior and Social Issues* 23, no. 1 (2014): 35–49.

Q2. IS THERE A SINGLE AGREED-UPON MEASURE OF SEXUAL ASSAULT IN THE UNITED STATES?

Answer: No. There is substantial variation in the way that sexual assault is measured across the major national sources of data on this topic, as well as in smaller samples (such as surveys of college students). Estimates of sexual assault occurrence are regularly provided by the Bureau of Justice Statistics (BJS), the Centers for Disease Control (CDC), and smaller-scale survey samples. The primary differences in how researchers define and measure "sexual assault" relate to which acts are included and how a lack of consent was established (e.g., through use of physical force, victim incapacitation). The most consensus seems to be in support of using the Sexual Experiences Survey (SES), an instrument designed and validated by psychologist and professor Mary Koss and colleagues and used by many researchers. At present, the SES is not employed in any of the regular national data collection efforts aimed at measuring sexual assault.

The Facts: Researchers in a range of academic disciplines, including criminal justice, public health, and psychology, are interested in understanding the occurrence of sexual assault in the United States and its consequences for victims. A fundamental area of concern is how many sexual assaults take place each year (what researchers call "incidence") and how many people are sexually assaulted (what researchers call "prevalence"). Incidence is typically higher than prevalence because if an individual is assaulted more than once, both assaults would count toward the total incidence of sexual assault (number of assaults), but the prevalence (number of victims) would not increase. There are two national crime data collection efforts published annually: the Uniform Crime Reports (UCR, overseen by the FBI) and the National Crime Victimization Survey (NCVS, overseen by the BJS). However, there are significant differences in the way that these two data sources are structured, the way that they define rape/sexual assault, and their resulting estimates of sexual assault frequency.

The UCR is compiled annually by the FBI based on reports from police jurisdictions throughout the United States. Any assaults that were not reported to law enforcement will not be recorded in the reports sent to the FBI and thus will not be reflected in the UCR data. Given the fact that most sexual assaults are not reported to law enforcement (Q11), the UCR is not a valid measure of sexual assault within the United States because it "is assembled in ways that make it vulnerable to major undercounting" (National Research Council, 2014). However, it is worth noting that the UCR has undergone a significant change in methodology by changing the way that "rape" is defined for data collection purposes. Historically, the UCR defined rape as "carnal knowledge of a female forcibly and against her will" (DOJ Archives, 2012), a very limited definition in that it included only penile-vaginal penetration, required physical force, and recognized only female victims of an assault by male perpetrators.

In 2012, the Department of Justice announced that the UCR would adopt a broader definition of rape to include, "penetration, no matter how slight, of the vagina or anus with any body part or object, or oral penetration by a sex organ of another person, without the consent of the victim" (DOJ Archives, 2012). This definition recognizes various forms of sexual assault beyond penile-vaginal penetration, committed both by male and female perpetrators, and against both male and female victims of sexual assault. However, even with this more expansive definition, the UCR consistently underestimates the incidence and prevalence of sexual assault in the United States because it includes only those assaults that are reported to law enforcement.

The UCR is being phased out and will be replaced by the National Incident-Based Reporting System (NIBRS). Although NIBRS will compile records of a larger variety of sexual crimes (i.e., statutory rape, forcible fondling), it is still limited by including only cases that are reported to law enforcement; it thus remains an incomplete measure of the frequency of sexual assault.

The NCVS overcomes this significant limitation by collecting data using a confidential study design that includes all incidents of criminal victimization regardless of whether they were reported to law enforcement. Survey respondents are asked whether they have "been forced or coerced to engage in unwanted sexual activity" as a screening question. If they answer affirmatively, the interviewer then asks a series of follow up questions to determine both the nature of the sexual activity and the type of force or coercion involved in the incident.

The NCVS differentiates between rape and sexual assault such that rape is defined as "Coerced or forced sexual intercourse. Forced sexual intercourse means vaginal, anal, or oral penetration by the offender(s). This category could include incidents where the penetration was from a foreign object such as a bottle." The NCVS definition recognizes both males and females as potential perpetrators or victims. In addition to this inclusive definition of rape, the NCVS also measures the occurrence of sexual assault, which they define as "a wide range of victimizations, separate from rape, attempted rape, or threatened rape. These crimes include attacks or threatened attacks involving unwanted sexual contact between the victim and offender. Sexual assaults may or may not involve force and include such things as grabbing or fondling."

The findings from this nationally representative annual survey of more than 40,000 households in the United States are used to generate national estimates of the occurrence of completed and attempted rape and sexual assault. However, the Panel on Measuring Rape and Sexual Assault in Bureau of Justice Statistics Household Surveys concluded that it was "highly likely that the NCVS is underestimating rape and sexual assault" (National Research Council, 2014). According to its findings, the BJS would be well served to create a new longitudinal survey instrument aimed specifically at measuring sexual assault (not a whole variety of crimes, as is the case with both the UCR and NCVS). Outside of the BJS, researchers may also refer to estimates provided by The National Intimate Partner Sexual Violence Survey (NISVS), which is conducted by the CDC.

The NISVS includes measures of the sexual acts covered by both the UCR and NCVS but with additional detail. The NISVS definition of rape includes the penetrative acts recognized by NCVS, but it also explicitly "includes times when the victim was drunk, high, drugged, or passed out and unable to consent"—circumstances that are not directly asked about in the NCVS. In addition to "rape," the NISVS also measures the occurrence of "being made to penetrate someone else," as well as unwanted or coercive sexual activity. Unwanted sexual contact in the NISVS refers to "unwanted sexual experiences involving touch but not sexual penetration, such as being kissed in a sexual way, or having sexual body parts fondled, groped, or grabbed," a definition largely consistent with the NCVS definition of sexual assault. Coercive sexual activity in the NISVS refers to, "unwanted vaginal, oral, or anal sex after being pressured in ways that included being worn down by someone who repeatedly asked for sex or showed they were unhappy; feeling pressured by being lied to, being told promises that were untrue, having someone threaten to end a relationship or spread rumors; and sexual pressure due to someone using their influence or authority" (Smith et al., 2018). The forms of psychological coercion measured here are generally not included in criminal justice measures of sexual assault occurrence because they do not meet most legal standards of sexual assault.

In summary, with regard to national data collection efforts, the UCR is a highly problematic measure of sexual assault because its collection strategy only includes assaults reported to law enforcement. Although NIBRS will improve on some aspects of the UCR, it is still limited to cases reported to law enforcement, which will once again produce a dramatic undercount of sexual assault frequency.

Both the NCVS and NISVS are informative and help to provide researchers and the general public with an understanding of sexual assault occurrence in the United States. However, a major national data collection effort is not feasible for every study and some research questions cannot be answered with these data sources. If a researcher wants to evaluate the empirical relationship between sexual assault victimization and some other factor not measured in the NCVS or NISVS (e.g., educational outcomes, specific physical and mental health diagnoses), they will need an accurate and methodologically defensible way to measure sexual assault victimization for the purposes of their study. Data have shown that simply asking a respondent, "Have you ever been raped/sexually assaulted?" will not yield accurate results, because many respondents do not recognize their experiences as sexual assault even when their experience meets a legal standard of this offense (Fisher & Cullen, 2000; Koss, 2011). To address these shortcomings of existing data sets, researchers have used various methods to more accurately measure sexual assault victimization (see Table 2.1). The SES is widely regarded as the most informative and frequently used of these instruments.

Table 2.1. A comparison of major data sources measuring sexual assault in the United States

	UCR—Legacy*	UCR—Revised*	NCVS	NISVS	SES
This data source includes sexual assaults that were:					
Reported to law enforcement	X	X	X	X	X
Not reported to law enforcement			X	X	X
This data source includes:					
Penile-vaginal penetration only	X				
Oral, anal, or vaginal penetration		X	X	X	X
Nonpenetrative sexual acts		X	X	X	X
This data source indicates whether sexual contact is:					
Forcible	X	X	X	X	X
Coercive				X	X
Unwanted				X	X
This data source indicates whether assaults involved:					
Physical force, violence	X	X	X	X	X
Threat of physical force, violence			X	X	X
Victim's inability to consent				X	X
Psychological coercion				X	X

* *Note:* The UCR is not a valid measure of sexual assault because it only includes assaults that were reported to law enforcement

The SES allows researchers to assess various forms of unwanted sexual contact including penetrative and nonpenetrative acts; offenses committed against male and female victims; offenses committed by male and female perpetrators; offenses committed when the victim was a child or an adult; and offenses carried out using various methods (e.g., physical force, threats, intoxication, psychological coercion). This level of nuance is important because it may help researchers and practitioners develop more effective prevention strategies, provide better context for first responders assisting victims, and predict different types and severity of mental health outcomes.

The SES is a simple survey in which respondents are asked whether anyone has committed a certain type of offense against them (i.e., "Someone fondled, kissed, or rubbed up against the private areas of my body [lips, breast/chest, crotch or butt] or removed some of my clothes without my consent . . .") and in what way (e.g., "by . . . Taking advantage of me when I was too drunk or out of it to stop what was happening," or "by . . . Using force, for example holding me down with their body weight, pinning my arms, or having a weapon"). There is room for respondents to report multiple victimization experiences, whether multiple types of offenses were committed (e.g., both vaginal and anal penetration), or if various types of force or coercion were used.

To summarize, multiple efforts exist to measure the incidence and prevalence of sexual assault in the United States. Although none provides a perfectly accurate count, comparing trends across multiple measures (what researchers call "triangulation") provides a clearer sense of the overall frequency of sexual assault. The more similar the trends across multiple forms of measurement (e.g., increases or decreases over time), the more confident researchers are in the accuracy of those trends.

FURTHER READING

Fisher, Bonnie S., and Francis T. Cullen. "Measuring the sexual victimization of women: Evolution, current controversies, and future research." *Criminal Justice* 4 (2000): 317–390.

Koss, Mary P. "Hidden, unacknowledged, acquaintance, and date rape: Looking back, looking forward." *Psychology of Women Quarterly* 35, no. 2 (2011): 348–354.

Morgan, Rachel E., and Barbara A. Oudekerk. *Criminal Victimization, 2018*. Washington, DC: Bureau of Justice Statistics (2019).

National Research Council. *Estimating the Incidence of Rape and Sexual Assault. Panel on Measuring Rape and Sexual Assault in Bureau of Justice Statistics Household Surveys*, edited by C. Kruttschnitt, W. D. Kalsbeek, and C. C. House. Committee on National Statistics, Division of Behavioral and Social Sciences and Education. The National Academies Press, 2014.

Smith, Sharon G., Xinjian Zhang, Kathleen C. Basile, Melissa T. Merrick, Jing Wang, Marcie-jo Kresnow, and Jieru Chen. "The national intimate partner and sexual violence survey: 2015 data brief–updated release." Atlanta, GA: National Center for Injury Prevention and Control, Centers for Disease Control and Prevention (2018).

U.S. Department of Justice (DOJ) Archives. "An updated definition of rape" (January 6, 2012). https://www.justice.gov/archives/opa/blog/updated -definition-rape

Q3. DO ALL STATES DEFINE CONSENT
IN THE SAME WAY?

Answer: No. In fact, most states do not provide a definition of consent. The more common approach is to define what does *not* constitute consent. Such statutes frequently refer to factors such as: physical force, verbal resistance, and inability to consent (e.g., due to being unconscious). Two states have recently passed legislation requiring public colleges and universities within their jurisdiction to have an affirmative consent standard. Each of these approaches is complex and is discussed more completely below.

The Facts: Despite its importance for establishing that a crime of sexual assault occurred, only nine states (California, Colorado, Florida, Illinois, Minnesota, Montana, Vermont, Washington, and Wisconsin) explicitly define consent (Wood, Rikkonen, & Davis, 2019). The legal definitions in Minnesota, Montana, and Wisconsin are nearly identical and call for participants to employ "words or overt actions" (in Minnesota, Montana, and Wisconsin) "indicating a freely given agreement to have sexual intercourse or sexual contact" (in Montana and Wisconsin).

Vermont provides a similar definition for consent: "words or actions by a person indicating a voluntary agreement to engage in a sexual act." While it covers the same concepts, the language in Washington's definition is slightly different: "at the time of the act of sexual intercourse or sexual contact there are actual words or conduct indicating freely given agreement to have sexual intercourse or sexual contact." The participant's knowledge is a key element in the definition of consent in California ("have knowledge of the nature of the act"), Colorado ("with knowledge of the nature of the act"), and Florida ("intelligent, knowing, and voluntary"). Across the nine states that provide definitions of consent, laws emphasize that the potential sexual partner needs to understand the sexual act and clearly express their desire to participate through words or actions.

However, rather than providing a definition of consent, the more common approach among the states has been to define what does *not* constitute consent (DeMatteo, Galloway, Arnold, & Patel, 2015). Alabama, for example, states that, "Lack of consent results from: (1) Forcible compulsion; or (2) Incapacity to consent." More specifically, "A person is deemed incapable of consent if he is: (1) Less than 16 years old; or (2) Mentally defective; or (3) Mentally incapacitated; or (4) Physically helpless" (Section 13A-6-70). The factors listed here are common considerations among those states that do not define consent. If force is used to compel the victim's participation in the sexual act (e.g., holding the victim down, physically restraining the victim, threatening the victim with a weapon), it indicates that the victim was not willing to participate and therefore it can be inferred that they did not consent to the sexual act. With regard to being deemed incapable of consent, a legal analysis of statutes concluded that:

> States define incapacity to consent based on roughly four categories of legal impairments: age, consanguinity, physical incapacity, and mental incapacity . . . often divided between temporary incapacitation because of intoxication (not unconsciousness) or the presence of a long-term or permanent mental disability. (Harris, 2018, pp. 513–514)

All states have an age of consent below which, regardless of desired participation, the individual may not legally agree to a sexual encounter. Young children (typically below the age of 13) cannot legally consent to sexual activities under any circumstances. Teenagers may be able to consent to sex with a similarly-aged partner, although the laws differ from state to state (Koon-Magnin, 2014). When below the age of consent (which ranges from 16 to 18 across states) most states provide a protected age-span. This means that in order to be prosecuted for statutory rape, many states require that the perpetrator be at least 3 to 4 years older than the adolescent victim (Koon-Magnin, 2014). In addition, numerous other reasons exist besides age that may make a person unable to provide consent: some mental, others physical, some temporary, others permanent.

Returning to the example of Alabama, the state code defines someone as mentally defective if they are "incapable of appraising the nature of his conduct," mentally incapacitated if they are "rendered temporarily incapable of appraising or controlling his conduct owing to the influence of a narcotic or intoxicating substance administered to him without his consent, or to any other incapacitating act committed upon him without his consent," and physically helpless if the victims is "unconscious or for any other reason is physically unable to communicate unwillingness to an act" (§ 13A-6-60). These three forms of incapacity to consent, as defined by the state of Alabama, include examples that are mental (mentally defective, mentally incapacitated), physical (physically helpless), temporary (mentally incapacitated), and permanent (mentally defective, physically helpless), but it does not mention all forms of incapacitation (Harris, 2018).

Arizona's definition of "Without consent" is more inclusive and recognizes all of the following circumstances:

(a) The victim is coerced by the immediate use or threatened use of force against a person or property. (b) The victim is incapable of consent by reason of mental disorder, mental defect, drugs, alcohol, sleep or any other similar impairment of cognition and such condition is known or should have reasonably been known to the defendant. For the purposes of this subdivision, "mental defect" means the victim is unable to comprehend the distinctively sexual nature of the conduct or is incapable of understanding or exercising the right to refuse to engage in the conduct with another. (c) The victim is intentionally deceived as to the nature of the act. (d) The victim is intentionally deceived to erroneously believe that the person is the victim's spouse. (13-1401)

In both Alabama and Arizona, a person who is unconscious, asleep, or in a coma is unable to provide consent to sexual activity. However, Arizona goes further than Alabama by prohibiting sexual acts in which the victim was intoxicated by drugs or alcohol even if they ingested these items willingly or in cases in which the perpetrator "intentionally deceived" the victim.

Intoxication is a complicated issue in consent legislation and is not addressed in many states' statutes. A 2015 analysis of sexual assault and consent statutes across the 50 states found that "only nine states includ(e) intoxication in the definition of temporary incapacity and only six states include voluntary intoxication within the definition of temporary incapacity" (DeMatteo et al., 2015, p. 235). This is highly problematic, the authors argue, in that it makes it very difficult for a prosecutor to prove a sexual assault took place if the victim was intoxicated. While there seems to be some broad societal consensus that impairment due to intoxication reduces a person's ability to make free, voluntary, and informed decisions (e.g., a drunk person cannot agree to a medical treatment, sign an informed consent to participate in research, or sign a binding lease for a new vehicle), many state statutes are "unclear as to whether intoxication itself negates consent, or whether intoxication negates consent only when that intoxication prevents an individual from resisting an attack" (Wood et al., 2019, p. 24). Moreover, the current legal definitions of consent (or lack of consent) do not adequately address the impact of intoxication, particularly when a person knowingly ingests drugs or alcohol, on a person's ability to consent.

Legal scholarship on how consent is defined suggests that "there is no coherent or consistent definition of consent, despite the fact that consent is the demarcation between rape and sex and remains a central concern of rape law and policies as well as scholarly inquiry into the problem of rape" (Pugh & Becker, 2018). A literature review and analysis of sexual coercion in obtaining consent points to many areas in which there is ambiguity or disagreement (Pugh & Becker, 2018). For example, if a person declines a sexual advance but then acquiesces after a partner pressures them to do so (perhaps with repeated nagging or strong statements expressing their own desire), has the person truly consented to the sexual act? The authors argue that because the initial response was "no" and agreement was only obtained following verbal sexual coercion, consent was not voluntarily given. However, most laws and policies do not recognize verbal sexual coercion as a form of "force" and would likely not consider the act just described as an assault.

Unlike state statutes that primarily focus on providing examples of what *does not* constitute consent, most institutions of higher education provide definitions of what *does* constitute consent. In a study of sexual assault policies at colleges and universities throughout the United States, large schools (compared to smaller schools), public schools (compared to private schools), and institutions where the student body was more than one-third female were particularly likely to include definitions of consent that went beyond the basic definition and provide additional context or information. However, a content analysis of these policies "showed that sexual consent definitions varied greatly across schools" (Graham et al., 2017, p. 249). A total of 30 concepts were recognized and recorded across the policies being studied and, in line with state-level legislation, the most common code recorded in these policies was incapacity to consent.

The broader theme of inability to consent mirrored state statutes in that most policies established by institutions of higher learning specifically mentioned mental incapacitation, physical incapacitation, intoxication, and being below the age of consent. Another common theme in this analysis of college and university policies was a discussion of how a partner may demonstrate consent—a clear desire and willingness to engage in the sexual act. This theme is in line with the minority of states that include a definition of consent (rather than lack of consent), but goes farther by describing what active participation from both parties may look like and describing the idea of affirmative consent.

Affirmative consent rejects the view that a lack of protest may indicate a person's willingness to engage in a sexual encounter. Instead, it requires that the participants freely and actively agree to each phase of a sexual encounter. These policies are relatively new but are in place in approximately one in five colleges and universities across the country and thus impact a substantial number of college students (Graham et al., 2017). Both California and New York have passed legislation requiring that institutions of higher education within their jurisdictions use an affirmative consent standard in their sexual assault policies. The impact of these policies will become clearer over time, but scholars have expressed concern about the potential pitfalls of an affirmative consent approach. They raise practical questions about what an ongoing consent process would look like during a sexual encounter and how its existence or violation could possibly be proven (see DeMatteo et al., 2015).

A final consideration when legally defining consent relates to relationships in which one individual is in a position of power or control over the other. If the power dynamic within a relationship is fundamentally imbalanced, many states do not recognize the consent of the person in the subordinate position. For example, correctional officers are in a position of authority over inmates. Therefore, even if both an officer and the inmate are adults willing to engage in a sexual act together, the inmate's "consent" would not be recognized. The potential for coercion or abuse of power is too high in such a situation to truly assess whether the agreement was free and voluntary; thus, the law generally prohibits such relationships. Other examples of inherently imbalanced relationships that are illegal in many states include those between teachers and students, foster parents and foster children, and doctors and patients.

To summarize, significant variation exists across states in terms of whether they provide a definition of consent, a definition of lack of consent, and what those definitions may entail. Common themes are age, incapacity (either temporary or permanent, physical or mental), and potential power imbalances. There is some variation in sexual assault policies across colleges and universities, but these policies seem to be more focused on what consent *is* rather than what it is not, while state statutes more often define lack of consent than consent. Areas in need of further scholarship and clarification include intoxication and affirmative consent.

FURTHER READING

DeMatteo, David, Meghann Galloway, Shelby Arnold, and Unnati Patel. "Sexual assault on college campuses: A 50-state survey of criminal sexual assault statutes and their relevance to campus sexual assault." *Psychology, Public Policy, and Law* 21, no. 3 (2015): 227.
Graham, Laurie M., Sarah Treves-Kagan, Erin P. Magee, Stephanie M. DeLong, Olivia S. Ashley, Rebecca J. Macy, Sandra L. Martin, Kathryn E. Moracco, and J. Michael Bowling. "Sexual assault policies and

consent definitions: A nationally representative investigation of US colleges and universities." *Journal of School Violence* 16, no. 3 (2017): 243–258.

Harris, Jasmine E. "Sexual consent and disability." *New York University Law Review* 93 (2018): 480.

Koon-Magnin, Sarah. "The fine line between statutory rape and consensual relationships." *Sexual Victimization: Then and Now* (2014): 103.

Pugh, Brandie, and Patricia Becker. "Exploring definitions and prevalence of verbal sexual coercion and its relationship to consent to unwanted sex: Implications for affirmative consent standards on college campuses." *Behavioral Sciences* 8, no. 8 (2018): 69.

Wood, Emily F., Kristina J. Rikkonen, and Deborah Davis. "Definition, communication, and interpretation of sexual consent." In *Handbook of Sexual Assault and Sexual Assault Prevention*, edited by William O'Donohue and Paul A. Schewe, 399–421. Springer, 2019.

Q4. IS SEXUAL ASSAULT A BIG PROBLEM IN THE UNITED STATES?

Answer: Yes. Hundreds of thousands (perhaps millions) of people are sexually assaulted every year in the United States. Consistent with the general decline in crime since the early 1990s, the rate of sexual assault has also declined (Planty, Langton, Krebs, Berzofsky, & Smiley-McDonald, 2013), but the crime of sexual assault continues to impact a substantial segment of the population. The long-term impacts of the assault on victims compound this significant problem. In addition, millions of people suffer indirectly when friends and family members are sexually victimized. Finally, the financial costs associated with sexual assault are substantial, exceeded only by homicide.

The Facts: As discussed in Q3, researchers use many different methods for measuring the frequency of sexual assault. At the national level, the most widely used instrument is the National Crime Victimization Survey (NCVS), which includes annual estimates, although scholars note that the NCVS is generally an underestimate of the true number of sexual assaults that take place in a given year (National Research Council, 2014). A report of NCVS data on the rate of sexual assault against female victims every year from 1995 through 2010 revealed a significant drop in victimization across that time period, coinciding with a broader crime drop throughout the United States (Planty et al., 2013). The significant decrease took

Table 4.1. Number and rate of sexual assaults according to the National Crime Victimization Survey

Year	Number of Sexual Assaults	Rate per 1,000 Females (Aged 12 or Older)
2005[1]	221,100	1.8
2006[1]	276,300	2.2
2007[1]	298,400	2.3
2008[1]	273,500	2.1
2009[1]	297,900	2.3
2010[1]	269,700	2.1
2011[2]	244,190	0.9
2012[3]	300,170	1.1
2013[3]	346,830	1.3
2014[4]	284,350	1.1
2015[4]	431,840	1.6
2016[4]	298,410	1.1
2017[4]	393,980	1.4
2018[4]	734,630	2.7

Notes: [1] Data reported in Planty et al., 2013
[2] Data reported in Truman, Langton, & Planty, 2013
[3] Data reported in Truman & Langton, 2015
[4] Data reported in Morgan & Oudekerk, 2019

place across the first 10 years of the data (1995–2005), and the rate of sexual violence remained relatively constant across the years 2005–2010 (see Table 4.1). Updates from additional years of NCVS data (Truman, Langton, & Planty, 2013; Truman & Langton, 2015; Morgan & Oudekerk, 2019) indicate that there was some variation in the years 2010–2017, followed by a notable jump in 2018. The number and rate of sexual assault in 2018 was significantly higher than the preceding years against which it was compared (2014, 2015, 2016, and 2017; Morgan & Oudekerk, 2019), although it is still substantially lower than the peak in the early 1990s.

Although the Bureau of Justice Statistics is capable of measuring victimization of both males and females using NCVS data, the major reports that it has published on sexual assault focus on female victims. The Center for Disease Control's National Intimate Partner and Sexual Violence Survey (NISVS) includes data on both male and female victims of sexual violence. According to the most recent available data (2015), 43.6 percent of women reported an experience with sexual violence in their lifetime, and 4.7 reported an experience with sexual violence within the past year (Smith et al., 2018). Using the sample collected for NISVS, researchers estimate that if these data were extrapolated to the national population of the United States, approximately 5,600,000 women would be victims of some form of sexual violence each year, of which 1,484,000 would be victims of rape. Among male respondents, 24.8 percent reported that they had been a victim of sexual violence in their lifetime, 3.5 percent in the past year. If the findings from this sample were extrapolated to the whole nation, approximately 3,916,000 men would be victims of sexual assault in a given year.

Unwanted sexual contact was the most common form of sexual violence reported in this sample for both men (estimated 2,188,000 victimizations per year) and women (estimated 3,260,000 victimizations per year). Sexual coercion was the second most common form of sexual violence reported by both men (estimated 1,769,000 victimizations per year) and women (estimated 2,899,000 victimizations per year). Although the estimates provided by the NCVS and NISVS do not perfectly align (largely because the NISVS includes more acts), it is clear that a large number of people are sexually assaulted each year and millions of Americans have been sexually assaulted at some point in their lives.

For millions of sexual assault survivors in the United States, the impact of the assault will be with them for years to come. For most survivors of sexual assault, there are long-term (potentially lifelong) consequences of the victimization (mental health consequences are discussed further in Q16). Data indicate that people who have been sexually assaulted are at an increased risk of a variety of problematic outcomes, including substance abuse, self-harm, eating disorders, sleep disorders, suicidal thoughts, sexual problems, and problems developing trust or intimacy with others (Campbell, Dworkin, & Cabral, 2009; Peterson, Voller, Polusny, & Murdoch, 2011). This wide variety of potential consequences following a sexual assault can impact multiple aspects of the victim's life—physical, psychological, social—which in turn impact factors including the victim's overall life satisfaction, feelings of pain and suffering, productivity, and personal and professional relationships (these outcomes will be discussed in detail in Chapter 4).

Millions of people are indirectly impacted by sexual assault in the United States as well. The current version of the Diagnostic and Statistical Manual of Mental Disorders (DSM–V), which provides the guidelines mental health professionals use to diagnose a mental illness, recognizes that people may develop posttraumatic stress disorder (PTSD) even if they did not directly experience the traumatic event. Specifically, those who hear about sexual assault frequently as first responders (e.g., rape crisis advocates, law enforcement) can suffer from vicarious trauma as the result of this repeated exposure to the point that they develop symptoms of PTSD. Furthermore, individuals may suffer if a close friend or family member is sexually assaulted. Learning about the traumatic event experienced by their loved one can lead to the individual developing PTSD themselves. The prevalence of sexual assault in the United States suggests that nearly everyone will know someone who is sexually assaulted in their lifetime. Millions of people are thus potentially exposed, either directly or indirectly, to sexual assault-related trauma and the mental and physical health consequences of trauma exposure.

Researchers have also identified significant financial costs associated with sexual assault. According to an analysis of both tangible and intangible costs of crime, the estimated cost per sexual assault in the United States is $240,776 (McCollister, French, & Fang, 2010), with $41,247 attributed to tangible expenses (e.g., criminal justice costs, medical expenses) and $199,642 attributed to intangible expenses (e.g., pain and suffering) that nonetheless have a financial impact. These intangible costs may include missed time or reduced productivity at work, for example. The only crime with a higher estimated tangible or intangible cost is murder.

In summary, a large number of people are sexually assaulted in the United States every year, impacting millions. This problem has an even broader impact when taking into account the first responders and loved ones who are indirectly exposed to the trauma of sexual assault.

FURTHER READING

Campbell, Rebecca, Emily Dworkin, and Giannina Cabral. "An ecological model of the impact of sexual assault on women's mental health." *Trauma, Violence, & Abuse* 10, no. 3 (2009): 225–246.

McCollister, Kathryn E., Michael T. French, and Hai Fang. "The cost of crime to society: New crime-specific estimates for policy and program evaluation." *Drug and Alcohol Dependence* 108, no. 1–2 (2010): 98–109.

Morgan, Rachel E., and Barbara A. Oudekerk. *Criminal Victimization, 2018.* Bureau of Justice Statistics, 2019.

National Research Council. *Estimating the Incidence of Rape and Sexual Assault. Panel on Measuring Rape and Sexual Assault in Bureau of Justice Statistics Household Surveys,* edited by C. Kruttschnitt, W. D. Kalsbeek, and C. C. House. Committee on National Statistics, Division of Behavioral and Social Sciences and Education. The National Academies Press, 2014.

Peterson, Zoë D., Emily K. Voller, Melissa A. Polusny, and Maureen Murdoch. "Prevalence and consequences of adult sexual assault of men: Review of empirical findings and state of the literature." *Clinical Psychology Review* 31, no. 1 (2011): 1–24.

Planty, Michael, Lynn Langton, Christopher Krebs, Marcus Berzofsky, and Hope Smiley-McDonald. *Female Victims of Sexual Violence, 1994–2010.* U.S. Department of Justice, Office of Justice Programs, Bureau of Justice Statistics, 2013.

Smith, Sharon G., Xinjian Zhang, Kathleen C. Basile, Melissa T. Merrick, Jing Wang, Marcie-jo Kresnow, and Jieru Chen. *The National Intimate Partner and Sexual Violence Survey: 2015 Data Brief–Updated Release.* National Center for Injury Prevention and Control, Centers for Disease Control and Prevention, 2018.

Truman, Jennifer, Lynn Langton, and Michael Planty. *Criminal Victimization, 2012 (NCJ 243389).* Bureau of Justice Statistics, U.S. Department of Justice, 2013.

Truman, Jennifer L., and Lynn Langton. *Criminal Victimization, 2014 (NCJ 248973).* Bureau of Justice Statistics, 2015.

Q5. ARE ALL FORMS OF SEXUAL ASSAULT TREATED EQUALLY SERIOUSLY BY THE CRIMINAL JUSTICE SYSTEM?

Answer: No. There are differences in how seriously a crime is treated based on characteristics of the assault itself—and of the victim. Across jurisdictions, penetrative assaults are treated more seriously than nonpenetrative sexual contacts. Generally, sexual crimes against children are treated very seriously and often result in more severe penalties than comparable crimes against adults. Differences in crime severity based on the nature of the assault and the age of the victim are typically written into state law. However, there are also differences in how cases involving violations of the same law tend to be treated. In adult cases, sexual assaults resulting in physical injury or those in which the assailant is a stranger are more likely to progress through the criminal justice system than cases in which no injury is documented or the assailant is known to the victim (assuming that the stranger assailant is identified).

The Facts: Generally speaking, penetrative acts of sexual assault are treated more seriously than nonpenetrative acts in the American legal system. While nonpenetrative forms of sexual assault (e.g., groping, fondling) are criminal and can result in punishment in many states, they tend to be classified as lower degrees of seriousness, thus resulting in less severe penalties. For example, in North Carolina, "A person is guilty of first-degree forcible rape if the person engages in vaginal intercourse with another person by force and against the will of the other person" (§ 14–27.21). This forcible rape statute applies solely to vaginal penetration. A separate statute prohibits oral and anal penetration as follows, "A person is guilty of a first degree forcible sexual offense if the person engages in (oral or anal penetration) with another person by force and against the will of the other person" (§ 14–27.26). The two statutes are nearly identical, with the key difference being the type of penetration involved. Both are categorized at the same level of severity, as a B1 Felony. By comparison, "sexual contact," which includes nonpenetrative acts, is classified as a significantly less severe A1 Misdemeanor. As the North Carolina statute reads, "A person is guilty of sexual battery if the person, for the purpose of sexual arousal, sexual gratification, or sexual abuse, engages in sexual contact with another person" (§ 14–27.33). The degree of classification of an offense typically varies by whether the act was penetrative or nonpenetrative.

However, the same sexual acts may be classified as more severe if the victim is a child. For example, in Virginia, the definition of rape is sexual intercourse, "accomplished (i) against the complaining witness's will, by force, threat or intimidation of or against the complaining witness or another person; or (ii) through the use of the complaining witness's mental incapacity or physical helplessness; or (iii) with a child under age 13 as the victim" (§ 18.2–61). Sexual intercourse with a victim who is younger than 13 is classified as rape based purely on age, regardless of whether force was used and regardless of whether the victim was incapacitated or physically helpless. Similarly, Minnesota has statutes that take both the act and the victim's age into account, by defining varying degrees of the same crime: criminal sexual conduct (see Table 5.1).

The most severe of these crimes, Criminal Sexual Conduct in the First Degree, prohibits, "sexual penetration with another person, or in sexual contact with a person under 13 years of age . . ." (MN 609.345). This law applies to a criminal incident that involved the fondling (i.e., molestation) of a child victim, but not the fondling of an adult victim. A nonpenetrative sexual contact crime against an adult would fall down one degree of severity and be covered in the statute titled, "Criminal Sexual Conduct in the Second Degree." Under this law, if the victim of the criminal sexual

Table 5.1. Age considerations in the Minnesota criminal sexual conduct statutes*

Criminal Sexual Conduct in the...	Age Considerations	Maximum Penalties
First Degree (609.342)	- Sexual penetration (regardless of victim age) - Sexual contact if victim is below the age of 13 and the offender is at least 36 months older than the victim	30 years in prison $40,000 fine
Second Degree (609.343)	- Sexual contact (regardless of victim age) - Sexual contact if victim is below the age of 13 and the offender is at least 36 months older than the victim; state is not obligated to prove coercion was used	25 years in prison $35,000 fine
Third Degree (609.344)	- Sexual penetration if victim is below the age of 13 and the offender's age is within 36 months of the victim's age	15 years in prison $30,000 fine
Fourth Degree (609.345)	- Sexual contact if victim is below the age of 13 and the offender's age is within 36 months of the victim's age	10 years in prison $20,000 fine

*Note: These Minnesota statutes also include considerations for other items (e.g., whether a weapon was used, physical injury sustained, provisions defining statutory rape), but the focus of this table is the impact of sexual act and victim age on degree of severity.

contact is less than 13 years old, "the state is not required to prove that the sexual contact was coerced" (MN 609.343). A further distinction is added in outlining the difference between Criminal Sexual Conduct in the First and Second Degrees compared to Criminal Sexual Conduct in the Third and Fourth Degrees: the age difference between the victim and the perpetrator. The elements of the criminal conduct are sexual penetration (Third Degree) or sexual contact (Fourth Degree) and the victim is described as being less than 13 years old. However, the severity of the crime drops from the First to Third Degree if "the actor is no more than 36 months older than the complainant" (MN 609.344) in a penetrative assault and from the Second to Fourth Degree in a sexual contact assault. As was the case in the Second Degree offense, in cases brought on the Fourth Degree offense, "the state is not required to prove that the sexual contact was coerced" (MN 609.345). Minnesota is just one example of what is typical across the United States: sexual crimes are generally treated with higher levels of severity when they involve penetration rather than contact and when they are committed against children rather than adults.

Even within a single state if the same laws were applied to all cases, there are differences in the way that cases progress through the criminal justice system. That is, once a case has been brought to the attention of law enforcement and the corresponding crime has been identified, some cases are more likely than others to result in a perpetrator being arrested, charges being filed, and a guilty verdict being rendered. As will be explored more fully in Q20, people tend to hold beliefs that "real" or "legitimate" rape is characterized by certain features. For example, a young, sober, and fully clothed woman walking to visit a relative who is violently attacked by a stranger would fit public stereotypes about "real" or "legitimate" rape (see Estrich, 1987). Physical resistance is not a legal requirement of sexual assault (e.g., someone who is paralyzed with fear or unconscious cannot resist an assault) and physical injury (cuts, stab wounds, ligature marks, etc.) are not present in most sexual assault cases (Planty, Langton, Krebs, Berzofsky, & Smiley-McDonald, 2013; see Q18). However, physical injury may be introduced as evidence to a jury that the victim struggled against the assailant, and thus did not consent to the sexual act. Given the weight of such evidence to jurors—who likely hold beliefs about "real" or "legitimate" rape and may be more persuaded by proof of physical resistance—it may not be a surprise to learn that such cases are more likely to result in an arrest by law enforcement (Spohn & Tellis, 2013) and filing of criminal charges by the prosecutor (Alderden & Ullman, 2012) than cases without signs of physical injury.

Another characteristic of the assault that may impact whether a case is processed through the full legal system is the prior relationship between the victim and the perpetrator. Most victims are sexually assaulted by someone they know (e.g., an acquaintance, a romantic partner, a family member), in contrast to the "real" rape scenario involving a stranger who pops out of the bushes. Stranger cases are far less common, but when they do occur, are more likely to be believed as credible (Estrich, 1987). If a suspect is identified, the case is more likely to be processed fully through the legal system compared to cases involving a known perpetrator (Tasca, Rodriguez, Spohn, & Koss, 2012; Alderden & Ullman, 2013).

Recent literature has also explored the impact of victim cooperation on case processing. Unsurprisingly, researchers have found that when victims withdraw participation from the criminal justice process, the case is less likely to lead to arrest or prosecution (Kaiser, O'Neal, & Spohn, 2017). "Due to the importance of victim cooperation—a practical constraint considered in the decision making process in both the decision to arrest and the prosecutor's decision to file charges—it is necessary to investigate the circumstances that surround willingness to cooperate," observed one such study (Kaiser et al., 2017).

Overall, there are differences in the way that cases are defined in statutes and in the way that cases are ultimately treated by law enforcement and prosecutors. Sexual assaults are generally treated as most severe when they involve sexual penetration rather than sexual contact and when they are committed against younger victims (i.e., children) rather than older victims (i.e., adults). When cases of penetrative assaults against adults are reported to law enforcement, those that involve physical injury, assaults committed by strangers, and cases in which the victim actively cooperates with the investigation are more likely to move forward than those cases in which there is no physical injury, the perpetrator was known to the victim, or the victim withdraws cooperation with the criminal justice system.

FURTHER READING

Alderden, Megan A., and Sarah E. Ullman. "Creating a more complete and current picture: Examining police and prosecutor decision-making when processing sexual assault cases." *Violence against Women* 18, no. 5 (2012): 525–551.

Estrich, Susan. *Real Rape*. Harvard University Press, 1987.

Kaiser, Kimberly A., Eryn N. O'Neal, and Cassia Spohn. "'Victim refuses to cooperate': A focal concerns analysis of victim cooperation in sexual assault cases." *Victims & Offenders* 12, no. 2 (2017): 297–322.

Planty, Michael, Lynn Langton, Christopher Krebs, Marcus Berzofsky, and Hope Smiley-McDonald. *Female Victims of Sexual Violence, 1994–2010*. U.S. Department of Justice, Office of Justice Programs, Bureau of Justice Statistics, 2013.

Spohn, Cassia, and Katharine Tellis. *Policing and Prosecuting Sexual Assault: Inside the Criminal Justice System*. Lynne Rienner Publishers, 2013.

Tasca, Melinda, Nancy Rodriguez, Cassia Spohn, and Mary P. Koss. "Police decision making in sexual assault cases: Predictors of suspect identification and arrest." *Journal of Interpersonal Violence* 28, no. 6 (2013): 1157–1177.

2

❖

Demographic Differences
in Sexual Assault Victimization

Sexual assault can impact anyone regardless of gender identity, sexual orientation, age, race, ethnicity, income level, occupation, religion, residence, veteran status, disability status, or any other variable. However, the risk of experiencing a sexual assault is not the same across all groups. Women are disproportionately victimized compared to men. There are also studies that indicate that the risk and experience of sexual assault victimization differ based on race. Members of the lesbian, gay, bisexual, transgender, queer (LGBTQ) community are more likely to be assaulted than their heterosexual or cisgender counterparts.

Scholars emphasize the fact that people experience the world differently based on identity characteristics. Being aware of intersectionality (i.e., the life experiences of a heterosexual White man and a bisexual Latina woman differ in many respects, for instance) provides a more complete sense of the lived experiences that researchers try to measure and understand. Research has also focused on sexual assault in certain locations where risk may be particularly high or populations may be particularly vulnerable (e.g., college campuses, correctional institutions). In short, demographic factors are associated with differences in the risk and experience of sexual assault victimization.

To better understand some of the more nuanced relationships between demographic variables and the risk of being sexually assaulted, this chapter addresses five questions. First, this section will establish that not all people are at equal risk of experiencing a sexual assault in their lifetime (Q6: Are all people at equal risk of being sexually assaulted?). Although it is possible for anyone to be assaulted (Q7: Can men be sexually assaulted?), the likelihood of experiencing sexual assault differs based on age (Q8: Are there differences in risk and experience of sexual assault victimization by age?), sexual orientation (Q9: Is the risk of sexual assault victimization greater for people with certain sexual orientations or gender identities?), and other variables (Q10: Do other factors impact the risk of sexual assault victimization or perpetration?).

By providing a more detailed view of who first responders in the United States are likely to encounter when responding to victims of sexual assault and what these victims may be experiencing, discussion of these five topics will help inform later sections of the book relating to how society and governmental agencies respond.

Q6. ARE ALL PEOPLE AT EQUAL RISK OF BEING SEXUALLY ASSAULTED?

Answer: No. Although any person can be a victim of sexual assault, the risk of victimization is much higher for women than men. There are also differences based on race/ethnicity, with Native Americans and Alaska Natives, in particular, at disproportionate risk of victimization. The results of large national data collection efforts underscoring these two findings will be discussed.

The Facts: Many researchers rely upon the National Crime Victimization Survey (NCVS) when reporting the prevalence of sexual assault in the United States. By interviewing participants from a large, nationally representative sample of the population, the NCVS provides estimates of how many sexual assaults take place each year in the United States. These data, which are collected by the Bureau of Justice Statistics, can then be examined in a variety of ways to better understand the context of sexual assault. For example, researchers may look at the demographic characteristics of the victim, where the assault took place, whether the assault was reported to the police, whether a weapon was used, and whether an injury was sustained. A clear trend that emerges from these data is that the frequency of sexual assault against female victims far exceeds the frequency of sexual assault against male victims. Table 6.1 includes the prevalence estimates of the total number of sexual assaults, sexual assaults against male victims, and sexual assaults against female victims, for all years 2000–2019, inclusive (Bureau of Justice Statistics, 2020). In 10 of the 20 years of data

Table 6.1. Number of rape/sexual assaults by sex, 2000–2019

Year[1]	Total Number of Sexual Assaults[1]	Male Victim[1]	Female Victim[1]	Percentage of Sexual Assaults Against Female Victims[2]
2000	366,747	14,768*	351,979	96.0%
2001	476,578	47,191*	429,387	90.1%
2002	349,805	46,861*	302,943	86.6%
2003	325,311	19,672*	305,639	94.0%
2004	255,769	6,201*	249,568	97.6%
2005	207,760	15,079*	192,682	92.7%
2006	463,598	103,750*	359,848	77.6%
2007	248,277	11,296*	236,980	95.4%
2008	349,691	39,589*	310,102	88.7%
2009	305,574	19,816*	285,758	93.5%
2010	268,574	15,020*	253,555	94.4%
2011	244,188	34,804*	209,384	85.7%
2012	346830	131,259	215,570	62.2%
2013	300,165	34,057	266,107	88.7%
2014	284,345	28,032*	256,313	90.1%
2015	431,837	62,916	368,921	85.4%
2016	298,407	45,860	252,547	84.6%
2017	393,979	30,586	363,393	92.2%
2018	734,632	81,956	652,676	88.8%
2019	459,306	52,336	406,970	88.6%

Notes: [1] Data provided by NCVS Victimization Analysis Tool at www.bjs.gov
[2] Calculation performed by author.
* Data marked with an asterisk included a warning from NCVS, "Interpret data with caution, based on 10 or fewer sample cases or the coefficient of variation is greater than 50%."

presented, female victims of sexual assault made up more than 90 percent of all victims. In only 3 years of data (2006, 2012, 2016) did female victims make up less than 85 percent of all victims. The findings of the NCVS unequivocally demonstrate that women are far more likely than men to report that they have experienced a sexual assault.

Another major data collection effort, begun in 2010 by the National Center for Injury Prevention and Control within the Centers for Disease

Control and Prevention, is the National Intimate Partner and Sexual Violence Survey (NISVS). A report of the most recent data (collected in 2015) indicates that 1 in 5 women and 1 in 14 men will be the targets of a completed or attempted sexual assault in their lifetime (Smith et al., 2018). As discussed in Q2, the NISVS has a more inclusive definition of sexual assault than the NCVS. The various forms of contact sexual violence studied in the NISVS as well as the percentage and number of men and women who are likely to experience each are shown in Table 6.2. Women were more likely to experience contact sexual violence (43.6 percent of women compared to 24.8 percent of men) overall as well as every component measure except being made to penetrate (men are more likely to be made to penetrate an assailant, 7.1 percent to 1.2 percent). Overall, women were more likely than men to experience completed forced penetration, attempted forced penetration, completed alcohol/drug-facilitated penetration, sexual coercion, and unwanted sexual contact in their lifetime. The findings of these major national studies demonstrating

Table 6.2. Estimates of lifetime experiences of sexual assault by sex according to the National Intimate Partner and Sexual Violence Survey, 2015

Type of sexual violence	Estimates of Lifetime Sexual Assault Experiences			
	Percentage of women	Number of women	Percentage of men	Number of men
Contact sexual violence				
	43.6	52,192,000	24.8	27,608,000
Completed forced penetration				
	13.5	16,169,000	0.8	943,000
Attempted forced penetration				
	6.3	7,568,000	0.5	583,000
Completed alcohol/drug-facilitated penetration				
	11.0	13,185,000	1.6	1,772,000
Made to penetrate				
	1.2	1,398,000	7.1	7,876,000
Sexual coercion				
	16.0	19,194,000	9.6	10,644,000
Unwanted sexual contact				
	37.0	44,349,000	17.9	19,883,000

the more frequent experience of sexual assault victimization among women than men are also present in samples of the general public (Elliot, Mok, & Briere, 2004) and undergraduates (Mellins et al., 2017). There is clear consensus among researchers that women are far more likely to be victims of sexual assault than men (men as victims of sexual assault are discussed further in Q7).

Another finding that has emerged is the disproportionately high risk of sexual assault victimization against Native American and Alaska Native women. The National Violence Against Women Survey, conducted in the late 1990s, reported that 34 percent of Native American and Alaska Native women had experienced a sexual assault in her lifetime compared to 18 percent of White women and 19 percent of Black women (Tjaden & Thoennes, 2006). Statistical analyses revealed that Native American and Alaska Native women "were significantly more likely than women from all other backgrounds to have been raped at some time in their lifetime" (Tjaden & Thoennes, 2006, p. 13). Results from the National Intimate Partner and Sexual Violence Survey (NISVS) also revealed significant differences in sexual assault prevalence based on race/ethnicity (see Table 6.3). Participants were asked to self-identify their race and among those women who identified as multiracial the reported lifetime experience of rape was 31.8 percent and lifetime experience of any form of contact sexual violence was 59.5 percent on average between 2010 and 2012. Women who identified as Native American or Alaska Native were also at high risk of experiencing a rape (28.9 percent) or contact sexual violence (45.6 percent) in their lifetime according to these data (see Table 6.3).

A review of literature on the prevalence of sexual assault against Native American and Alaska Native women was consistent with this finding, suggesting that the rate of sexual assault among this group is disproportionately high (Bachman, Zaykowski, Lanier, Poteyeva, & Kallmyer, 2010). Using 13 years of NCVS data (collected between 1992 and 2005), researchers assessed the frequency of sexual assault among Native American and Alaska Native women and tested for differences in the characteristics of sexual assault (Bachman et al., 2010). This study did not find substantial differences in prevalence of sexual assault by race/ethnicity, with 40 percent of Native American and Alaska Native women, 38 percent of Black women, and 36 percent of White women reporting a sexual assault during the study period (Bachman et al., 2010). However, they did find significant variation in the characteristics of the assaults. Specifically, "[Native American and Alaska Native] women were over two times more likely to face armed offenders and to be physically hit during the sexual assault

Table 6.3. Average estimates of lifetime experiences of sexual assault by race/ethnicity according to the National Intimate Partner and Sexual Violence Survey, 2010–2012

Race/Ethnicity		Estimates of Lifetime Sexual Assault Experiences	
	Type of sexual violence	Percentage of women	Confidence intervals
Hispanic			
	Contact sexual violence	26.9%	(24.0, 30.0)
	Rape	15.0%	(12.8, 17.6)
Non-Hispanic			
Black			
	Contact sexual violence	35.5%	(32.8, 38.4)
	Rape	20.7%	(18.5, 23.2)
White			
	Contact sexual violence	38.9%	(37.8, 40.0)
	Rape	19.9%	(19.0, 20.9)
Asian or Pacific Islander			
	Contact sexual violence	22.9%	(18.1, 28.5)
	Rape	9.5%	(6.3, 14.1)
Native American or Alaska Native			
	Contact sexual violence	45.6%	(36.9, 54.5)
	Rape	28.9%	(21.3, 37.9)
Multiracial			
	Contact sexual violence	49.5%	(43.4, 55.6)
	Rape	31.8%	(26.5, 37.5)

compared to either White or African American women. [Native American and Alaska Native] women were also slightly more likely to suffer physical injuries in addition to the rape injuries and more likely to require medical care for these injuries than other women" (Bachman et al., 2010, p. 211). These findings indicate that sexual assaults committed against Native American and Alaska Native women were more violent than sexual assaults committed against Black or White women reported to NCVS. Furthermore, "Although victimisations against [Native American and Alaska Native] women are more likely to come to the attention of police, they are much less likely to result in an arrest compared to attacks against either White or African American victims" (Bachman et al., 2010, p. 199).

In another report from 2008, the same group of researchers attributed the low rates of arrest on tribal lands to organizational issues within the criminal justice system that relate specifically to Native American and Alaska Natives (Bachman, Zaykowski, Kallmyer, Poteyeva, & Lanier, 2008). The authors explain:

> Complicated jurisdictional issues still produce unique barriers to American Indian and Alaska Native women seeking help from a criminal justice authority on tribal lands. When an act of violence occurs on tribal lands, there are several possible law enforcement officials who may respond including tribal officers, Federal Bureau of Investigation officers, Bureau of Indian Affairs officers, and in PL-280 states, state police officers. Deciding who has jurisdictional authority is dependent on several factors including the crime that was committed, whether the offender or the victim was an American Indian and Alaska Native, and whether the crime was committed exclusively on tribal land. The jurisdictional confusion that may ensue when an act of violence occurs sometimes produces an inadequate and delayed response to female victims. Importantly, some tribes have worked out cross-deputization agreements with state police authorities, which serve to alleviate the jurisdictional confusion over authority. (Bachman et al., 2008, pp. 8–9)

These important contextual differences require further study to better understand the dynamics of the sexual assault, reporting to police, and the criminal justice investigation, particularly with regard to Native American and Alaska Native women. Bachman et al. (2010) suggest oversampling Native American and Alaska Native survey participants in future iterations of major national data collections to provide a sufficient sample size to make meaningful statistical comparisons across race/ethnicity and allow examination of victimization experiences within racial/ethnic groups.

In summary, not all people are at equal risk of sexual assault. Women are far more likely to be sexually assaulted than are men. There are also differences based on race/ethnicity indicating that some populations, particularly Native American and Alaska Native and multiracial women, experience a disproportionate rate of sexual assault. These national survey estimates focus exclusively on the frequency of occurrence of sexual assault, but community-based research helps understand the dynamics more specifically (please note that differences in reporting of sexual assault based on race will be discussed in Q11).

FURTHER READING

Bachman, Ronet, Heather Zaykowski, Rachel Kallmyer, Margarita Poteyeva, and Christina Lanier. *Violence Against American Indian and Alaska Native Women and the Criminal Justice Response: What Is Known.* National Criminal Justice Reference Service, 2008.

Bachman, Ronet, Heather Zaykowski, Christina Lanier, Margarita Poteyeva, and Rachel Kallmyer. "Estimating the magnitude of rape and sexual assault against American Indian and Alaska Native (AIAN) women." *Australian & New Zealand Journal of Criminology* 43, no. 2 (2010): 199–222.

Black, Michele, Kathleen Basile, Matthew Breiding, Sharon Smith, Mikel Walters, Melissa Merrick, Jieru Chen, and Mark Stevens. *National Intimate Partner and Sexual Violence Survey: 2010 Summary Report.* Centers for Disease Control and Prevention, 2011.

Bureau of Justice Statistics. Number of rape/sexual assaults by sex, 2000–2019. Generated using the NCVS Victimization Analysis Tool at www.bjs.gov. Accessed Sept. 27, 2020.

Elliott, Diana M., Doris S. Mok, and John Briere. "Adult sexual assault: Prevalence, symptomatology, and sex differences in the general population." *Journal of Traumatic Stress: Official Publication of the International Society for Traumatic Stress Studies* 17, no. 3 (2004): 203–211.

Mellins, Claude A., Kate Walsh, Aaron L. Sarvet, Melanie Wall, Louisa Gilbert, John S. Santelli, Martie Thompson et al. "Sexual assault incidents among college undergraduates: Prevalence and factors associated with risk." *PLoS One* 12, no. 11 (2017): e0186471.

Smith, Sharon G., Kathleen C. Basile, Leah K. Gilbert, Melissa T. Merrick, Nimesh Patel, Margie Walling, and Anurag Jain. *National Intimate Partner and Sexual Violence Survey (NISVS): 2010–2012 State Report.* Centers for Disease Control and Prevention, 2017.

Smith, Sharon G., Xinjian Zhang, Kathleen C. Basile, Melissa T. Merrick, Jing Wang, Marcie-jo Kresnow, and Jieru Chen. *The National Intimate Partner and Sexual Violence Survey (NISVS): 2015 Data Brief—Updated Release.* National Center for Injury Prevention and Control, Centers for Disease Control and Prevention, 2018.

Tjaden, Patricia G., and Nancy Thoennes. *Extent, Nature, and Consequences of Rape Victimization: Findings from the National Violence Against Women Survey.* U.S. Department of Justice, Office of Justice Programs, National Institute of Justice, 2006.

Q7. CAN MEN BE SEXUALLY ASSAULTED?

Answer: Absolutely. Each year in the United States, men are victims of various types of sexual assaults that can be committed by perpetrators of any gender identity. The name of the statute applied to that assault differs based on the act, but also differs across states (as discussed in Q1). There are some states that maintain a statutory definition of rape that requires a male perpetrator of a female victim. However, even in those states that do not apply the term "rape" to the assault, there are other serious felony sexual assault statutes that would apply to a sexual assault committed against a man. Men, however, are less likely to acknowledge themselves as a victim; reporting a crime to the police or seeking help services following an assault are lower for male victims than female victims. This trend is likely due to social pressures on men to be "tough" and common perceptions of men as being sexually aroused easily and often. The myths surrounding male sexual assault and their potential harm to male survivors are discussed.

The Facts: Some disagreement as to whether men can be "raped" may be attributable to legal codes. In fact, even the definition used by the FBI in reporting the frequency of rape across states in the Uniform Crime Reports was limited to "carnal knowledge of a woman forcibly and against her will" until 2012. Starting in 2013, the FBI's Uniform Crime Reports presented two sets of statistics: "Rape—Legacy Definition" and "Rape—Revised." The new definition is far more inclusive and recognizes the potential for either males or females to be either victims or perpetrators. It reads, "The penetration, no matter how slight, of the vagina or anus with any body part or object, or oral penetration by a sex organ of another person, without the consent of the victim." It also recognizes multiple forms of penetration as rape, which has not traditionally been reflected in many statutes.

Until quite recently, many states did not recognize men as potential victims of rape. Prior to September 2019, Alabama limited the act recognized as rape to vaginal penetration, defining rape in the first degree as "sexual intercourse with a member of the opposite sex by forcible compulsion" (13a-6-61). Other states were more explicit in defining women as victims of rape. For example, in Mississippi, the law against "Rape; assault with intent to ravish," refers to "an assault with intent to forcibly ravish any female of previous chaste character" (§ 97-3-71). However, statutes prohibiting "sexual battery" in Mississippi do not specify that the victim be of a particular sex (i.e., "A person is guilty of sexual battery if he or she engages in sexual penetration with: (a) Another person without his or her consent"

[§ 97-3-95]). In other words, even when a state's definition of "rape" was exclusive to female victims, there were typically additional laws that could be applied when men were sexually victimized. These latter laws were called other names such as Forcible Sodomy (e.g., Alabama) or Involuntary Deviate Sexual Intercourse (e.g., Pennsylvania). As in Mississippi's "sexual battery" statute, these laws generally described acts that could be committed against either a man or a woman such as oral or anal penetration. This approach (defining vaginal penetration as a separate statute from oral or anal penetration) meant that in cases in which the defendant had penetrated the victim in multiple ways, the prosecution could charge the defendant with multiple felony charges related to the incident. And because these laws typically involved equally severe penalties, the punishment for the offender could be enhanced. However, it also meant that many states' definitions of "rape" did not include or apply to cases in which the victim was a man. For some male victims, the idea of a penetrative sexual violation not being labeled as "rape" was invalidating and left them feeling like their assault was not being taken seriously or somehow did not count.

Regardless of the name of the crime at the federal or state level, data clearly demonstrate that men can be victims of sexual assault and that millions of men in the United States have experienced sexual assault in their lifetime (Smith et al., 2018). A comprehensive statute describing various forms of sexual assault is necessary to capture the variety of acts that may be reported. As shown in the data collected by the National Intimate Partner and Sexual Violence Survey (see Table 6.2, Q6) respondents report a variety of types of sexual assault. While for women, the rate of being "made to penetrate" is very low (1.2 percent), the risk among men is substantially higher (7.1 percent). This 7.1 percent of men who were made to penetrate another person in his lifetime (1.6 percent completed using force, 1.4 percent attempted using force, and 5.5 percent facilitated by alcohol or drugs) is approximately 1 in 14 men in the United States (Smith, et al., 2018). Thus, to adequately capture the different experiences of sexual assault, laws defining sexual assault must be inclusive of multiple acts. In an effort to accurately capture experiences of sexual assault against male victims, most jurisdictions in the United States (Caringella, 2009) and governments of other Western nations (Lowe & Rogers, 2017) have made changes to their statutes such that now anyone can be charged as a perpetrator of rape and anyone can be recognized as a victim of rape.

However, not all disagreement about whether men can be victims of rape is based in legal codes. There are strong and pervasive societal beliefs relating to men's sexuality and masculinity that make it harder to study male victims of sexual assault. Researchers refer to these inaccurate beliefs about sexual assaults, its victims, and its perpetrator as "rape myths" (see Q20). A 2018 study of myths relating to male sexual assault found that, "One in three respondents believed a man's resistance to be crucial in determining whether he was raped, would doubt a man who was raped by a woman, and thought that male rape was committed by homosexuals. Slightly less (25%) endorsed rape myths based on male sexual insatiability: Men can enjoy forced sex and would enjoy being raped by a woman" (Walfield, 2018, p. 13). The more strongly that an individual holds these ideas, the more resistant they will be to the possibility that a man (particularly a heterosexual man) can be raped. As discussed by psychologist and professor Nicola Gavey, a widespread ideology known as the "male sex drive discourse" suggests that a healthy man would generally never turn down sex from a woman. Although commonly held, Gavey discusses reasons this belief is problematic in her work, *Just Sex? The Cultural Scaffolding of Rape*. Specifically, individuals who believe in the male sex drive discourse assume blanket consent given by the man for all sexual encounters involving a man and a woman. Support for this belief would discredit the possibility of a nonconsensual sexual encounter, and thus would not allow the believer to recognize that a man could be raped by a woman. In short, it trivializes the experience of sexual assault by implying that it is a wanted or consensual encounter.

However, most researchers (including Gavey) emphasize the existence of a great deal of evidence that disputes claims about a "male sex drive discourse." Researchers emphasize that men absolutely have the ability to turn down sexual encounters and often do so. They also caution that men should not be assumed to be consenting participants in every sexual scenario involving a woman. If an encounter is forcible, if the victim is incapacitated, if there is an inherent power imbalance (e.g., teacher and student, correctional officer and inmate), or if the act is otherwise nonconsensual, it can be categorized as rape regardless of the sex of the victim.

Another commonly held myth is that because men are tough and strong, a man can or should be able to fight off any attacker. People who strongly believe this may argue that if the man failed to adequately defend himself against the assault, he must have actually wanted or consented to the sexual activity and thus could not be a victim of rape. Again, this myth is not reality. There are plenty of reasons why a man might not be able to fight off an attacker, none of which should be construed as consent to the sexual act. The man may be asleep, unconscious, intoxicated, outnumbered, infirm, physically overpowered, or frozen in fear (a state known as tonic immobility). Indeed, male victims of sexual assault often do not label the act as a sexual assault. These individuals are known as "unacknowledged victims." Men are particularly unlikely to label an act as sexual assault if it took place in adulthood rather than childhood (Artime, McCallum, & Peterson, 2014). The authors argue that:

> Lack of acknowledgment of victimization among men may be, in part, a reflection of commonly held myths about male rape. These myths promote a traditional view of masculinity that portrays "real" men as strong, invulnerable, and always in the mood for sex. Given these cultural messages, men who are victimized may avoid labeling their experiences as abuse or rape because doing so implies a failure of their masculinity. (Artime, McCallum, & Peterson, 2014, p. 9)

Recent research suggests that male survivors of sexual assault are less likely than women to recognize their experiences as assaults (Reed et al., 2020). The authors demonstrate that the rate of rape myth acceptance is significantly higher among men than women, which indirectly reduces the likelihood that men will acknowledge their assaults. This is in line with prior literature on male rape myth acceptance, but it underscores the need for practitioners and first responders to address rape myth attitudes with men who seek services relating to an unwanted sexual encounter, even if the victim is not referring to that encounter as an assault (Reed et al., 2020). Victim blaming based on social conceptions of masculinity and the corresponding fear of being disbelieved also may decrease the likelihood of disclosure, help-seeking, and reporting assaults to the police (see Schulze, Koon-Magnin, & Bryan, 2019, for a discussion of the impact of both the perpetrator's and victim's gender identity on understanding sexual assault).

Another point of confusion for some people, including some survivors of sexual assault, is that they may experience sexual arousal or even orgasm during a sexual assault. Some survivors and first responders to sexual assault erroneously interpret this to mean that they must have "enjoyed" the assault and thus agreed to it. Erection in males is a physiological reaction, for example, and physical arousal is not a proxy for consent (Bullock & Beckson, 2011). In a review of research on sexual arousal and consent, researchers conclude, "the induction of arousal and even orgasm does not permit the conclusion that the subjects consented to the stimulation. A perpertrator's defence against the alleged assault built solely on the evidence that genital arousal or orgasm in the victim proves consent has no intrinsic validity and should be disregarded" (Levin & van Berlo, 2004, p. 87). If medical professionals, criminal justice personnel, or other service providers discount an experience of sexual assault in which there was physical arousal, it will not only limit the possibility of pursuing criminal charges, it will likely have a significant psychological impact on the victim.

Being disbelieved, questioned, or doubted is a form of secondary victimization (see discussion in Q16 and Q17) that enhances the risk of several negative psychological consequences for survivors of sexual assault. Legal codes that exclude sexual assault experiences committed against men, myths relating to male victimization, and misunderstandings of physiological indicators of arousal all discount the experience of sexual assault that a man may experience. Although adequate response services are not present in every community, sexual assault of male victims impacts millions of men throughout the United States.

FURTHER READING

Artime, Tiffany M., Ethan B. McCallum, and Zoë D. Peterson. "Men's acknowledgment of their sexual victimization experiences." *Psychology of Men & Masculinity* 15, no. 3 (2014): 313.

Bullock, Clayton M., and Mace Beckson. "Male victims of sexual assault: Phenomenology, psychology, physiology." *Journal of the American Academy of Psychiatry and the Law Online* 39, no. 2 (2011): 197–205.

Caringella, Susan. *Addressing Rape Reform in Law and Practice.* Columbia University Press, 2009.

Gavey, Nicola. *Just Sex?: The Cultural Scaffolding of Rape.* Routledge, 2018.

Levin, Roy J., and Willy van Berlo. "Sexual arousal and orgasm in subjects who experience forced or non-consensual sexual stimulation–a review." *Journal of Clinical Forensic Medicine* 11, no. 2 (2004): 82–88.

Lowe, Michelle, and Paul Rogers. "The scope of male rape: A selective review of research, policy and practice." *Aggression and Violent Behavior* 35 (2017): 38–43.

Reed, Rebecca A., Jordan T. Pamlanye, Hannah R. Truex, Madeleine C. Murphy-Neilson, Kristen P. Kunaniec, Amie R. Newins, and Laura C. Wilson. "Higher rates of unacknowledged rape among men: The role of rape myth acceptance." *Psychology of Men & Masculinities* 21, no. 1 (2020): 162.

Schulze, Corina, Sarah Koon-Magnin, and Valerie Bryan. *Gender Identity, Sexual Orientation, and Sexual Assault: Challenging the Myths.* Lynne Rienner Publishers, 2019.

Smith, Sharon G., Xinjian Zhang, Kathleen C. Basile, Melissa T. Merrick, Jing Wang, Marcie-jo Kresnow, and Jieru Chen. *The National Intimate Partner and Sexual Violence Survey (NISVS): 2015 Data Brief—Updated Release.* National Center for Injury Prevention and Control, Centers for Disease Control and Prevention, 2018.

Walfield, Scott M. "'Men cannot be raped': Correlates of male rape myth acceptance." *Journal of Interpersonal Violence* (2018): https://doi.org/10.1177%2F0886260518817777

Q8. ARE THERE DIFFERENCES IN RISK AND EXPERIENCE OF SEXUAL ASSAULT VICTIMIZATION BY AGE?

Answer: Yes, definitely. The risk of experiencing sexual assault is highest before the age of 25 and drops significantly as an individual goes deeper into adulthood. However, there are important differences in the relationship between age and risk of victimization based on gender. For example, men are more likely to be assaulted as children rather than in adulthood, whereas women are equally likely to be assaulted as minors or adults. The experience of sexual assault also varies by age, most notably in the relationship between the victim and the offender, tactics used to complete the assault, and the level of injury sustained.

The Facts: When studying the experience of sexual assault based on age, statistics clearly demonstrate that the risk is highest in the teenage years and early adulthood (roughly between the ages of 16 and 24). The risk of sexual assault drops substantially into adulthood, such that the risk of being assaulted after the age of 30 is relatively low. However, because the majority of sexual assault victims are women, findings relating to the relationship between age and sexual assault largely represent the experience of women. When exploring the relationship between age and sexual assault victimization separately for women and men, two different relationships emerge. Both the National Intimate Partner and Sexual Violence Survey (NISVS; Smith et al., 2018) and the National Violence Against Women Survey (NVAWS; Tjaden & Thoennes, 2006) present the percentage of victims who experienced sexual assault(s) during their lifetime based on the age at first assault. The two surveys report their findings using different age group divisions and their percentages differ slightly, but the trends are consistent.

In the NISVS, female survey participants who reported a lifetime experience of being assaulted in the form of a completed or attempted rape were most likely to have been first assaulted was 18 to 24 years old (38.1 percent), followed by 11 to 17 years old (30.5 percent). The likelihood of being the victim of a first completed or attempted rape was approximately equal for women between the ages of 25 and 34 (12.4 percent) and girls aged 10 or younger (12.7 percent). These findings are consistent with the primary

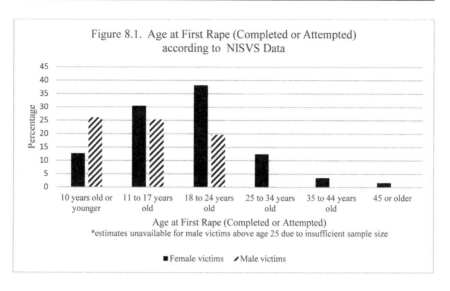

Figure 8.1. Age at First Rape (Completed or Attempted) according to NISVS Data

Age at First Rape (Completed or Attempted)
*estimates unavailable for male victims above age 25 due to insufficient sample size

■ Female victims   ⁄ Male victims

age-related findings that the risk of assault is highest in a female's teens and early twenties, as described above. However, among male participants in the NISVS, a different pattern emerged. Specifically, the most common age at which male victims experienced their first completed or attempted rape was 10 or younger (26.0 percent), followed closely by 11 to 17 years old (25.3 percent). Another 19.6 percent of men who have been sexually assaulted experienced a first completed or attempted rape between the ages of 18 to 24. In short, men who reported a completed or attempted rape during their lifetime were much more likely to experience a first assault as a child than as an adult (see Figure 8.1).

The NVAWS presented its findings by gender across four age groups, but the general pattern was the same. Female victims of sexual assault in the NVAWS were most likely to report their first completed or attempted rape between the ages of 12 and 17 (32.4 percent) or in early adulthood, between the ages of 18 and 24 (29.4 percent). Another 21.6 percent of women who have been sexually assaulted reported that they first experienced a completed or attempted rape when they were younger than 12 years old, while 16.8 of victims reported that they were first assaulted at the age of 25 or older. However, among the male victims of sexual assault in the NVAWS, the most commonly reported age of completed or attempted rape was in childhood, before the age of 12 (48 percent). Within each following age group, the percentage of male victims reporting a first completed or attempted rape decreased to 23 percent during the ages of 12 to 17, 16.6 percent from ages 18 to 24, and 12.3 percent at age 25 or older. Like

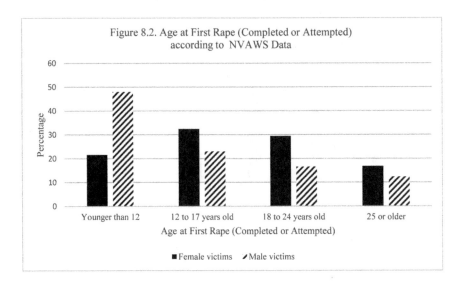

Figure 8.2. Age at First Rape (Completed or Attempted) according to NVAWS Data

the NISVS, the NVAWS data suggest that the risk for males to be victimized by sexual assault is highest in childhood (see Figure 8.2).

The data presented thus far has focused on the age at first sexual assault, but because some victims experience assault more than once in their lifetime, it is important to consider additional time periods when assessing the overall risk of sexual assault associated with age. "Although most rape victims identified by NVAWS were under 18 when they were first raped, the survey found that more women were raped as adults than as children or adolescents. . . . Specifically, 9.1 percent of all women surveyed said they were raped before their 18th birthday, while 9.6 percent said they were raped since they turned 18" (Tjaden & Thoennes, 2006, pp. 18–19). On the other hand, "men were nearly twice as likely to be raped as children than as adolescents or adults" (Tjaden & Thoennes, 2006, p. 19).

To be clear, the number of women (or girls) who were raped at every age exceeded the number of men (or boys) who were raped at that age. Women or girls are more likely than men or boys to be raped at every age. But among women and men who are rape victims, the likelihood of risk based on age follows a different trend. For men who are sexually assaulted, the assault is most likely to take place in early childhood; whereas for women who are sexually assaulted, the assault is most likely to take place in their teens or early adulthood (Smith et al., 2018; Tjaden & Thoennes, 2006).

The experience of sexual assault may differ in important ways based on the age of the victim. An impactful study published in 2000 evaluated sexual crimes against children that were recorded in the National Incident-Based Reporting System (NIBRS; Snyder, 2000). This descriptive study included cases that were reported to law enforcement in 12 states between the years of 1991 through 1996. A major finding of this study, one that runs contrary to much public opinion on the nature of sexual assault, was that sex crimes at the hands of strangers were exceptionally rare among children. Fewer than 5 percent of sexual assaults committed against children younger than 12 years old were committed by strangers (Snyder, 2000). The risk of assault by a stranger increased gradually with age, peaking at 30.1 percent of assaults involving adults over the age of 25. The reverse trend was present for assaults committed by a family member, which were most common among the youngest children (over 40 percent of assaults against children younger than 12 were committed by a family member) and generally declined into adulthood. The most consistent risk was posed by acquaintances, who accounted for 48.3 percent of assaults against children younger than 5 and more than 50 percent of assaults against victims in all other age groups (see Figure 8.3).

While these data are old, the findings presented have been generally supported by subsequent additional research, which shows that strangers account for very few cases of sexual assault and that family members are rarely the culprits of sexual crimes committed against people after they have reached adulthood (Planty, Langton, Krebs, Berzofsky, & Smiley-McDonald, 2013).

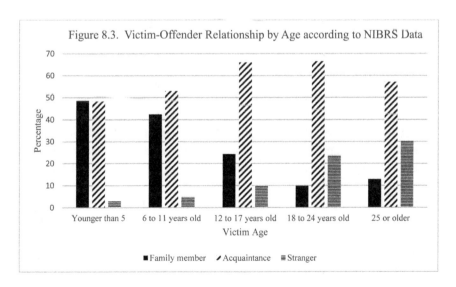

Figure 8.3. Victim-Offender Relationship by Age according to NIBRS Data

There are also important differences in how assailants carry out their crimes based on the victim's age. Many offenders who commit acts of sexual violence against children engage in a practice known as "grooming," which refers to tactics the offender uses to complete the assault and minimize the likelihood of detection. While there is substantial variation in what exactly constitutes "grooming" (Bennett & Donohue, 2014), one definition is, "the use of nonviolent techniques by one person to gain sexual access to and control over potential and actual child victims" (Lanning, 2018, p. 12).

The specific form that this grooming takes may differ based on the nature of the predatory adult's relationship to the child (e.g., a member of the extended family, a babysitter, a coach), but across studies, there tend to be similar steps recognized within the grooming process. One review of research noted key themes: (1) "identifying potential victims," (2) "the use of attention, bribery, and coercion," (3) "sexual desensitization," (4) "boundary violations," and (5) "grooming the child's environment" (Bennett & Donohue, 2014). Other scholars have concluded, "Through a review of literature, there appears to be a series of stages the offender utilizes in sexual grooming, including selecting a vulnerable victim, gaining access to the child, developing a trusting relationship, and desensitizing the child to touch" (Winters & Jeglic, 2017, p. 727). The early steps in this process involve the offender working to gain the trust of both the potential victim (the child) and the child's parents or other caretakers. This is often achieved through seemingly innocuous actions like becoming involved in shared activities (e.g., a club, sport) or locations (e.g., a school, church). Once the offender and the potential victim share a social space, the offender will likely seek out a vulnerability within the child (e.g., the child may feel they are not getting enough attention from adults at home, which the offender then provides; the child may be insecure about a specific personal characteristic that the offender compliments or says is special; the offender provides clothing, jewelry, sports gear, tickets to events, or other items the child may not be able to afford). By reaching out to a specific vulnerability within the child, the offender seeks to gain the potential victim's trust and fill a role in that child's life that the child views as valuable.

After developing this sense of trust, the offender typically violates some form of boundary such as allowing the child to break a well-established rule or asking the child to keep a secret. This step serves two purposes for the offender: first, it tests whether the child will keep a secret from their parents or caregivers if directed by the offender; second, it gives the offender some leverage over the child (e.g., "I didn't tell your mom that you saw that movie you aren't allowed to see so you wouldn't get in trouble, so now I need you to keep this secret so that I don't get in trouble"). Increased awareness of this grooming process is reflected in tips for parents to teach their children, like identifying safe adults for children to reach out to if they feel scared or need help and which parts of the body are private. Warning signs of potential sexual abuse are outlined in Figure 8.4 and tips for talking to children about recognizing potential threats identified by the National Child Advocacy Center are outlined in Figure 8.5.

Figure 8.4. National Child Advocacy Center: Child Sexual Abuse: Perpetrators—Manipulation—Disclosure—Prevention

---

How do Perpetrators manipulate children and families?

- Perpetrators are patient! They work to gain trust and friendship of the child and often of the entire family.
- Perpetrators pay attention to what a child likes and dislikes, to find ways to interact with the child.
- Perpetrators find ways to be alone with the child.
- Perpetrators often "test" a child's ability to protect himself/herself by engaging in touching activities such as hugs and kisses, back rubs, horseplay, etc.
- Perpetrators take advantage of a child's natural curiosity. If a child seems comfortable and/or curious about touching, then slowly increases the sexual contact.

Why do only 16% of child victims tell about the abuse?

- Many child victims don't understand that what is happening to them is sexual or is wrong.
- The "touches" may feel good to the child and because it "didn't hurt," the child is less likely to tell.
- Child victims may feel guilty or embarrassed about the abuse, or think it is their fault.
- Perpetrators may give the child alcohol, drugs, or pornography and later threaten to expose the child's use of these items.
- Perpetrators may threaten to hurt the child, the child's family members, or pets.
- Child victims often fear they will not be believed by family members, especially caregivers.

Source: National Children's Advocacy Center. "Child Sexual Abuse." 2018. Reprinted with permission. https://www.nationalcac.org/wp-content/uploads/2018/02/CSA-Perpetrators.pdf

Figure 8.5. National Child Advocacy Center: "Parents Can Help Prevent Child Sexual Abuse"

How do you talk to children about sexual abuse?

- Start at an EARLY AGE.
- Keep discussions DEVELOPMENTALLY APPROPRIATE, with an awareness of normal behaviors.
- REPEAT the message.
- Promote HEALTHY SEXUALITY by teaching respect and value of body and gender.
- Teach CORRECT NAMES FOR BODY PARTS, to reduce children's vulnerability.
- Establish TOUCHING BOUNDARIES so children understand they can say "no" to unwanted touch.
- Establish PRIVACY RULES in the home and away from home.
- Talk about SECRETS/TRICKS/THREATS that a perpetrator may use to keep children from telling.
- Educate children on VULNERABLE SITUATIONS, including social media and online activities.
- Educate children BEYOND "STRANGER DANGER" because approximately 90% of sexual abuse is perpetrated by someone the child knows.
- Give children PERMISSION to tell about anything happening to them.

Source: National Children's Advocacy Center. "Child Sexual Abuse." 2018. Reprinted with permission. https://www.nationalcac.org/wp-content/uploads/2018/02/CSA-Parents -Talk.pdf

Strategies from the advocacy group Stop It Now! to promote awareness of sexual abuse and recognize and respond to potential abuses are outlined in Figure 8.6.

These stages of the grooming process are used by the perpetrator to increase their odds of completing a sexual assault against a child and reduce their risk of detection, which may allow for repeated victimizations of the same child over time. Once the offender is satisfied that the child will keep a secret, or once the offender feels that they have enough lever-age to use against the child as a form of control, they will often introduce a sexual element to their interactions with their victim, such as discussing explicitly sexual things or placing their hand high on the child's thigh. This stage in the grooming process may extend over a long period of time, progressing and escalating to the first criminal sexual encounter.

In one study, researchers wrote a series of vignettes depicting various stages of the grooming process and presented them to undergraduate

Figure 8.6. Stop It Now! "Every Day Actions To Keep Kids Safe"

Here are some things that you and your family can do to protect children from sexual abuse, right now.

Set and respect clear guidelines

- Set and respect family boundaries. All members of the family have rights to privacy in dressing, bathing, sleeping and other personal activities. If anyone does not respect these rights, an adult should clearly enforce the family rules.
- Demonstrate boundaries by showing in your own life how to say "no." Teach your children that their "no" will be respected, whether it's in playing or tickling or hugging and kissing. For instance, if your child does not want to give Grandma a kiss, let the child shake hands instead. And make sure, too, that Grandma understands why a child's ability to say "no" is important for the safety of the child.
- Use the proper names of body parts. Just as you teach your children that a nose is a nose, they need to know what to call their genitals. This knowledge gives children the correct language for understanding their bodies, for asking questions and for telling about any behavior that could lead to sexual abuse.
- Be clear with adults and children about the difference between "okay touch" and inappropriate touch. For younger children, teach more concrete rules such as "talk with me if anyone—family, friend or anyone else—touches your private parts." Also teach kids that it is unacceptable to use manipulation or control to touch someone else's body.
- Explain the difference between a secret and a surprise. Both the adults and children in your life need to know how secrets may make kids unsafe. Surprises are joyful and generate excitement in anticipation of being revealed after a short period of time. Secrets exclude others, often because the information will create upset or anger. When keeping secrets with just one person becomes routine, children are more vulnerable to abuse.

Watch out for signs

- Watch for any inappropriate behaviors in other adults or older youth because children, especially young ones, are not as able to recognize these behaviors or to protect themselves.
- Stay on top of your children's use of technology—Internet, email, instant messaging, webcam use, peer-to-peer/social networking sites, and cell phones, including photo exchanges. The illusion of anonymity on these electronic mediums often leads to a breakdown of social rules and expectations, ones that would be assumed if the interactions were face-to-face. Whenever possible, make sure the child's interactions are visible and public. Kids, and even adults, can easily stumble into inappropriate or even dangerous situations and exchanges.

Figure 8.6. (Continued)

Speak up

- Practice talking before there's a problem. Say the "difficult" or "embarrassing" words out loud so that you become more comfortable using those words, asking those questions, and confronting those behaviors. Having stress-free conversations about difficult issues with both the adults and children in your life gets everyone in the habit of talking openly and honestly. Show those people in your life that you will listen to anything they have to say, even if it's about something embarrassing or something they've done wrong.
- Speak up when you see, or are subject to, any inappropriate behaviors. Interrupt and talk with the person who is making you uncomfortable. If you feel you can't do this, find someone who is in a position to intervene. The person behaving inappropriately might need help to stop these behaviors.
- Report anything you know or suspect might be sexual abuse. If nobody speaks up, the abuse will not stop.

Support your kids

- Make it clear that you will support your children when they request privacy or say "no" to an activity or a kind of touch that makes them uncomfortable.
- Talk to your kids about who you/they trust. Give your kids permission to talk to these trustworthy adults whenever they feel scared, uncomfortable or confused about someone's behavior toward them.

Be prepared

- Create a clear and easy-to-follow Family Safety Plan. Make sure that as adults, you know how to challenge each other when you see any inappropriate behaviors.
- Create a list noting both who to talk to when you see behavior you are unsure about and who to call if you believe you need to report sexual abuse. Teach the children about what to do and who to talk with if they are sexually threatened or touched by someone.
- Make a list of people and organizations you can call for advice, information, and help. You can be a resource to your family and friends about how to report abuse and how to get help for everyone involved. If you know that a child has been sexually abused, be sure to get help for the child quickly, so the harm can be stopped and healed.

Source: Stop It Now! 2020. Reprinted with permission. https://www.stopitnow.org/ohc -content/everyday-actions-to-keep-kids-safe

research participants. The researchers "hypothesized that the sexual grooming stages involving gaining access and physical touch would be more easily recognized than the stages of victim selection and trust development. Overall, the results revealed that participants were unable to recognize sexual grooming behaviors for any of the stages of grooming" (Winters & Jeglic, 2017, p. 729).

By design, the grooming process is subtle and if it is executed well by the offender it can be turned back on the victim if they are accused of inappropriate behavior (e.g., "You took my expensive gift/hours of attention/ hug and kiss to mean that I wanted to hurt you? What is the matter with you that you would interpret my kind and loving actions in that way?"). In this type of "gaslighting," the child is made to feel paranoid or crazy or ashamed of their instincts and feelings.

Because they so often rely on grooming, sexual crimes committed against children are less likely to involve physical violence or intoxicants than sexual crimes committed against teenage and young adult victims. In these older age groups, the offender often selects a victim based on opportunity rather than a carefully plotted grooming process that pivots on building trust over the course of weeks or months. It is common for assailants of adolescents and adults to use actual or threatened physical force to complete the assault, or to facilitate the assault by plying the intended victim with drugs or alcohol.

A 2019 statewide study of cases reported to law enforcement in Massachusetts and in which a sexual assault forensic exam was collected looked for differences among victims of four age groups: children (11 or younger), younger adolescents (below the age of consent; aged 12–15), older adolescents (above the age of consent; aged 16–17), and adults (18 or older). Consistent with findings of other work, there were significantly more male victims in the child group (31 percent of child victims were male) compared to the older age groups. Compared to the other age groups, child victims were at significantly lower risk of having a nongenital injury (Cross & Schmitt, 2019). Lower rates of physical injury among young children are consistent with prior literature and may be explained by the fact that children more often experience nonpenetrative assaults (i.e., fondling, molestation) that result in less tissue damage. Another factor may be that, due to delayed disclosure, children are often examined after a longer period has elapsed since the assault (Smith, Raman, Madigan, Waldman, & Shouldice, 2018). The Massachusetts study found that no cases involving child victims were labeled as "unfounded" (see discussion in Q13), a significant difference when compared to cases involving victims of other age groups. Finally, the researchers documented a significant increase in the likelihood of an arrest being made when the victim was younger than the age of consent compared to older than the age of consent: "We found significant differences by victim age in the results of forensic medical examination and in law enforcement action, but greater similarity between adolescent and adult cases than might have been anticipated. Both younger and older adolescents may be at higher risk of experiencing physical violence during sexual assault than has been previously recognized" (Cross & Schmitt, 2019, p. 109).

To summarize, there are important differences in the risk and experience of sexual assault based on age. The risk of victimization based on age is modified by gender, such that men are at greater risk as young children whereas women are at highest risk in the teens and early adult years. Regardless of gender, children and young teens who are sexually assaulted are more likely to have experienced grooming prior to that assault, a phenomenon that is not generally discussed with regard to assaults against older adolescents or adults.

FURTHER READING

Bennett, Natalie, and William O'Donohue. "The construct of grooming in child sexual abuse: Conceptual and measurement issues." *Journal of Child Sexual Abuse* 23, no. 8 (2014): 957–976.

Cross, Theodore P., and Thaddeus Schmitt. "Forensic medical results and law enforcement actions following sexual assault: a comparison of child, adolescent and adult cases." *Child Abuse & Neglect* 93 (2019): 103–110.

Lanning, Kenneth. "The evolution of grooming: Concept and term." *Journal of Interpersonal Violence* 33, no. 1 (2018): 5–16.

Planty, Michael, Lynn Langton, Christopher Krebs, Marcus Berzofsky, and Hope Smiley-McDonald. *Female Victims of Sexual Violence, 1994–2010.* U.S. Department of Justice, Office of Justice Programs, Bureau of Justice Statistics, 2013.

Smith, Sharon G., Xinjian Zhang, Kathleen C. Basile, Melissa T. Merrick, Jing Wang, Marcie-jo Kresnow, and Jieru Chen. *The National Intimate Partner and Sexual Violence Survey (NISVS): 2015 Data Brief—Updated Release.* National Center for Injury Prevention and Control, Centers for Disease Control and Prevention, 2018.

Smith, Tanya D., Sudha R. Raman, Sheri Madigan, Judy Waldman, and Michelle Shouldice. "Anogenital findings in 3569 pediatric examinations for sexual abuse/assault." *Journal of Pediatric and Adolescent Gynecology* 31, no. 2 (2018): 79–83.

Snyder, Howard N. *Sexual Assault of Young Children as Reported to Law Enforcement: Victim, Incident, and Offender Characteristics: A Statistical Report Using Data from the National Incident-Based Reporting System.* U.S. Department of Justice, Office of Justice Programs, Bureau of Justice Statistics, 2000.

Tjaden, Patricia G., and Nancy Thoennes. *Extent, Nature, and Consequences of Rape Victimization: Findings from the National Violence Against Women Survey.* U.S. Department of Justice, Office of Justice Programs, National Institute of Justice, 2006.

Winters, Georgia M., and Elizabeth L. Jeglic. "Stages of sexual grooming: Recognizing potentially predatory behaviors of child molesters." *Deviant Behavior* 38, no. 6 (2017): 724–733.

Q9. IS THE RISK OF SEXUAL ASSAULT VICTIMIZATION GREATER FOR PEOPLE WITH CERTAIN SEXUAL ORIENTATIONS OR GENDER IDENTITIES?

Answer: Yes. Members of the lesbian, gay, bisexual, transgender, and queer (LGBTQ) community are at higher risk of sexual assault than their heterosexual and cisgender counterparts. Samples of undergraduates and community-based samples had suggested this trend for years, but the first major national study of sexual assault victimization that accounted for sexual orientation, the National Intimate Partner and Sexual Violence Survey (NISVS) conducted by the Centers for Disease Control in 2010, confirmed these findings (Walters, Chen, & Brieding, 2011). Bisexual and transgender individuals are at particularly high risk of sexual assault victimization. Furthermore, members of the LGBTQ community face additional barriers to reporting their assaults and obtaining victim support services after an assault.

The Facts: As the phenomenon of sexual violence rose to an issue of public concern in the 1970s and 1980s, it was framed, discussed, and responded to as a crime of violence perpetrated by (presumably heterosexual) men against (presumably heterosexual) women. While this is certainly the most common dynamic, it is not the only dynamic of sexual assault. In the 1990s, research began to focus on the experiences of men as victims of sexual assault (Davies, Pollard, & Archer, 2006). However, research on the phenomenon of sexual assault against members of the LGBTQ community has more recently gained attention in the academic literature. A review of all 71 published studies on sexual violence against members of the gay, lesbian, or bisexual communities between the years of 1989 and 2009 demonstrated that the risk of experiencing a sexual assault was higher among these groups than within the heterosexual community (Rothman, Exner, & Baughman, 2011).

Many of these studies focused specifically on childhood sexual abuse, but among the studies that focused on adult sexual assault, gay or bisexual males and lesbian or bisexual females reported high rates of these experiences. Specifically, the samples used in these studies resulted estimates ranging from 10.8 percent to 44.7 percent of gay or bisexual males reporting a sexual assault, with a median of 14.7 percent. The numbers were higher for samples of lesbian and bisexual women, ranging from 11.3 percent to 53.2 percent, with a median of 23.2 percent. Expanding the analysis to include all experiences of lifetime sexual assault (i.e., those that occurred in childhood or in adulthood), the rates among these groups again demonstrated a high prevalence. Across the review of 71 studies, the estimate of lifetime history of experiencing sexual assault among gay or bisexual males was a median of 30.4 percent (range: 11.8–54.0 percent) and among lesbian or bisexual females, the median was 43.4 percent (range: 15.6–85.0 percent). In other words, Rothman and colleagues' (2011) analysis of prior studies suggest that 3 out of every 10 gay or bisexual men and 4 out of every 10 lesbian or bisexual women experience a sexual assault in their lifetime. These findings led the authors to conclude that "the currently available literature suggests that (gay, lesbian, and bisexual) people are likely at elevated risk for lifetime sexual violence victimization" (Rothman et al., 2011, p. 9).

As the first major review of its kind, this widely cited and important study led to further research on the experience of sexual assault within the LGBTQ community. However, there are two important limitations of this work that should be noted. First, this study combined the experiences of bisexual victims with gay or lesbian victims, respectively. This methodological choice reflected the studies being reviewed, because some of the original studies combined these groups, but there may be differences in the prevalence of sexual assault among these sexual orientations that are masked by combining responses across them. Second, although there was substantial variation in the locations and communities included in this review, they did not provide nationally representative estimates, thus limiting the generalizability of the findings.

The first nationally representative study of the prevalence of sexual violence that provided estimates of lifetime sexual assault experience by sexual orientation was a report from the NISVS, published in 2011 (Walters et al., 2011). Moreover, these findings supported prior literature suggesting that sexual minorities are at an increased risk of sexual assault. However, they also revealed an important difference based on sexual orientation, visible once the bisexual respondents were treated as a unique category rather than being combined with either gay or lesbian respondents. Bisexual women reported higher rates of rape in their lifetime (46.1 percent) than did either lesbian (13.1 percent) or heterosexual women (17.4 percent). Bisexual women also reported strikingly high lifetime rates (74.9 percent) of other forms of sexual violence (such as nonpenetrative acts or coerced acts) compared to lesbian (46.4 percent) or heterosexual (43.3 percent) women. Among male respondents, the rate of experiencing sexual violence (other than rape, which was experienced by too few male participants to provide reliable estimates) was significantly higher among bisexual (47.4 percent) and gay (40.2 percent) men compared to heterosexual (20.8 percent) men. These findings (Walters et al., 2011), consistent with prior work (Rothman et al., 2011), clearly demonstrate that individuals who identified as bisexual or gay were at greater risk of being sexually assaulted. While researchers have not reached a definite consensus about why these two groups are at particularly high risk, some explanations have been offered. One potential explanation is that some offenders are motivated by hate or homophobia and use sexual assault as a way to assert dominance, instill shame or fear, or punish the victim (Javaid, 2018). Qualitative research reveals concerns that the bisexual community is hypersexualized and objectified (Schulze, Koon-Magnin, & Bryan, 2019). It is possible that labeling a group as promiscuous leads some offenders to erroneously assume that their targets will automatically consent to their sexual advances. Regardless of the precise reasons, these differences across groups that fall within the LGBTQ umbrella also underscore the need to address sexual assault experiences separately across sexual orientations rather than lumping people into broad categories like heterosexual and non-heterosexual.

At present, there are no nationally representative estimates of the prevalence of sexual assault victimization against members of the transgender community. A 2009 discussion of researchers' ability to measure sexual violence against the transgender community noted, "Despite the growing anecdotal knowledge that violence is a significant problem in the transgender community, data about this issue are not readily available. There are currently three possible sources for information about the violence and harassment that transgender people experience: I. Self-report surveys," "II. Hotline calls and social service reports," and "III. Police reports" (Stotzer, 2009, p. 171). Although all three of these sources of data have substantial limitations, taken together, they can help provide a clearer picture of the prevalence of crime against members of the transgender community. Specifically,

> When combining all three forms of violence reporting it becomes clear that among transgender people, known others are physically and sexually assaulting transgender people at high rates, and strangers are physically and sexually assaulting transgender people, but also harassing them and causing other types of violence and abuse. These acts of violence are not single incidents, but happen across a lifetime, and often a single individual experiences multiple acts of violence or intolerance on a daily basis. (Stotzer, 2009, p. 177)

A major self-report survey effort known as the National Trans Survey suggests that the rate of sexual victimization in this population is high (James et al., 2016). Almost half of all respondents (47 percent) to that survey reported experiencing a sexual assault in their lifetime, with 10 percent of respondents reporting such an experience in the past year. The likelihood of experiencing a sexual assault in one's lifetime was even more pronounced among transgender people of color, with particularly high rates reported by Native American (71 percent), Middle Eastern (67 percent), and multiracial (58 percent) respondents. While the sexual assaults reported here were most likely to be committed by a known perpetrator (e.g., acquaintance, intimate partner), 30 percent of respondents reported a sexual assault perpetrated by a stranger (James, 2016).

Although not nationally representative, the findings of the National Trans Survey are in line with findings from a major literature review of the prevalence of sexual assault crimes against trans individuals (McKay, Lindquist, & Misra, 2019). This review included 102 studies spanning 20 years, and the findings generally suggest that the trans community is at a disproportionately high risk of sexual assault victimization as well as a variety of other forms of assault and harassment (McKay et al., 2019). Although there are methodological challenges for researchers who seek to quantify the occurrence of sexual assault against the trans community, a growing body of data suggest that this community is at an increased risk of sexual assault compared to the cisgender community (Langenderfer-Magruder, Walls, Kattari, Whitfield, & Ramos, 2016).

After researchers established the disproportionately high likelihood of sexual assault in the LGBTQ community, a line of scholarship emerged to attempt to better understand and respond to this group of survivors. A theoretical review by psychologists argued that,

> Thus far, prevention, treatment, and risk reduction interventions in the area of sexual violence have focused almost exclusively on male perpetrators and female victims. Although this may serve the needs of the majority, such approaches to sexual violence may overlook and minimize the clinical needs of the minority. Available research suggests that male victims and GLBT victims face less public and provider understanding of issues related to sexual violence that is not male to female, more barriers to care, fewer available treatment resources, and less advocacy. (Turchik et al., 2016, p. 143)

A key barrier to members of the LGBTQ community reporting their sexual assault is the erroneous belief held by many people that sexual assault is a crime that happens to only women and is perpetrated by only men (Schulze, Koon-Magnin, & Bryan, 2019). This incorrect, although widely held, belief (see also Q7) is discussed at length in a 2019 book featuring qualitative interviews with 15 members of the LGBTQ community who disclosed being victims of sexual assault to the researchers. Only two victims brought their assaults to the attention of law enforcement: "Of the two participants who did speak to law enforcement, only one did so by choice. The other was identified by another victim of the same offender and contacted by a detective. Both of these participants received negative reactions from law enforcement and felt judged, shamed, or worse off after the report" (Schulze et al., 2019, p. 84). A shared theme among these participants was the sentiment that reporting to law enforcement would not yield any positive outcome. In the words of one participant:

> I have had female friends who have been assaulted and who have gone to the police and tried to report it, and had the police tell them, "That's not enough evidence for us to prove that anything happened." And so when I had my experience I was like, "Well what are they going to say if I go to them?" Especially since we have talked about before with it being female on female how are they going to perceive that? What are they going to consider to be assault, or not assault? If my friends who were raped by penetrative sex couldn't hold their attackers accountable for their actions then and I didn't feel like I really had the chance to. I figured that it would be more of a headache to go through that than anything else so I just never did anything about it. (Schulze et al., 2019, p. 83)

This quote hits on key elements of the LGBTQ experience. First, it addresses the concern that if sexual assault is not well-handled in most cases (see Q13) even among the most privileged groups of victims, individuals from marginalized communities will almost certainly feel uncomfortable coming forward. Second, it reflects great concern among victims whose cases do not fit the most common sexual assault scenario (i.e., male perpetrator, female victim) that their assaults will not be taken seriously or believed. This would introduce the possibility of secondary victimization (Q16) and increase the risk of further trauma to the survivor. Third, this quote closes with a reference to the "headache" that reporting an assault to law enforcement would entail. For victims to cooperate as their case moves through the criminal justice system is a major emotional commitment that can stretch across years. Because this participant did not expect that her offender would be held accountable for the assault in the end, she did not think it would be a worthwhile investment of her emotional resources.

Another theme that emerged from participant interviews was LGBTQ discomfort with accessing support services designed for victims of sexual assault. Unless a medical clinic, counseling center, or other agency specifically advertised that it was LGBTQ-friendly, participants assumed it would not welcome them (Schulze et al., 2019). These results were consistent with findings reported in a qualitative survey a decade earlier (Todahl, Linville, Bustin, Wheeler, & Gau, 2009). Researchers in Canada surveyed representatives from the healthcare industry and community organizations within the region to gauge interest in and feasibility of developing a network of providers to help break down barriers to access among the trans community (Du Mont, Hemalal, Kosa, Cameron, & Macdonald, 2020). Three specific barriers to service provision were noted, consistent with prior literature: poor knowledge base among potential service providers, insufficient resources, and lack of access. Respondents also identified barriers to developing a network of inclusive services, including lack of interest among some providers in developing trans-friendly services as well as inadequate training, staff, and other resources. However, responses from these service providers indicated that focusing on trans advocates within the community along with providing a safe space for representatives from various organizations to meet, collaborate, and support each other, could work to overcome some of these barriers and promote a more inclusive response to trans victims of sexual assault. Members of the LGBTQ community are at an increased risk of having experienced various forms of trauma (James, 2016; McKay et al., 2019) regardless of sexual violence history. Thus, there is an emphasis on protection from further trauma, which can easily be introduced by insensitive medical professionals, mental health providers, or advocates. As a result, unless the provider is trusted and known to provide culturally competent care, members of the LGBTQ community are less likely than their heterosexual and cisgender counterparts to make use of whatever services are offered.

When LGBTQ victims do decide to come forward with an experience of sexual assault, they sometimes find a lack of services available to assist with their particular needs. For example, if a male victim were to enter a medical clinic or hospital to have a sexual assault forensic exam (Q15) only to be told that they have to go to a women's center because that is where such services are housed, that extra barrier to treatment could increase the likelihood that the victim decides to not get the exam. Or if a woman who was assaulted by a female perpetrator decided to attend a group counseling session and all references to the perpetrator were to a male, that therapy session may lead the victim to feel further marginalized. These examples illustrate the types of concerns that led one study to conclude that "adopting a gender inclusive framework and using theory to guide future research and clinical intervention are important pieces of the complex puzzle needed in ongoing efforts to eliminate sexual violence against both men and women" (Turchik, Hebenstreit, & Judson, 2016, p. 143). In short, there are significant and substantial differences in sexual assault victimization by both sexual orientation and gender identity.

FURTHER READING

Davies, Michelle, Paul Pollard, and John Archer. "Effects of perpetrator gender and victim sexuality on blame toward male victims of sexual assault." *Journal of Social Psychology* 146, no. 3 (2006): 275–291.

Du Mont, Janice, Shilini Hemalal, Sarah D. Kosa, Lee Cameron, and Sheila Macdonald. "The promise of an intersectoral network in enhancing the response to transgender survivors of sexual assault." *PLoS One* 15, no. 11 (2020): e0241563.

James, Sandy, Jody Herman, Susan Rankin, Mara Keisling, Lisa Mottet, and Ma'ayan Anafi. *The Report of the 2015 US Transgender Survey.* National Center for Transgender Equality, 2016.

Javaid, Aliraza. "'The penis is a weapon of power': a feminist and hate crime interpretation of male sexual victimisation." *NORMA* 13, no. 1 (2018): 23–40.

Langenderfer-Magruder, Lisa, N. Eugene Walls, Shanna K. Kattari, Darren L. Whitfield, and Daniel Ramos. "Sexual victimization and subsequent police reporting by gender identity among lesbian, gay, bisexual, transgender, and queer adults." *Violence and Victims* 31, no. 2 (2016): 320–331.

McKay, Tasseli, Christine H. Lindquist, and Shilpi Misra. "Understanding (and acting on) 20 years of research on violence and LGBTQ+ communities." *Trauma, Violence, & Abuse* 20, no. 5 (2019): 665–678.

Rothman, Emily F., Deinera Exner, and Allyson L. Baughman. "The prevalence of sexual assault against people who identify as gay, lesbian, or bisexual in the United States: A systematic review." *Trauma, Violence, & Abuse* 12, no. 2 (2011): 55–66.

Schulze, Corina, Sarah Koon-Magnin, and Valerie Bryan. *Gender Identity, Sexual Orientation, and Sexual Assault: Challenging the Myths.* Lynne Rienner Publishers, 2019.

Stotzer, Rebecca L. "Violence against transgender people: A review of United States data." *Aggression and Violent Behavior* 14, no. 3 (2009): 170–179.

Todahl, Jeffrey L., Deanna Linville, Amy Bustin, Jenna Wheeler, and Jeff
    Gau. "Sexual assault support services and community systems: Under-
    standing critical issues and needs in the LGBTQ community." *Violence
    against Women* 15, no. 8 (2009): 952–976.
Turchik, Jessica A., Claire L. Hebenstreit, and Stephanie S. Judson. "An
    examination of the gender inclusiveness of current theories of sexual
    violence in adulthood: Recognizing male victims, female perpetrators,
    and same-sex violence." *Trauma, Violence, & Abuse* 17, no. 2 (2016):
    133–148.
Walters, Mikel, Jieru Chen, and Matthew Breiding. *National Intimate Part-
    ner and Sexual Violence Survey 2010: Findings on Victimization by Sexual
    Orientation.* Center for Victim Research, 2011.

Q10. DO OTHER FACTORS IMPACT THE RISK OF SEXUAL ASSAULT VICTIMIZATION OR PERPETRATION?

Answer: Yes, but not all of the relationships are equally well understood or empirically validated at this point. There are a variety of factors that researchers believe may increase the risk of experiencing sexual assault ("risk factors") as well as a variety of factors that researchers believe may decrease the risk of experiencing sexual assault ("protective factors"). Similarly, studies have identified factors that increase or decrease the likelihood that someone will perpetuate sexual assault and other offenses against others. The mechanisms that relate these variables (e.g., history of abuse, substance abuse) to sexual victimization or perpetration are complex and still under exploration by researchers. However, there are some factors that have been studied more fully than others and those will be the focus of this discussion.

The Facts: Researchers have worked to identify and empirically investigate any characteristics or situations that increase the likelihood of sexual assault occurring; these are known as "risk factors." On the other hand, characteristics or circumstances associated with a decrease in the likelihood of sexual assault occurring are known as "protective factors." In line with the development of targeted programming to address sexual assault on college campuses, a great deal of research on identifying both risk and protective factors have focused on undergraduate populations.

For example, a 2020 study focused on sexual assault at colleges and universities discussed three types of risk factors: contextual, demographic, and behavioral (Rogers & Rogers, 2020). Contextual characteristics are those relating to the larger community, not simply the individual victim or perpetrator. Examples would include the size of the campus, whether the campus has a "party culture" promoting alcohol use, and the availability of resources for victims of sexual assault. Demographic factors are individual level characteristics like gender, race, ethnicity, age, and sexual orientation. As discussed elsewhere (Q6–Q9), demographic characteristics are associated with differential risk of sexual assault in a variety of ways. Finally, behavioral characteristics refer to any activities that a person engages in that may be associated with an increase or decrease in risk. These may include factors such as substance use, consensual sexual activities, or participation in a specific group (e.g., a sports team, a fraternity, or sorority).

The aforementioned study included more than 27,000 students at 44 institutions of higher education in the United States. Researchers considered a variety of each type of factor (contextual, demographic, and behavioral) to determine their relative impacts on the risk of sexual assault victimization. In line with prior literature, they found that, "Overall, respondents who were younger, unmarried, women, not in a relationship, and identified as non-heterosexual were significantly more likely to report experiencing sexual victimization" (Rogers & Rogers, 2020, p. 14).

Furthermore, their analyses suggest that:

Respondents who perceived "typical" students as drug users were more likely to report experiencing sexual victimization, as well as respondents who were interested in information on sexual assault prevention, and who used alcohol, marijuana, and other drugs within the last 30 days were also more likely to report sexual victimization. Finally, respondents who were in a sorority or fraternity, had lower GPAs, and who had multiple sexual partners were also more likely to report experiencing sexual victimization. (Rogers & Rogers, 2020, p. 14)

Additionally, statistical analyses indicated that behavioral characteristics had a more substantial impact on predicting sexual assault victimization than did either contextual or demographic characteristics (Rogers & Rogers, 2020). An analysis by economists looked at the frequency of sexual assaults reported among 17–24-year-olds as a function of the division 1 college football schedule. "Our results indicate that Division 1 college football games significantly increase reports of rape involving college-aged victims. The estimates are largest for rapes in which offenders are also college-aged and are unknown to the victim. The effects are also comparatively large for schools with prominent teams (those playing in Division 1A) and for prominent games (rivalry games and games against ranked teams)" (Lindo, Siminski, & Swensen, 2018, p. 261). The authors link their findings to increased alcohol use on game days, particularly on dates with high-profile games that attract even more watch parties, tailgates, and other game-related social events.

These findings are consistent with prior work that has found alcohol use to be associated with an increased risk of sexual assault, particularly among undergraduate women (McGraw, Tyler, & Simons, 2020). A potential explanation that has been offered for this relationship is that a perpetrator may target an intoxicated person as a potential victim because they view them as more vulnerable. While under the influence of drugs or alcohol, a person may be less aware of their surroundings and thus unable to identify or respond to a potential threat as quickly as usual. Furthermore, if a victim is highly intoxicated at the time of an assault, they may be less able to recall the event clearly. A perpetrator may therefore seek out intoxicated people as potential victims in hopes that they would be able to successfully complete the sexual assault and be less likely to be detected after the fact (McGraw et al., 2020). Multiple studies have also found "risky behaviors" (i.e., casual sexual encounters, multiple sexual partners) to be associated with both the experience and severity of sexual assault (McGraw et al., 2020). Specifically, these studies found that more sexual risk-taking behavior increased the risk of experiencing an assault—and of that assault being rape rather than another type of sexual violation (Turchik & Hassija, 2014).

Although the precise mechanisms remain under investigation, researchers have also demonstrated a link between experiencing sexual abuse as a child and being assaulted later in life (as an adolescent or adult) (Scoglio, Kraus, Saczynski, Jooma, & Molnar, 2021). Researchers suggest that an increased sense of self-blame associated with the childhood experience of sexual abuse may lead to an increase in substance abuse. Problems with substance abuse can, in turn, increase one's vulnerability to drug or alcohol-facilitated sexual assault (Mokma, Eshelman, & Messman-Moore, 2016). Scholars have also explored the potential impact of child sexual abuse on a victim's ability to regulate emotions (what psychologists refer to as "emotion dysregulation"). According to one study, "Given that better skills [at regulating emotions] are associated with more refusal assertiveness, improving emotion dysregulation in CSA survivors may help them also improve their self-protective abilities" (Ullman & Vasquez, 2015, p. 311). Again, the relationship between these variables requires additional exploration.

Researchers have also sought to identify experiences or characteristics that may reduce the risk of sexual assault; these are known as "protective factors." They have identified factors including social support, attachment and support from the mother, and individual religious beliefs or practices (McGraw et al., 2020). Although findings remain preliminary, researchers suggest that these protective factors may reduce exposure to risk factors such as alcohol use.

Another line of literature focuses on factors that increase the risk that an individual will engage in sexual assault or other sex-related crimes and offenses. A meta-analysis of 16 studies of undergraduates in the United States published across 17 years revealed that the effects of a variety of risk factors were consistent across multiple studies (Steele, Martin, Yakubovich, Humphreys, & Nye, 2020). Four of the included studies assessed the impact of a prior experience of sexual violence and found that, "History of sexual violence was associated with an increase of risk of sexual violence perpetration by 297%" (Steele et al., 2020, p. 11). Five studies measured the impact of being intoxicated; they demonstrated that, on average, a "one-unit increase in men's alcohol consumption was associated with 13% higher odds of perpetrating sexual violence" (Steele et al., 2020, p. 7). Other significant risk factors included holding hostile attitudes toward women and high acceptance of rape myth attitudes, both of which are positively associated with higher odds of committing a sexual assault. However, the studies used to assess the findings relating to these attitudes contained substantial variation in estimates, so the authors note that they should be interpreted cautiously. Three other factors were significant predictors of sexual assault perpetration: prior delinquency, fraternity membership, and peer approval, each across two studies (Steele et al., 2020).

In summary, sexual assault is a complex phenomenon impacted by individual, situational, and societal characteristics. While some risk factors seem to be associated with sexual assault, the exact nature and strength of the relationships remains unclear. Other risk or protective factors may have impacts on sexual assault occurrence, but further research is needed to clarify these relationships.

FURTHER READING

Lindo, Jason M., Peter Siminski, and Isaac D. Swensen. "College party culture and sexual assault." *American Economic Journal: Applied Economics* 10, no. 1 (2018): 236–65.

McGraw, Lora K., Kimberly A. Tyler, and Leslie G. Simons. "Risk factors for sexual assault of heterosexual and sexual minority college women." *Journal of Interpersonal Violence* (2020): 0886260520976224.

Mokma, Taylor R., Lee R. Eshelman, and Terri L. Messman-Moore. "Contributions of child sexual abuse, self-blame, posttraumatic stress symptoms, and alcohol use to women's risk for forcible and substance-facilitated sexual assault." *Journal of Child Sexual Abuse* 25, no. 4 (2016): 428–448.

Rogers, Sarah A., and Baker A. Rogers. "Expanding our view: demographic, behavioral, and contextual factors in college sexual victimization." *Journal of Interpersonal Violence* (2020): 0886260520905076.

Scoglio, Arielle AJ, Shane W. Kraus, Jane Saczynski, Shehzad Jooma, and Beth E. Molnar. "Systematic review of risk and protective factors for revictimization after child sexual abuse." *Trauma, Violence, & Abuse* 22, no. 1 (2021): 41–53.

Steele, Bridget, Mackenzie Martin, Alexa Yakubovich, David K. Humphreys, and Elizabeth Nye. "Risk and protective factors for men's sexual violence against women at higher education institutions: A systematic and meta-analytic review of the longitudinal evidence." *Trauma, Violence, & Abuse* (2020): 1524838020970900.

Turchik, Jessica A., and Christina M. Hassija. "Female sexual victimization among college students: Assault severity, health risk behaviors, and sexual functioning." *Journal of Interpersonal Violence* 29, no. 13 (2014): 2439–2457.

Ullman, Sarah E., and Amanda L. Vasquez. "Mediators of sexual revictimization risk in adult sexual assault victims." *Journal of Child Sexual Abuse* 24, no. 3 (2015): 300–314.

3

❖

Reporting Sexual Assault

The criminal justice system has historically failed victims of sexual assault. For decades, many acts that are now recognized as sexual assaults were legal (e.g., rape of a spouse), the onus was on the victim to prove that a rape happened (e.g., to demonstrate that they had provided strong physical resistance to the assailant), and victims were judged, blamed, and further traumatized after reporting their rapes to law enforcement. This history of interaction between law enforcement and victims of sexual assault is frequently cited as a contributing factor in the low rates of reporting of sexual assault and related offenses that we see in society today. As will be discussed in Q11 ("Do most victims report their assaults to law enforcement?"), most experts believe that only about one in every three rapes that takes place in the United States is reported to law enforcement, with the reporting rates among some demographic groups much lower.

However, if a case is reported to law enforcement, there are many potential paths it may take through the criminal justice system. It is common for statements taken right after a sexual assault to be incomplete, because victims are still dealing with the chemical effects of the hormonal release that takes place in the body during a traumatic event. As the hormones subside and the victim is able to recall the events in a more complete and chronological way, they may add additional information to their statement. Recent work on the neurobiology of trauma indicates that this is a completely normal bodily response, but a change to the victim's initial statement is sometimes interpreted as deceptive or dishonest, which will be discussed in Q12 ("Do inconsistencies in victim's statements to police mean that their claims are false or exaggerated?"). Many cases that are reported to law enforcement are never solved. The investigations may remain open but become cold. Others are labeled "unfounded," a classification with a particular meaning in law enforcement. However, this label is often misunderstood by the public and may be misused or misapplied in sexual assault cases, as will be discussed in Q13 ("If a claim of sexual assault does not result in an arrest, does that mean the assault did not happen?").

Finally, there is frequent debate within society about the rates of false reports of sexual assault. As discussed in Q14 ("Are false reports of sexual assault a common problem in the United States?"), false reports of sexual assault are quite rare. But the impact of these uncommon events can be substantial, both to the wrongly accused person and to the vast majority of victims who come forward and truthfully report their assaults to law enforcement. This chapter will also address the potential forensic evidence that may be recorded during a sexual assault forensic exam (often called a "rape kit"). While much scientific evidence may be recovered during such an exam, in most cases, they do not provide a definitive answer as to whether a sexual assault took place, as will be discussed in Q15 ("Can a sexual assault forensic exam ['rape kit'] prove whether someone was raped?").

Q11. DO MOST VICTIMS REPORT THEIR ASSAULTS TO LAW ENFORCEMENT?

Answer: No, most victims do not report their assaults to law enforcement. In fact, only about one-third of sexual assaults are reported to law enforcement. The likelihood of reporting has varied somewhat over time and differs based on the victim's demographic characteristics, including race, gender identity, and sexual orientation.

The Facts: The National Crime Victimization Survey (NCVS) contacts a nationally representative sample of the United States population directly and asks about their experiences of various crimes (see further discussion in Q2). Because it includes all offenses, not only those reported to law enforcement, it is considered a more accurate measure of sexual assault prevalence than official reports. If a survey respondent replies that they were sexually assaulted in the previous 6 months (the typical length of coverage of an NCVS interview), the interviewer will then ask a series of follow-up questions, including whether the victim reported the assault to police. Two reports of NCVS data compiled by the Bureau of Justice Statistics that show longitudinal trends in reporting among female survivors of sexual assault are discussed below.

A study of NCVS data collected across 17 years (1994–2010) demonstrated consistently low rates of reporting (Planty, Langton, Krebs, Berzofsky, Smiley-McDonald, 2013). Between 1994 and 1998, 29 percent of cases were reported to police, leaving 71 percent unreported. Between 1999 and 2004, the rate grew to 41 percent of cases reported, with 59 percent of cases unreported. However, between 2005 and 2010, the rate dropped again to 36 percent of cases reported, 64 percent of cases unreported. Notably, the frequency of the victim being the source of the report increased at each time point (50 percent in 1994–1998 data, 57 percent in 1999–2004 data, 64 percent in 2005–2010 data). If a case was brought to the attention of law enforcement by someone other than the victim, it was often another member of the person's household (e.g., a parent, sibling, spouse).

If a case was reported to the police, the NCVS interviewer followed up with a question as to why the report was made. Among those who reported, there were four primary reasons that were indicated as a reason for the report: "To improve police surveillance/duty to tell police/because it was a crime" (21–27 percent of reporting respondents across time periods), "To protect respondent and household from further crimes by the offender" (18–28 percent of reporting respondents across time periods), "To stop incident or prevent recurrence or escalation" (15–25 percent of reporting respondents across time periods), and "To catch/punish/prevent offender from reoffending" (14–20 percent of reporting respondents across time periods). The least common response across all three time periods was, "To get help or recover loss," which never exceeded 3 percent of responses. A nontrivial percentage of respondents reported an "Other/unknown/not one most important reason" for reporting (6–22 percent of reporting respondents across time periods).

If a victim disclosed during the NCVS interview that they had experienced a sexual assault but that they did not report it to the police, the interviewer followed up with a question as to why no report was made. Among those who did not report their assaults to police, there were two primary reasons: (1) a desire to treat the assault as a "Personal matter" (13–23 percent of nonreporting respondents across time periods) and (2) "Fear of reprisal" (16–20 percent of nonreporting respondents across time periods). Less common responses included: "Reported to different official" such as a teacher, healthcare worker, or social worker (8–10 percent of nonreporting respondents across time periods), a belief that "Police would not do anything to help" (6–13 percent of nonreporting respondents across time periods), "Not important enough to respondent" (7–8 percent of nonreporting respondents across time periods), and "Did not want to get offender in trouble with the law" (4–7 percent of nonreporting respondents across time periods). The two least common responses across all three time periods were, "Advised not to report," (never exceeded 1 percent of responses) and a belief that "Police could not do anything to help" (never exceeded 2 percent of responses). The largest category of responses was "Other/unknown/not one most important reason" for reporting (29–34 percent of nonreporting respondents across time periods), with nearly one-third of nonreporting respondents indicating this answer at each of the three time periods. This nationally representative data, collected across 17 years, show a consistently low rate of reporting sexual assault among women in the United States. However, studies of specific demographic groups demonstrate differences in likelihood of reporting based on individual characteristics.

A study of NCVS covering the years 1995–2013 was data limited to women between the ages of 18 and 24 and compared the experiences of sexual assault and reporting decisions of college students and noncollege students (Sinozich & Langton, 2014). The study found that college students were less likely than their similarly aged peers who were not enrolled in college to report an assault. Only 20 percent of college student respondents who had been victims of sexual assault reported it, whereas 32 percent of nonstudents in the same age group reported the crime to authorities. Among both groups, the two most common reasons for nonreporting were "Personal matter" (26 percent of students and 23 percent of nonstudents) and "Fear of reprisal" (20 percent across both groups). The analysts compared the reasons provided by students and nonstudents who did not report their assaults to the police and found several significant differences. Nonstudents were more likely than college students to indicate that, "The police would not or could not do anything to help" (19 percent of nonstudents vs. 9 percent of college students) and that they "Reported to different official" such as a teacher, healthcare worker, or social worker (14 percent of nonstudents vs. 4 percent of college students). College students were more likely than nonstudents to report that they did not report because they perceived that it was "Not important enough to respondent" (12 percent of college students vs. 5 percent of nonstudents). Approximately one-third of all participants (both students and nonstudents) indicated "Other reason" for not reporting.

Nationally representative studies typically have not recruited sufficient samples of each demographic group to make comparisons between the rates of reporting across race, gender, and sexual orientation. However, many community-level studies provide insight into these experiences and how they may differ.

A literature review of the experience of sexual assault and reporting among Black women indicates that there are several barriers to reporting that specifically impact this group (Tillman, Bryant-Davis, Smith, and Marks, 2010). These barriers include stereotypes relating to Black female sexuality that may lead to disbelief or distrust of victims' accounts (potentially introducing fear of secondary victimization), the desire of some victims to fulfill the role of a "Strong Black Woman" (Tillman et al., 2010, p. 64) who can handle adversity on her own without relying on an outside authority, and negative impressions of government institutions such as law enforcement, including beliefs that these institutions are tainted by or perpetuate systemic racism. The literature review states that:

> To date, researchers have suggested that African American sexual assault survivors are less likely to seek help from dominant society for several reasons. Notably, experiences with oppression, both intergenerational and societal trauma, require that members of the African American community protect themselves from mistreatment by establishing psychological and social boundaries that ensure problems and conflicts stay within the community thereby decreasing the exposure to risk, ridicule, and racism. (Tillman et al., 2010, p. 64)

Due to low rates of sexual assault victimization against men in many large samples, nationally representative data on the reporting experiences of male survivors of sexual assault is very limited. However, because of the strength of beliefs within society that men cannot be sexually assaulted (see Q7), many male survivors feel that there is an extra stigma attached to their experiences and thus choose not to report (Davies, 2002). They may also live in an area where no services are available to male survivors or fear that law enforcement would not be helpful to them if they did choose to report. Overall, although precise rates are difficult to obtain, the estimates of male victims' rates of reporting of sexual assault are far lower than the estimates of female victims' rates of reporting (Davies, 2002).

Unique barriers to reporting also exist within the lesbian, gay, bisexual, transgender, queer (LGBTQ) community. These barriers were explored in 2019 in a qualitative study of LGBTQ experiences of sexual violence, the disclosure and reporting process, and the societal beliefs that delegitimize these experiences (Schulze, Koon-Magnin, & Bryan, 2019). As one female participant in that study explained:

> Part of my problem is that I tend to be more masculine . . . I have short hair, I dress in boys' clothes typically, I just like bigger clothes, it's more comfortable. So when I tell people I've been assaulted, they tilt their heads because usually they would expect me to 'wear the pants', kind of a thing. I am usually the more masculine partner, but both of my partners that assaulted me tended to be more feminine. That's part of my problem, too. They look at me and they're like, 'But how? Shouldn't you be in control?' type of thing. (Schulze et al., 2019, p. 73)

Beyond the concerns cited by respondents to the NCVS surveys discussed above, an LGBTQ victim of sexual assault may also fear that their assault may not be recognized by law enforcement or that their sexual orientation or gender identity may put them at risk of being shamed or ridiculed upon making a report. As the identities discuss here intersect differently (e.g., a Black gay man's experience of reporting will likely differ from that of a White transwoman), the likelihood of reporting and the experience of reporting may change depending on a host of variables.

FURTHER READING

Davies, Michelle. "Male sexual assault victims: A selective review of the literature and implications for support services." *Aggression and Violent Behavior* 7, no. 3 (2002): 203–214.

Planty, Michael, Lynn Langton, Christopher Krebs, Marcus Berzofsky, and Hope Smiley-McDonald. *Female Victims of Sexual Violence, 1994–2010.* U.S. Department of Justice, Office of Justice Programs, Bureau of Justice Statistics, 2013.

Schulze, Corina, Sarah Koon-Magnin, and Valerie Bryan. *Gender Identity, Sexual Orientation, and Sexual Assault: Challenging the Myths.* Lynne Rienner Publishers, 2019.

Sinozich, Sofi, and Lynn Langton. *Rape and Sexual Assault among College-Age Females, 1995–2013.* Bureau of Justice Statistics, 2014.

Tillman, Shaquita, Thema Bryant-Davis, Kimberly Smith, and Alison Marks. "Shattering silence: Exploring barriers to disclosure for African American sexual assault survivors." *Trauma, Violence, & Abuse* 11, no. 2 (2010): 59–70.

Q12. DO INCONSISTENCIES IN VICTIMS' STATEMENTS TO POLICE MEAN THAT THEIR CLAIMS ARE FALSE OR EXAGGERATED?

Answer: No. If a sexual assault survivor's account of the assault changes over time, it does not necessarily indicate deception. Developments in understanding the biological impacts of trauma have provided clear scientific explanations for why people may provide an incomplete narrative of a traumatic event shortly after the event, but then provide additional (and accurate) details of the event later. These scientific explanations, which researchers may broadly refer to as, "the neurobiology of trauma," explain the recall of memories in a gradual and nonlinear fashion following a traumatic event. However, such memories may be accurately recalled (i.e., not fabricated) after at least these three conditions are met: (1) the individual is in a safe environment, (2) at least 24 to 48 hours have passed, and (3) the victim has had sufficient opportunity to rest.

The Facts: When experiencing a traumatic event, a series of uncontrollable events may take place in the body including substantial (but temporary) hormonal changes. During a traumatic threat, the HPA Axis (the hypothalamus, the pituitary gland, and the adrenals) is activated and releases a series of hormones to promote survival (Campbell, 2012). Specific examples include catecholamines (what people commonly refer to as "adrenaline") to aid in a "fight" or "flight" response, natural opioids to help manage physical pain, and oxytocin to respond to the psychological pain of the situation (Campbell, 2012). With regard to a sexual assault:

> The information that's coming into the victim's brain and body during a sexual assault is traumatic. It is threatening. It is horrifying. It is one of the most psychologically damaging forms of crime that anybody could experience. The amygdala [the organ responsible for activating the body's response in cases of potential danger] is going to recognize this as a threat to the sustainability of the organism, okay, much like an attempted murder is. The amygdala processes it at that level of severity. It is going to signal to the hypothalamus, "We have a threat to the sustainability of the organism coming in." The hypothalamus is now going to signal to the pituitary and the HPA axis is going to kick in, and there is going to be a hormonal flood in the victim's body. (Campbell, 2012)

Scientists have established that the large release of this combination of hormones is a natural response to a traumatic event. These releases seek to keep the body alive and limit the experience of pain during the trauma. However, these hormones have further temporary impacts on behavior, reasoning ability, and memory.

The presence of these hormones in the body, particularly the cate-cholamines, make it difficult for the brain to complete the processing and storing of information. If not given sufficient time for the hormones to abate, the victim will likely be unable to recall details of the event. After the body perceives that the threat to life is over and thus stops releasing such large quantities of these hormones, the body needs time for the hormones to leave its system and then for the brain to do the work of consolidating the memories. During this period, all of the elements of the memory are stored in the brain but not in a way that can be readily accessed by the victim. After a chance to rest (two sleep cycles are typically suggested, which may be completed in one long period of sleep), the victim's ability to recall the memory and discuss it in a linear way (i.e., first this happened, then this happened) is greatly enhanced (Hopper, Lonsway, & Archambault, 2020). However, many survivors of sexual assault are interviewed very shortly after the assault, when their systems are still flooded with hormones triggered by the attack on them. As a result, the details that they provide may be incomplete and may not make sense to the individual conducting the interview. For example, a victim may jump from recounting bits of conversation that took place in one location to describing a physical act that took place in a different location without explaining when or how they changed locations. This does not mean that they are creating the account, but that only certain memories are available to them at the time. As researcher Rebecca Campbell explains:

> The story may come out as fragmented or sketchy. How are law enforcement and prosecutors trained to handle something that looks fragmented and sketchy? They're trained to believe that that is something that is not truthful, and their job is to hone in on it and look at it from multiple points of views and keep cycling back on it to try to ferret out what is true and what is false. And again, they interpret this victim's behavior as evasiveness or lying. And again, what it really is, most often, is that the victim is having difficulty accessing the memories. Again, the content of the memory the research tell us very clearly is accurate. It's just going to take some time and patience for it to come together. (Campbell, 2012)

Such impacts of trauma on memory are not unique to sexual assault victims. In fact, guidelines provided by the International Association of Chiefs of Police Psychological Services Section recommend "delaying personal interviews (of law enforcement officers who witness or are involved with a shooting) from 48 to 72 hours in order to provide the officer with sufficient recovery time to help enhance recall." The bodily response to trauma has a significant impact on the processing and storage of memory, which requires time (after the traumatic event has ended) to reconcile. Once the individual has returned to a sense of safety and had sufficient rest, giving their brain a chance to do the important work of memory encoding, they should be able to better recollect the event in question. This new information may be perceived as created to try and fit the evidence, but in fact, it is information that the victim could not access during the initial interview.

A 2020 webinar for End Violence Against Women International (EVAWI) explored these issues. Rather than focusing on the impact of hormones, this webinar stated a broad view of the neurobiology of trauma, describing it as a "multidisciplinary field that draws upon scientific disciplines including anatomy, physiology, molecular biology, mathematical modeling, and psychology to understand the fundamental and emergent properties of neurons (i.e., brain cells) and neural circuitries" (Hopper, 2020a, p. 5). While recognizing that "Neurobiology helps to explain human experience, thinking, emotions, memories, and behavior in terms of brain structures and processes," the webinar emphasized that researchers and practitioners can understand a great deal of victim experience and behavior using traditional social and behavioral sciences (e.g., psychology and sociology). As social scientists have been saying for decades, people respond to trauma differently. Neurobiology has helped to demonstrate why that might be, but there are still no definitive rules as to how anyone who experiences a traumatic event (including sexual assault) "should" or "will" behave. According to clinical psychologist Jim Hopper:

> If we know common characteristics of traumatic memories, we can recognize them in victim accounts: vivid central details; vague, inconsistent, and missing peripheral details; and missing time sequencing of details—especially later in the assault, when the memory circuitry tends to go into a minimal-encoding mode. We'll know to keep listening, without bias or assumptions about whatever else the victim may disclose, with greater confidence that we're unlikely to miss or misunderstand valuable information. (Hopper, 2020a, p. 7)

This information can be used to guide the timing and nature of an inter-view (see Q24).

> So when we think about first-response care from nurses, the frenetic pace of the emergency room—slowing that down—a safe space, a little time and a little patience. We think about the first interview with the patrol officer or with the sex crimes unit detective. Slow it down. A little time, a little patience, and it will go a long way in help-ing the victim recover, and it will go a long way in terms of the inves-tigation itself. (Campbell, 2012)

Specifically, Hopper recommends that authorities "ask non-leading ques-tions about central details, which often elicit remarkable and unexpected information that may line up with other evidence and make for very com-pelling testimony. We can avoid pushing for peripheral details that may never have been encoded, or may have rapidly faded from memory, and thereby prevent inaccuracies and inconsistencies that can be weaponized later" (Hopper, 2020a, p. 8). As the victim returns to a sense of safety, their ability to recall the event improves. Furthermore, sleep can give the victim time for stress to abate and give the brain a chance to complete the encod-ing process (which in turn allows someone to recall the memory). Although it may be frustrating to the investigators and to the victim, "Just because information is stored in someone's brain, this doesn't necessarily mean it is accessible to recall. That's because stress impairs the brain's ability to retrieve memories that have been encoded and stored" (Hopper et al., 2020, p. 8).

EVAWI (see Figure 12.1 and Figure 12.2) provides recommendations for investigators of sexual assault claims based on the science outlined by Camp-bell, Hopper, and others. As the scientific literature demonstrates, and in line with the recommendations provided by EVAWI, if a victim's account of a sexual assault changes over time it does not mean that the individual was initially lying. "In short, memories can get better over time," emphasized Hopper. "And when they do, there's no scientific basis for assuming that the person's later (and more complete) memories are less reliable or credible than their earlier (and less complete) memories" (Hopper et al., 2020, p. 6).

Figure 12.1. End Violence Against Women International

We inspire and educate those who respond to gender-based violence, equipping them with the knowledge and tools they need to support victims and hold perpe-trators accountable. We promote victim-centered, multidisciplinary collabora-tion, which strengthens the response of the criminal justice system, other professionals, allies, and the general public—making communities safer.

Figure 12.1. (Continued)

We work to achieve our mission by:

- Formulating policies and best practices to guide reforms
- Hosting live and online training programs for professionals
- Providing technical assistance and expert consultation
- Developing and disseminating resource materials
- Educating policymakers, media representatives, and the public
- Conducting and translating research for practitioners
- Promoting multidisciplinary collaboration
- Partnering with organizations that share our vision

Working with professionals inside and outside the criminal justice system, we seek to improve outcomes for victims and pursue accountability for their assailants. Our goal is to protect victims, prevent future attacks, and keep our communities safe.

We envision a world where gender-based violence is unacceptable on every level—where victims receive the compassion, support and justice they deserve.

When we create a system that helps victims not only to heal, but to thrive, they will transform our world with strength, hope, and joy.

Source: End Violence Against Women International, 2021. Reprinted with permission. https://evawintl.org/about/

Figure 12.2. End Violence Against Women International Best Practice FAQs

---

Question: Based on the research, is there a recommended time frame for investigators to wait before conducting a detailed interview of a sexual assault victim? What time is needed for the victim's neurochemistry to return to a more normal state?

Answer: It can take days or weeks for a person's neurochemistry to return to normal following a traumatic experience. However, the acute phase subsides within a matter of days. Therefore, we generally recommend waiting 2 or 3 days following a sexual assault to conduct a detailed interview of the victim. Yet, these are simply the most general recommendations; the actual decision must be made on a case-by-case basis.

For example, victims are often sexually assaulted late at night. By the time the police are involved, or victims seeks medical assistance, they have often been up all night. Victims may also wait some time for officers to respond, to begin the preliminary interview, or for forensic examiners to arrive to start the medical forensic exam. By the time the process is complete, and victims finally arrive home, they are likely to be physically and emotionally exhausted. If the investigator then calls in the morning, shortly after receiving the case, the victim will have had little to no sleep.

Figure 12.2. (Continued)

Clearly, victims need some time to rest and recover after reporting and partici-pating in the preliminary interview and/or medical forensic exam. The morning after is not the appropriate time to ask them to come into the police station for a detailed follow-up interview. Yet this is often exactly what happens. Law enforce-ment has historically been trained to believe that the detailed interview must be done as quickly as possible, to gather information while it is still fresh in the mind of the victim – and to question the victim about any statements that might appear inconsistent or otherwise problematic. Given this all-too-common scenario, it really shouldn't be surprising that so many victims are unable to participate effec-tively in the detailed interview. If we push them to do the impossible, they will not be able to provide information that is as helpful as it could be – or they will fail to show up and withdraw their participation altogether.

A better approach is to provide victims time to rest and recover, and have the investigator only make an initial contact by calling the victim within 24 hours. The purpose of this initial contact is for investigators to introduce themselves and schedule the detailed interview at a time and place that is most convenient for the victim. The timeframe for this interview can be flexible. While 2-3 days following the initial report is offered as a general guideline, the actual schedule will depend on the individual victim.

The investigator can then use the intervening days to prepare for the detailed interview, by reviewing the initial reports from the preliminary investigation and the medical forensic examination, as well as any crime scene reports, evidence, and/or witness statements that were documented. The timeframe can thus be help-ful for the investigator as well as the victim – both will be better able to success-fully contribute in the detailed follow-up interview when it eventually takes place.

Source: End Violence Against Women International, 2021. Reprinted with permission. https://evawintl.org/best-practices/faqs/

FURTHER READING

Campbell, Rebecca. "The neurobiology of sexual assault: Implications for first responders in law enforcement, prosecution, and victim advocacy." In *NIJ Research for the Real World Seminar*, December 2012. https://www.ojp.gov/ncjrs/virtual-library/abstracts/neurobiology-sexual-assault-implications-first-responders-law

Hopper, J. *Important Things to Get Right, and Avoid Getting Wrong, About the "Neurobiology of Trauma." Part 1: Benefits of Understanding the Sci-ence.* End Violence Against Women International, 2020a.

Hopper, J. *Important Things to Get Right About the "Neurobiology of Trauma." Part 2: Victim Responses During Sexual Assault.* End Violence Against Women International, 2020b.

Hopper, J., K. A. Lonsway, and J. Archambault. *Important Things to Get Right About the "Neurobiology of Trauma." Part 3: Memory Processes.* End Violence Against Women International, 2020.

Spohn, Cassia, Clair White, and Katharine Tellis. "Unfounding sexual assault: Examining the decision to unfound and identifying false reports." *Law & Society Review* 48, no. 1 (2014): 161–192.

Q13. IF A CLAIM OF SEXUAL ASSAULT DOES NOT RESULT IN AN ARREST, DOES THAT MEAN THE ASSAULT DID NOT HAPPEN?

Answer: No. As with most other crimes, most reported cases of sexual assault do not result in an arrest. This does not mean that the crime did not take place.

The Facts: After a detective is assigned a case, it will likely remain an active case under investigation until some outcome is reached that leads to case closure. It is worth noting that some cases may remain open and under investigation for many years and some cases may go "cold." Cold cases may be revisited for further investigation at a future date but they are not actively assigned to a detective in the primary unit. However, most cases are ultimately concluded and labeled using a form of what law enforcement calls "clearance." The best-known form of case clearance is "cleared by arrest," in which an investigation turns up evidence that the crime took place and that a certain individual (or individuals) was responsible for that crime, leading to arrest of that individual (or those individuals). Lesser known but other important "clearance" labels are "unfounded" or "cleared by exceptional means."

According to guidance from the International Association of Chiefs of Police, a case can be labeled "unfounded" when it is determined to be either false or baseless. While these terms are sometimes used interchangeably by the general public, they have different meanings. A case is "false" if the report was a deliberate lie (see Q14). A case is "baseless" if the report was made in good faith, but an investigation reveals that no crime took place (Weiser, 2017). For example, if someone suffering from mental illness makes an assault claim based on sincerely held but false or distorted memories of events or people, their claim would be classified as baseless. The complainant may have been sincere in their belief that the assault took place, but it did not. Another example of a baseless case would be if someone woke up after attending a party, had hazy or incomplete memories from the night before, felt physically uncomfortable, and sought a sexual assault forensic exam (Q15). If the exam showed no sign of sexual activity and an investigation indicated that no sexual activity took place, the report would be labeled "baseless." Again, the individual who came forward did not deliberately lie (in which case the report would be labeled "false") but after investigation, law enforcement concluded that there was no crime to investigate.

In both scenarios just described, law enforcement would clear the case as "unfounded." However, research into when and how law enforcement officers apply the label "unfounded" to cases, thus closing them, suggests that this classification is sometimes used for claims that were neither false or baseless (Weiser, 2017).

> For example, cases are often erroneously classified as either false or unfounded because victims refused to cooperate with the investigation, alcohol was involved, the victim and suspect are known to each other and have a previous sexual relationship, the victim changes his or her account or is uncertain about details, the victim does not seem sufficiently emotional or is overly emotional, there are no signs of physical injury, or the victim did not report the assault immediately (Archambault & Lonsway, 2012; Lisak et al., 2010). Research indicates that these circumstances are common among individuals who experienced sexual assault and are not evidence of a false report (IACP, 2004a). Rather, these patterns of behaviors are indicative of individuals who have experienced trauma and are processing it in diverse ways. (Weiser, 2017, p. 48)

Notably, two studies conducted in the 2010s suggest that the label of "unfounded" is being applied less frequently than in the past (De Zutter, Horselenberg, & van Koppen, 2017) and generally in an accurate manner (Spohn, White, & Tellis, 2014). In a major study of sexual assault case processing in Los Angeles, Spohn and colleagues analyzed 81 cases that were reported to the Los Angeles Police Department (LAPD) in 2008 and ultimately labeled "unfounded." Working as independent coders, three researchers reviewed each of the 81 files to determine whether the case should be labeled false (in which case it would be appropriate to classify as unfounded), baseless (in which case it would be appropriate to unfound), not false (in which case it would be inappropriate to unfound), or whether additional information was required to reach a conclusion. The researchers' conclusions were generally consistent with the labels applied by LAPD, suggesting that this jurisdiction was correctly "unfounding" sexual assault cases. A small percentage of all cases reported to LAPD in 2008 were false (4.5 percent of the total number of reported cases, $n = 55$) and even fewer were baseless (a total of 5 cases). Researchers found that the "strongest predictor of unfounding was whether the victim recanted the allegations" (Spohn et al., 2014, p. 182). Other significant predictors that a claim might ultimately be classified as unfounded included assaults in which the attack was committed by a stranger (rather than a known assailant) and when the person making the claim suffered from a mental illness. Cases were less likely to be unfounded if the victim was injured or if there was physical evidence to inform the investigation.

Some cases do not lead to an arrest but are also not false or baseless and thus should not be labeled as unfounded. In addition to investigations that remain open, there is another method of case clearance known as "cleared by exceptional means." For a case to be cleared by exceptional means, according to guidance provided by the IACP, it must meet four criteria: (1) the offender has been identified, (2) there is sufficient evidence to arrest and charge the offender, (3) law enforcement know where the offender is, and (4) some circumstance beyond the control of law enforcement prevents an arrest from being made. The clearest example of appropriate use of this type of case closure is if the offender is deceased. The offender is known, an arrest would be supported by evidence, and law enforcement officials are aware of the offender's location (i.e., cemetery or morgue), but they cannot arrest or charge the offender.

However, research indicates that this clearance is sometimes applied in cases in which considerable ambiguity exists as to whether an arrest could reasonably be made. In an analysis of more than 23,000 reported cases of sexual assault in a large Midwestern jurisdiction from 1999 to 2014, researchers examined how case outcomes were classified (i.e., whether the case was unfounded, cleared by arrest, or cleared by exceptional means; Venema et al., 2019). The researchers found that "Older cases were more likely to be exceptionally cleared . . . Regarding incident characteristics, those without victim injury had higher odds of exceptional clearance. Those with a witness, and those involving an acquaintance or former/current romantic partner, had higher odds of exceptional clearance." Another study found that this form of clearance was being overused by the LAPD and that it was common for detectives to apply an exceptional clearance when the case did not fit definition of these types of cases (Spohn and Tellis, 2013). As the authors explain:

> The use—or misuse—of the exceptional clearance when a suspect is arrested but the DA refuses to file charges is based on an

LAPD policy stating that a case can be cleared by arrest only if felony charges are filed . . . The fact that the LAPD clears a case by arrest only if felony charges are filed by the DA means that—practically speaking—their arrest practices are based upon a prosecutorial standard of proof beyond a reasonable doubt, rather than the police standard of probably cause. (Spohn & Tellis, 2013, p. 178)

They continue by explaining,

In short, if the agency has an identified suspect and probable cause to make an arrest, the agency should clear the case by arrest as it is within their control to arrest, charge, and turn the suspect over to the DA for prosecution. To do otherwise is not only counter to the FBI's guidelines, but it becomes an avenue through which to prematurely dispose of the nonstranger sexual assault cases, which are the most common type of sexual assault and require specialized investigation to overcome the consent defense. (Spohn & Tellis, 2013, p. 179)

Moreover, there appears to be significant variation across jurisdictions in terms of when cases are closed and how they are labeled (Lonsway & Archambault, 2012). Because statistics are often presented in aggregate form (i.e., not separately by what type of closure was applied), they may indicate that many more sexual assault cases are solved and ultimately lead to arrest than is actually the case. The FBI's Uniform Crime Reports, for example, list cases simply as, "cleared." Lay readers may interpret this to mean an arrest was made (i.e., "cleared by arrest") when in fact a substantial number of these cases were "cleared by exceptional means" (Walfield, 2015). Not only does this mean that no arrest was made, but critics assert that this label is often overused to close cases that could be investigated further (Spohn & Tellis, 2014; Walfield, 2016; Walfield, McCormack & Clarke, 2020). The trend in applying this type of clearance too broadly varies significantly by jurisdiction; many jurisdictions reserve the use of an exceptional clearance for truly exceptional circumstances whereas others apply the label much more loosely and widely. Scott Walfield, a leading scholar on this issue, has advocated for presenting data separately by type of clearance and promoting more accurate use of the label "cleared by exceptional means," perhaps through additional training or oversight.

FURTHER READING

De Zutter, A. W. E. A., Robert Horselenberg, and Peter J. van Koppen. "The prevalence of false allegations of rape in the United States from 2006–2010." *Journal of Forensic Psychology* 2, no. 2 (2017): 1–5.

Lonsway, Kimberly A., and Joanne Archambault. "The 'justice gap' for sexual assault cases: Future directions for research and reform." *Violence against Women* 18, no. 2 (2012): 145–168.

Spohn, Cassia, and Katharine Tellis. *Policing and Prosecuting Sexual Assault: Inside the Criminal Justice System.* Lynne Rienner Publishers, 2013.

Spohn, Cassia, Clair White, and Katharine Tellis. "Unfounding sexual assault: Examining the decision to unfound and identifying false reports." *Law & Society Review* 48, no. 1 (2014): 161–192.

Venema, Rachel M., Katherine Lorenz, and Nicole Sweda. "Unfounded, cleared, or cleared by exceptional means: Sexual assault case outcomes from 1999 to 2014." *Journal of Interpersonal Violence* (2019): 0886260519876718.

Walfield, Scott M. "When a cleared rape is not cleared: A multilevel study of arrest and exceptional clearance." *Journal of Interpersonal Violence* 31, no. 9 (2016): 1767–1792.

Walfield, Scott M., Philip D. McCormack, and Kaitlyn Clarke. "Understanding case outcomes for male victims of forcible sexual assaults." *Journal of Interpersonal Violence* (2020): 0886260520967154.

Weiser, Dana A. "Confronting myths about sexual assault: A feminist analysis of the false report literature." *Family Relations* 66, no. 1 (2017): 46–60.

Q14. ARE FALSE REPORTS OF SEXUAL ASSAULT A COMMON PROBLEM IN THE UNITED STATES?

Answer: No. Many people believe that false reports of sexual assault are very common. However, public perceptions of the frequency of false reports are generally inflated toward a much higher rate of occurrence than rigorous studies show. Of course, even one false report is too many, with potentially life-altering consequences for the individual who is wrongly accused. Although only a very small percentage of reported claims are actually false, the perception that accusations of sexual assault are often erroneous, exaggerated, or outright lies is problematic for victims who fear that they will be disbelieved when coming forward with truthful accounts of traumatic assaults.

The Facts: According to the International Association of Chiefs of Police:

> The determination that a report of sexual assault is false can be made only if the evidence establishes that no crime was committed or attempted. *This determination can be made only after a thorough investigation.* This should not be confused with an investigation that fails to prove a sexual assault occurred. In that case the investigation would be labeled unsubstantiated. *The determination that a report is false must be supported by evidence that the assault did not happen . . .*

As was the case with other labels that may be applied to criminal cases (see Q13), the "false" label is not always accurately applied. The term "false" report should only be applied to cases in which there was an intentional lie, whereas a good faith report that turns out to be inaccurate should be classified as "baseless" (Weiser, 2017). If a victim recants their initial statement, this is not, on its own, sufficient cause to label a case "false." Many victims who recant initial statements do so after being threatened or out of fear of retaliation by the perpetrator (Spohn, White, & Tellis, 2014). It is also not sufficient cause to label a case "false" because a victim decides not to participate in the criminal justice process or because a prosecutor declines to file charges. Either of these situations may ultimately lead law enforcement to decide to close the case—but they are not required to do so.

Although published work suggests that there is substantial variation in the rate of false reports of rape and other forms of sexual assault, those studies that are methodologically strong present a fairly small range of estimates (O'Donohue, 2019; Lisak, Gardinier, Nicksa, & Cote, 2010). Furthermore, even in studies in which the scientific methods are questionable (for example, a frequently cited 1994 study by Kanin), *most* reports of sexual assault were determined to be truthful reports. The studies outlined below include only those that scholars have identified as methodologically rigorous and thus more likely to produce valid results.

In a meta-analysis of seven studies that measured false reports of rape (four conducted in the United States, one in Canada, one in the United Kingdom, and one in Australia), researchers presented a common definition utilized by researchers attempting to study false reporting. "In its simplest terms, most who choose to define a false allegation (also referred to as a false accusation or report) refer to it as an allegation made to police, either directly or through a third party, which the complainant knows to be untrue" (Ferguson & Malouff, 2016, p. 1186).

These authors pointed out an important methodological limitation of some prior research efforts that chose to rely on the labels law enforcement assigned to the case. This approach is problematic because law enforcement can make mistakes and their labels may be applied incorrectly or inappropriately across cases (Ferguson & Malouff, 2016; Lisak et al., 2010). A preferred approach is for researchers to study the case files directly to make a determination as to whether the case was in fact a false report. All studies included in the meta-analysis utilized this preferred approach.

Overall, across the seven studies included in the meta-analysis, approximately 5 percent of all cases reported to police were false (Ferguson & Malouff, 2016). This percentage is consistent with another study that found a 5 percent rate of false reports in five years of U.S. sexual assault data (De Zutter, Horselenberg, & van Koppen, 2017). Other studies that aim to identify the rate of false reporting and meet the standards of methodological rigor outlined by scholars tend to cluster around this estimate, with percentages ranging from 2.1 percent to 10.9 percent (Lisak et al., 2010). Conversely, this means that 90 percent or more of reported sexual assault are truthful reports (O'Donohue, 2019). And as discussed in Q11, these cases reported to the police represent only a fraction of the total number of assaults actually taking place, because the majority are not reported to law enforcement.

Scholars emphasize that generally truthful accounts may still contain inaccurate or incomplete information. For example, incomplete information may be provided as the result of trauma (see Q12). People who are not aware of the impacts of trauma on memory may interpret omissions from the initial statement as dishonesty indicating deception. Inaccurate information in the form of intentional omissions or misstatements may also occur in instances in which the victim is embarrassed or fears being judged or disbelieved. When omissions or misstatements do occur, they often revolve around the victim's drinking or drug use prior to the assault, or interactions with the assailant following the assault (e.g., they got a ride home from the offender after the assault or texted with them the next day) that the victim fears will lead to judgment, blame, or doubt. These fears are the result of victim blaming, a common occurrence in which people implicitly or explicitly suggest that the victim's behaviors prompted or led to the assault, taking culpability away from the perpetrator and instead placing it on the victim. They may also indicate a general sense of embarrassment surrounding sexuality, because some victims have difficulty acknowledging or describing the specific details of the assault. To be clear, though, researchers believe that the vast majority of reported sexual assaults (approximately 95 percent) are truthful.

Researchers who seek to better understand false reports have identified several factors that may lead an individual to lie to the police about the occurrence of a sexual assault. In a review of 30 cases of crimes against adults (not exclusively sex crimes) that were "confirmed false allegation cases" that had been referred to the FBI's National Center for the Analysis of Violent Crime (NCAVC), the most common motive for making a false accusation was to gain attention. The review found that half of false sexual assault claims could be ascribed to this motivation (McNamara, McDonald, & Lawrence, 2012). The work of criminology professor Eryn O'Neal has focused specifically on police perceptions of why someone may falsely report a sexual assault. In a review of 55 cases of sexual assault that were reported to LAPD and ultimately determined to be false, five distinct motivations emerged (O'Neal, Spohn, Tellis, & White, 2014). A report may have been motivated by more than one factor, but the five most common motivations included: (1) to gain attention or sympathy from others (23 of 55 cases), (2) to give the individual an alibi for their whereabouts or otherwise avoid getting into trouble (22 of 55 cases), (3) the presence of a mental illness (18 of 55 cases), (4) to seek revenge against a target of anger (13 of 55 cases), and (5) out of guilt (7 of 55 cases).

The motivations identified in O'Neal's empirical work were consistent with prior theorizing on why someone may falsely report a crime (Engle & Donohue, 2012). In a study focused particularly on sexual assaults against adolescent victims, law enforcement perceived false reports to be an important and significant problem (O'Neal & Hayes, 2020). More specifically, 73 percent of respondents in a survey of Los Angeles Police Department (LAPD) sex crimes detectives reported that teenagers lie about sexual assault, most commonly for "self-serving reasons" such as "to excuse age-inappropriate behavior" (O'Neal & Hayes, 2020, p. 34). These perceptions and attitudes can be sensed by victims who report to police and are received with skepticism, because qualitative interviews with adolescent victims of sexual assault indicated that some teenagers feel distrusted and blamed by law enforcement (Greeson, Campbell, & Fehler-Cabral, 2016).

A 2021 study discussed three levels of influence on how law enforcement respond to cases: (1) societal influences (e.g., prevalence of rape myths throughout society), (2) institutional influences (e.g., department culture and expectations communicated by leadership and other agencies), and (3) individual influences (e.g., personal attitudes about rape, victims, women) (Dewald & Lorenz, 2021). If these influences lead a detective to assume that a victim is being dishonest, it may create a cycle in which victims sense that they are being disbelieved and therefore withdraw. This withdrawal is sometimes perceived by the detective as evidence that the individual is uncooperative or perhaps even engaging in deception. A vicious cycle of escalating mistrust of motives can then take hold between the victim and the investigator, causing the victim to further withdraw from participation with the investigation (Dewald & Lorenz, 2021).

Understanding drivers of false reports of sexual assault is a vital task because "unfortunately, false reports wreak havoc on the innocent people involved, and often losses to their reputation, livelihood, and mental health are not recoverable even when the falsity of the claim is uncovered" (Ferguson & Malouff, 2016, p. 1192). At the same time, however, it has been pointed out that "the greater concern exhibited for perpetrators' ruined reputations than for a sexual assault victim's well-being and trauma helps explain the paranoia surrounding false allegations" (Weiser, 2017, p. 47).

FURTHER READING

Dewald, Stacy, and Katherine Lorenz. "Lying about sexual assault: a qualitative study of detective perspectives on false reporting." *Policing and Society* (2021): 1–21.

De Zutter, A. W. E. A., Robert Horselenberg, and Peter J. van Koppen. "The prevalence of false allegations of rape in the United States from 2006–2010." *Journal of Forensic Psychology* 2, no. 2 (2017): 1–5.

Engle, Jessica, and William O'Donohue. "Pathways to false allegations of sexual assault." *Journal of Forensic Psychology Practice* 12, no. 2 (2012): 97–123.

Ferguson, Claire E., and John M. Malouff. "Assessing police classifications of sexual assault reports: A meta-analysis of false reporting rates." *Archives of Sexual Behavior* 45, no. 5 (2016): 1185–1193.

Greeson, Megan R., Rebecca Campbell, and Giannina Fehler-Cabral. "'Nobody deserves this': Adolescent sexual assault victims' perceptions of disbelief and victim blame from police." *Journal of Community Psychology* 44, no. 1 (2016): 90–110.

Kanin, Eugene J. "False rape allegations." *Archives of Sexual Behavior* 23, no. 1 (1994): 81–92.

Lisak, David, Lori Gardinier, Sarah C. Nicksa, and Ashley M. Cote. "False allegations of sexual assault: An analysis of ten years of reported cases." *Violence against women* 16, no. 12 (2010): 1318–1334.

McNamara, James J., Sean McDonald, and Jennifer M. Lawrence. "Characteristics of false allegation adult crimes." *Journal of Forensic Sciences* 57, no. 3 (2012): 643–646.

O'Donohue, William T. "Understanding False Allegations of Sexual Assault." In *Handbook of Sexual Assault and Sexual Assault Prevention*, pp. 537–549. Springer, 2019.

O'Neal, Eryn Nicole, Cassia Spohn, Katharine Tellis, and Clair White. "The truth behind the lies: The complex motivations for false allegations of sexual assault." *Women & Criminal Justice* 24, no. 4 (2014): 324–340.

O'Neal, Eryn Nicole, and Brittany E. Hayes. "'Most [false reports] involve teens': Officer attitudes toward teenage sexual assault complainants—A qualitative analysis." *Violence against Women* 26, no. 1 (2020): 24–45.

Spohn, Cassia, Clair White, and Katharine Tellis. "Unfounding sexual assault: Examining the decision to unfound and identifying false reports." *Law & Society Review* 48, no. 1 (2014): 161–192.

Weiser, Dana A. "Confronting myths about sexual assault: A feminist analysis of the false report literature." *Family Relations* 66, no. 1 (2017): 46–60.

Q15. CAN A SEXUAL ASSAULT FORENSIC EXAM ("RAPE KIT") PROVE WHETHER SOMEONE WAS RAPED?

Answer: No. Generally speaking, a sexual assault medical forensic examination, commonly known as a "rape kit" exam or sexual assault kit (SAK), cannot definitively determine whether an assault took place. This physical examination is completed by a medical professional and documents all injuries to the victim, collects any evidence left on or inside of the victim's body, on the victim's clothing, in their hair, blood, etc. Some findings may be strongly suggestive of sexual assault, such as bruising, evidence consistent with the victim being restrained or beaten, or evidence of a tranquilizer found in the victim's blood or urine. However, there are many assaults in which no drugs are detected in the victim's system and in which no significant physical injury is documented. These findings (or lack of findings) do not indicate that an assault did not take place, however. Since a sexual assault can be completed without leaving clear evidence, a rape kit exam cannot prove whether an assault took place.

The Facts: The Office on Violence Against Women provides specific recommendations for conducting a thorough and victim-centered sexual assault medical forensic examination with guidelines that can be applied by city, county, state, and tribal authorities throughout the country (Office on Violence Against Women, 2013). In 2017, the Office of Justice Programs published, "National Best Practices for Sexual Assault Kits: A Multidisciplinary Approach" with additional recommendations representing a variety of perspectives and considerations. While different jurisdictions have their own procedures for what evidence should be collected, where it should be sent, and when it should be forensically tested, the steps outlined below, summarizing the national protocols, are typically included in a thorough exam.

It is common for a victim to come to a medical facility on their own (or with a friend), but they may also be brought by a law enforcement officer, arrive in an ambulance, or be escorted by a rape crisis advocate. Upon arrival at the emergency room or other medical facility, the victim is to be prioritized among emergency cases and brought to a private room to wait for the exam to be conducted. Sometimes, there are pressing medical issues that must be addressed before the exam takes place (if the victim has been stabbed and requires treatment for the wound, for example), but once any acute medical needs have been accounted for, the medical professional conducting the forensic exam will take over. It is preferable to have a sexual assault nurse examiner (SANE) conduct the exam, but this is not always possible due to lack of availability in some areas (see Q32 for more information on SANEs). It is also recommended that a rape crisis advocate be present during the exam, but again, this is not possible in all locations.

Once all relevant parties are present in the exam room, the medical professional will ask for a medical history and a narrative account of the assault to guide the exam. This is a crucial step because it provides important information about the patient (e.g., do they have a latex allergy?) as well as the potential evidence that may have been left during an assault. For example, if the victim reports that the offender bit her shoulder, the medical professional will likely swab that location for DNA evidence. Without the sharing of this detail during a narrative account, that potential evidence might otherwise be missed, since the shoulder may not be considered a typical point of contact during a sexual assault. According to the Office on Violence against Women,

> An accurate but brief description is crucial to detecting, collecting, and analyzing physical evidence. The description should include any:
>
> - Penetration of genitalia (e.g., vulva, hymen, and/or vagina of female patient), however slight, including what was used for penetration (e.g., finger, penis, or other object);
>
> - Penetration of the anal opening, however slight;

- Oral contact with genitals (of patients by suspects or of suspects by patients);

- Other contact with genitals (of patients by suspects or of suspects by patients);

- Oral contact with the anus (of patients by suspects or of suspects by patients);

- Nongenital act(s) (e.g., licking, kissing, suction injury, strangulation, and biting); Other act(s) including use of objects;

- If known, whether ejaculation occurred and location(s) of ejaculation (e.g., mouth, vagina, genitals, anus/rectum, body surface, on clothing, on bedding, or other); and

- Use of contraception or lubricants.

These questions require specific and sometimes detailed answers and can feel invasive to victims. Some may be especially difficult for patients to answer. Examiners should explain that these questions are asked during every sexual assault medical forensic exam. They should also explain why each question is being asked. (Office on Violence Against Women, 2013, p. 89)

After all necessary documents are collected and history questions answered, the physical exam begins. This exam should follow a checklist, often provided by the state in which the exam is taking place (see, for example, the detailed guidelines provided by the state of Massachusetts at https://www.mass.gov/doc/adultadolescent-kit-forms-0/download). Note that every step in the examination is conducted only if the victim consents to it. A victim may decide to skip any portion of the exam and cannot be forced to undergo any steps or procedures.

All bodily injuries should be documented in photographs as well as in the examiner's notes and forms. The victim's clothes are collected, including any items that may have been in contact with the assailant such as jewelry or hair bands. The body is then subject to a thorough external search in which any foreign objects are collected (e.g., if the assault was outdoors, there may be grass or leaves in the victim's hair). If the assailant left a hair on the victim, it should be collected during this process as well. The examiner will swab any bodily location with which that the assailant had contact potential DNA. If there is any blood present, it should be swabbed and collected. The victim's mouth will be swabbed, their hair (facial, head, and pubic) combed, and the underside of their fingernails scraped in case any DNA or other trace evidence can be found. Some jurisdictions also require reference samples of pubic hair that are collected from the victim by plucking to include an intact hair follicle. Items collected from the victim (e.g., their DNA, hair samples) are stored with kit.

Once the external exam is complete, an internal exam is completed. This is the most invasive portion of the exam and will include both a physical examination and photographic documentation using a special camera that can be inserted into the vagina or anus to capture photographs of tears to the tissue. The narrative account of the assault guides this portion of the exam (e.g., if there was no anal penetration, an anal exam may not be conducted). The examiner will visually examine the genital area for evidence of trauma and swab the area to collect any DNA that may have been left by the assailant. An internal swab may also be taken from the vagina or anus, depending on the victim's gender and account of events. A blood sample may also be drawn from the victim.

If the assault involved (or is suspected to have involved) drugs or alcohol as a means to incapacitate the victim, samples of blood and urine should be sent to a toxicologist for analysis. Because the victim likely will not know their assailant's medical history, the exam typically includes an offer of medications to minimize the risk of the victim acquiring a sexually transmitted infection. The risk of pregnancy following the assault is also typically addressed with female victims. With regard to both STI-contraction and pregnancy, the examiner may make referrals for follow-up appointments, medications, or tests with other medical professionals. At discharge, the examiner is also encouraged to provide information on any rape crisis advocacy services available to the victim, as well as any other services that might be helpful to them in recovering from the assault.

The steps outlined in this protocol written by a federal office may not be followed exactly in each jurisdiction (they are recommendations) and any step(s) may be omitted, if the victim does not wish to consent to that step. Massachusetts has a very detailed description of what evidence is collected (see Table 16.1).

The national protocol recommends developing a "coordinated team approach" that recognizes the roles of all relevant parties in responding to sexual assault and encourages cooperation and collaboration between these parties. The key stakeholders may differ from community to community, but they typically include law enforcement and rape crisis advocates, in addition to the medical professionals (see discussion of Sexual Assault Response Teams in Q31).

Table 16.1. Steps in the Commonwealth of Massachusetts' Executive Office of Public Safety Protocol, "Sexual Assault Evidence Collection Instructions"

Step 1	Consent form and reports
Step 2	Control swabs
Step 3	Toxicology testing
Step 4	Known blood sample
Step 5	Head hair combings
Step 6	Oral swabs and smears
Step 7	Fingernail scrapings
Step 8	Foreign material collection
Step 9	Clothing
Step 10	Bite marks
Step 11	Additional swabs
Step 12	Pubic hair combings
Step 13	External genital swabs
Step 14	Perianal swabs
Step 15	Vaginal swabs and smears
Step 16	Anorectal swabs and smears
Step 17	Completion forms

Source: Commonwealth of Massachusetts Executive Office of Public Safety, Sexual Assault Evidence Collection Kit Instructions, https://www.mass.gov/doc/adultadolescent -kit-forms-0/download

A key emphasis of these protocols is to provide victim-centered care, always prioritizing the needs and desires of the victim. This includes keeping the victim informed during each step of the examination as to what is being done, why it is being done, and providing them an opportunity to consent or decline to consent to every individual portion of the exam. Victim-centered care also takes into account any circumstances that may impact the victim's experience, such as fear of shaming, retribution, or discrimination, and requires providing a culturally competent response (e.g., gender identity, sexual orientation, disability status, active duty military status, as they may fear discrimination or retribution). Finally, the physical safety, privacy, and confidentiality of a victim are to be prioritized at all times during and after the exam. The protocol also includes information regarding the specific facilities and equipment that are necessary to conduct a forensic exam, the training and skills necessary for an individual to conduct the exam, and how to safely collect and store evidence to maintain its integrity.

While the evidence collected during these exams can be immensely valuable to investigators in some cases, rape kits cannot always prove whether someone was raped. First, oftentimes, no DNA is recovered. Perhaps the perpetrator (if male) did not ejaculate or wore a condom. Perhaps the victim showered or otherwise washed away the evidence before coming in for an exam. Even when DNA is recovered, it only establishes that sexual activity took place. It does not address the more central question relevant to sexual assault, which is whether the victim consented to that sexual activity. Such cases are commonly referred to in the media as, "He said/ she said" cases. In other words, there is evidence that sex took place but one party says it was an assault and the other party says that it was a consensual sexual encounter. The rape kit may provide insights on whether an encounter was consensual or forced, but it is not definitive. For example, as discussed in Q18, most sexual assaults do not result in serious physical injury. Thus, there may be no physical evidence of trauma. Even if external bruises or internal tears are present, a defense attorney may argue (and a jury may believe) that they originated from consensual rough sex.

If there is evidence that the victim was drugged, that also supports the conclusion that the sexual encounter was nonconsensual. However, a defense attorney may argue that the victim knowingly ingested the drug for recreational purposes and that it was not used to facilitate a sexual assault.

To summarize, a rape kit exam can provide a great deal of information if it is conducted in a reasonable period following the assault and by a trained medical professional. Rape kit exams can be conducted up to 120 hours after an assault, but the sooner it is conducted, the greater likelihood of recovering evidence. However, this evidence can usually only be used to support the charges of sexual assault, not to definitively prove that one took place.

FURTHER READING

National Institute of Justice (NIJ), U.S. Department of Justice, Office of Justice Programs, and United States of America. *National Best Practices for Sexual Assault Kits: A Multidisciplinary Approach.* NIJ, 2017.

Office on Violence Against Women. *National Protocol for Sexual Assault Medical Forensic Examinations: Adults/Adolescents.* OVW, 2013.

4

❖❖❖

The Impact of Sexual Assault on Victims

The mental, emotional, physical, and social impacts of sexual assault on victims is the focus of this chapter. Q16 addresses, "Is someone who is sexually assaulted likely to suffer negative mental health consequences?" and Q18 addresses, "Are most victims of sexual assault physically injured?" Researchers have found that for most victims, the psychological toll of sexual assault is far more common, severe, and long-lasting than physical injury (although of course there are some cases of sexual assault that result in serious or lifelong physical injuries). The negative health consequences that a survivor experiences following a sexual assault can be exacerbated if they are judged, blamed, and disregarded by others. This topic is discussed fully in Q17 ("Does the reaction that someone receives following a disclosure of sexual assault impact the recovery process?") These individual experiences—the occurrence of psychological injury, physical injury, and disclosure of a sexual assault—are important for understanding the impact of a sexual assault on an individual. However, there are also more macrolevel considerations.

On a broader scale, the persistence of rape myths (e.g., relating to believability or seriousness of the assault, perpetrator culpability) and the ubiquity of victim blaming (e.g., the assault was the victims' "fault" for being out late, drinking alcohol) in the United States have substantial impacts on survivors. These two issues are discussed in Q19 ("Is victim blaming a problem in the United States?") and Q20 ("Do rape myths impact sexual assault survivors?"). The chapter closes by considering the impact of the Me Too movement that gained national recognition in 2017 and increased public discourse on sexual assault victimization significantly. Although the full impact of Me Too remains to be seen over time, Q21 discusses preliminary findings to the question, "Has the Me Too movement had an effect on sexual assault survivors?"

Q16. IS SOMEONE WHO IS SEXUALLY ASSAULTED LIKELY TO SUFFER NEGATIVE MENTAL HEALTH CONSEQUENCES?

Answer: Yes. There is an abundance of data establishing the link between experiencing sexual assault and a variety of negative mental health consequences including depression, anxiety, substance abuse, self-harm, and suicidality. This relationship is robust across different samples, measurement techniques, and demographic groups. Furthermore, recent research on the impact of trauma over the life course demonstrates that sexual assault survivors are likely to experience a variety of psychological harms even years following the assault. A more extensive discussion of the relationship between sexual assault and negative mental health consequences follows.

The Facts: As sexual assault became an issue of public concern in the 1970s, research quickly arose to assess the relationship between such traumatic events and the psychological suffering of victims. A major review and meta-analysis that included studies published across 44 years (between 1970 and 2014) demonstrated a clear link between sexual assault victimization and mental health suffering (Dworkin, Menon, Bystrynski, & Allen, 2017). The authors found that sexual assault "was associated with increased risk for all forms of psychopathology assessed, and relatively stronger associations were observed for posttraumatic stress and suicidality" (Dworkin et al., 2017, p. 65).

These relationships were present across a variety of demographic groups and the magnitude of the effects were considerable, suggesting that the risk of experiencing negative mental health consequences was significantly and substantially higher among sexual assault survivors compared to individuals who had not experienced a sexual assault. Across studies, this meta-analysis found that being the target of a sexual assault increased the likelihood of posttraumatic stress disorder (PTSD), suicidal ideation (thoughts about killing oneself), suicide attempts, bipolar disorder, and obsessive-compulsive disorder. Although all traumatic events can increase the risk of experiencing negative mental health outcomes such as PTSD, "these results also suggest that [sexual assault] has a stronger association with psychopathology than other forms of trauma" (Dworkin et al., 2017, p. 77). The effects were especially large in sexual assaults committed by strangers (rather than known assailants) or assaults that involved a weapon or physical injury to the victim. This meta-analysis is important because it includes so many studies across more than four decades and addresses key limitations in prior literature on this issue (i.e., using different definitions of sexual assault). However, the authors acknowledge that sexual assault is a complex crime and that the personal responses to the experience, including later mental health consequences, can differ based on many factors (Dworkin et al., 2017).

A separate meta-analysis of studies of sexual assault and mental health functioning revealed significant differences in lifetime experience of multiple forms of mental health disorders based on the experience of sexual assault (Dworkin, 2020). Specifically:

> Nearly every study included found a higher prevalence for mental disorders among people who had been sexually assaulted than in people who had not been assaulted. Significantly higher risk associated with SA was identified for all anxiety disorders (except for specific phobia and lifetime agoraphobia), all depressive disorders, lifetime bulimia nervosa, OCD, PTSD, and all substance use disorders. Among people who have been sexually assaulted, depressive disorders and PTSD appear to be particularly common. About one third of people exposed to SA evidenced lifetime (36%) or past-year (26%) PTSD, more than one third evidenced lifetime depressive disorders (39%), and almost a quarter evidenced past year depressive disorders (24%). (Dworkin, 2020, p. 1018)

An earlier and highly impactful review of the mental health consequences of sexual assault was "An Ecological Model of the Impact of Sexual Assault on Women's Mental Health" (Campbell, Dworkin, & Cabral, 2009). This work took a broad view of the issue by utilizing an ecological approach, which takes into account how the various levels of personal and social influences can impact the way people experience certain events. With regard to sexual assault, these authors identify the following levels of influence: individual-level, microsystem, meso-exosystem, macrosystem, and chronosystem. Each of these levels is explained below, with examples of factors at each level that impact the risk of suffering mental health consequences from a sexual health.

Individual-level factors that may impact the relationship between sexual assault and mental health may relate to the specific victim or to characteristics of the assault. For example, if someone who has struggled with depression throughout their life is sexually assaulted, they are more likely to experience additional mental health consequences to a greater extent than another victim who has no preexisting mental health conditions (Campbell et al., 2009). This is an example of a victim-level characteristic. An example of an assault-level characteristic that impacts the likelihood of mental health suffering is whether the victim's life was threatened during the assault through the use of a weapon or physical violence. When assaults involve threat to life, the risk of negative mental health consequences is exacerbated (Campbell et al., 2009).

A microsystem refers to an individual's close personal relationships, such as friends, family members, and romantic partners. As discussed elsewhere (Q17), the disclosure experience has a significant impact on an individual's recovery following a sexual assault. If an individual perceives their close personal network (i.e., members of their microsystem) as generally unsupportive of sexual assault victims, they may feel silenced and thus not disclose their experience. If they do disclose an assault to a friend or family member and receive a harmful response (e.g., doubt, blame), it increases the risk of negative mental health consequences for that individual (Dworkin, Brill, & Ullman, 2019).

A level further removed from the close contacts that make up an individual's microsystem are the individuals and institutions that comprise the meso/exosystem. In cases of sexual assault, likely contacts at this level would include sexual assault nurse examiners, victim advocates, law enforcement officers, or prosecutors. These individuals and institutions may reflect community norms and values, but they are not members of the victim's intimate personal community of friends or family. Members of the meso/exosystem often play important gatekeeper roles that require the victim to interact with them prior to accessing services for victims of sexual assault. If an individual lives in a community in which there is no strong meso/exosystem (such as advocacy or counseling) available to respond to victims of sexual assault, this lack of adequate support may increase their risk of negative mental health consequences. Notably, prior research indicates that contact with a formal source of support (e.g., law enforcement or others within the meso/exosystem level) increases the risk of experiencing secondary victimization (Filipas & Ullman, 2001). "Secondary victimization" refers to the additional trauma experienced by sexual assault survivors who are treated poorly by others. Being judged, blamed, or subjected to anger and other negative emotions can leave the survivor feeling further victimized by the assault. This level of the ecological model is a current focus of research initiatives on the impact of providing a trauma-informed response (see Q33), but is certainly both complex for victims to navigate and impactful for their ultimate healing and recovery (Campbell et al., 2009; Rich, 2019).

The broadest level of social influence, the macrosystem, includes societal influences and cultural practices that impact victim recovery. For example, if victim blaming rape myths are prevalent within a society, that may increase the psychological suffering of sexual assault survivors who internalize these beliefs. If a culture has established a code of silence surrounding sexual assault, it increases the likelihood that the victim keeps the assault secret and does not report to police or seek help services. The final level, chronosystem, takes into account the impact of repeat victimization over the course of one's life. For example, if two victims were assaulted at the age of 21, but one of them had been assaulted as a child and the other had not, the victim with a prior sexual assault history would likely suffer more substantial mental health problems following the assault than the victim with no prior sexual assault history (Campbell et al., 2009). The impact of repeat victimization is an example of a chronosystem-level effect.

Finally, the authors argue that "self-blame" is a meta-construct that impacts all levels of the ecological model. That is, an individual who experiences self-blame is more likely to experience negative mental health consequences. If they are also blamed by their micro or mesosystems, the experience of self-blame is enhanced, as is the resultant risk of negative mental health outcomes. Victim-blaming societies (i.e., macrolevel) enhance the risk of victims experiencing self-blame, thereby increasing their risk of mental health suffering. Finally, research has shown that victims who experience more than one assault in their lifetime experience higher levels of self-blame, thus also impacting the chronosystem (Campbell et al., 2009).

One occurrence that has been reported as a source of self-blame, shame, and confusion among some survivors of sexual assault is being frozen during the attack; not fighting back or attempting to run away. Support for the belief that all victims should physically fight against their assailant is so strong that it was once a part of the law. Known as a "resistance requirement," victims would need to prove that they had earnestly demonstrated their lack of consent by attempting to escape from or fight back against the perpetrator. While such a requirement has been removed from modern laws governing sexual assault, many people still believe that victims should always physically resist sexual assault. When a survivor froze during an assault and did not fight back against their assailant it was, for some survivors, a potential source of shame. They could not understand why they had not fought back or attempted to flee the situation, which left them confused and in a state of self-blame. However, researchers in the neurobiology of trauma (see Q12) have identified and explained a phenomenon known as "tonic immobility." This term refers to a temporary state of complete paralysis brought on by extreme fear. A person who perceives that their life is being threatened, as may be the case during a sexual assault, may react by entering a state of shutdown in which the body is unable to move and the reasoning center of the brain is temporarily unavailable. In a state of tonic immobility, a victim cannot process the fact that there are people nearby and they could be heard if they screamed out. Even if they were able to process that set of information, they would be unable to scream due to the state of paralysis. Importantly, tonic immobility is an unconscious, involuntary response. In other words, people may not be able to choose whether they will, "fight, flight, or freeze"—the body may choose for them. As awareness of tonic immobility has increased, some survivors have expressed relief that they now understand why they reacted the way they did during the assault. Tonic immobility is an involuntary reaction that impacts many people during violent, traumatic experiences and is no cause for shame. Recognizing the complexity of the experience of sexual assault and the social reactions to it is a critical step in understanding how this type of trauma can lead to the experience of multiple negative mental health consequences.

FURTHER READING

Campbell, Rebecca, Emily Dworkin, and Giannina Cabral. "An ecological model of the impact of sexual assault on women's mental health." *Trauma, Violence, & Abuse* 10, no. 3 (2009): 225–246.

Dworkin, Emily R. "Risk for mental disorders associated with sexual assault: A meta-analysis." *Trauma, Violence, & Abuse* 21, no. 5 (2020): 1011–1028.

Dworkin, Emily R., Charlotte D. Brill, and Sarah E. Ullman. "Social reactions to disclosure of interpersonal violence and psychopathology: A systematic review and meta-analysis." *Clinical Psychology Review* 72 (2019): 101750.

Dworkin, Emily R., Suvarna V. Menon, Jonathan Bystrynski, and Nicole E. Allen. "Sexual assault victimization and psychopathology: A review and meta-analysis." *Clinical Psychology Review* 56 (2017): 65–81.

Filipas, Henrietta H., and Sarah E. Ullman. "Social reactions to sexual assault victims from various support sources." *Violence and Victims* 16, no. 6 (2001): 673.

Rich, Karen. "Trauma-informed police responses to rape victims." *Journal of Aggression, Maltreatment & Trauma* 28, no. 4 (2019): 463–480.

Q17. DOES THE REACTION THAT SOMEONE RECEIVES FOLLOWING A DISCLOSURE OF SEXUAL ASSAULT IMPACT THE RECOVERY PROCESS?

Answer: Absolutely. When a victim tells another person that they have been sexually assaulted, the nature of that interaction is critical to the survivor's mental health outcomes, their help-seeking behavior, and ultimately to the individual's healing process. If a victim receives positive social reactions such as support, compassion, and belief, it often makes it easier for them to tell other people about the assault and seek help from medical professionals or counseling services. However, a negative reaction like disbelief, blame, or judgment decreases the likelihood that the victim will disclose their assault again or seek help services. This latter phenomenon is known as "silencing." Furthermore, silencing increases the risk of negative mental health outcomes, including self-blame, depression, and anxiety (Dworkin, Brill, & Ullman, 2019).

The Facts: "Disclosure" refers to a personal interaction in which a survivor of sexual assault tells someone, typically a trusted friend or family member, that they have experienced a sexual assault. The response received during this single interaction is vital to the healing process of the victim. Perhaps the best-known scholar in the area of sexual assault disclosure is Sarah Ullman, creator of the Social Reactions Questionnaire (SRQ), a survey instrument that measures the types of responses that an individual may receive after they disclose an assault (Ullman, 2000). Analysis of this instrument revealed seven types of reactions that an individual may receive following a sexual assault: victim blame, treat differently, take control, egocentric, distraction, emotional support/belief, and tangible aid/information support. Five of these types of reactions (victim blame, treat differently, take control, egocentric, and distraction) are considered negative reactions. Examples of each type of negative social reaction, why these reactions may be harmful to victims, and the frequency with which victims of sexual assault experience these reactions are discussed below.

A response can contribute to *victim blame* if it sends the message that the victim was at fault for the assault. Sample items from this factor in the SRQ include, "Told you that you were irresponsible or not cautious enough" or "Told you that you could have done more to prevent this experience from occurring." These statements both imply that the victim contributed to their own assault, which sends the message that they should feel guilty or ashamed about the event. Such statements also ignore the culpability of the assailant, the person who is ultimately responsible for the sexual assault. Victim blaming reactions are quite common during a disclosure of a sexual assault, and is anticipated if the victim discloses to a formal source of social support such as law enforcement or health professionals (Filipas & Ullman, 2001; Griffin, Wentz, & Meinert, 2021). Blaming a victim is sometimes categorized as a "turning against" social reaction because it introduces a sense of judgment and separation between the individual making and the individual receiving the disclosure. While not directly measured on the SRQ, a victim may feel that they are being blamed if they are asked questions like, "Why were you out that late?" "How much did you drink?" Or, "What were you wearing?" All of these questions suggest that the victim made choices that make their rape acceptable or justifiable in some way and can lead to a variety of negative consequences (see Q19 for more on victim blaming).

If, following a disclosure, a friend or family member begins to treat the victim differently, it is considered a negative and potentially harmful reaction. *Treat differently* examples in the SRQ include "Avoided talking to you or spending time with you," and "Acted as if you were damaged goods or somehow different now." This type of withdrawal sends the victim a message that they are less worthy of care, friendship, and attention because they have been sexually assaulted. Treating a victim differently is another form of a "turning against" social reaction because of the emotional (or perhaps physical) distance it creates between the victim and the individual to whom they are disclosing their assault experience. In addition to harming the individual's relationship with the person who is now treating them in a more cold and distant way, victims who are treated differently often feel an increased sense of shame and greater reluctance to confide in others about their experience. "Silencing" refers to keeping a sexual assault private out of fear of being blamed, disbelieved, or otherwise diminished for an extended period of time—typically years, but potentially forever (Ahrens, 2006).

Though often employed by well-intentioned friends or family members, another form of negative social reaction is *take control*. The SRQ measures take control with items such as "Made decisions or did things for you" and "Told others about your experience without your permission." Following the traumatic experience of enduring a sexual assault, it is important for the survivor to have the opportunity to reassert control over their own body and experience and make decisions for themselves. These decisions include whether to undergo a sexual assault forensic exam, whether to report to law enforcement, and when and to whom they disclose the sexual assault. If a loved one receives a disclosure and immediately starts telling the victim what they "need" to do or starts calling other friends or family members to share the story, the victim continues to feel a lack of control over their own circumstances. Importantly, if the victim asks for a ride to the hospital, invites another to join them while making a report to law enforcement, or requests that they inform a third party about the assault (e.g., an undergraduate who has been assaulted asks a friend to go and tell the resident advisor), those actions completed on behalf of the survivor are instances of providing tangible aid/support, not of taking control. Rather, take control behaviors are completed without the victim's input and may send the message that the victim cannot make decisions for themselves. Victims may interpret such interventions as implying that they are irresponsible or incapable of taking care of themselves. This behavior, even if well-meaning, is classified as "unsupportive acknowledgment" of the assault. It recognizes that the victim has experienced something traumatic but it does not ultimately help them to recover, heal, or move forward. As with the other negative reactions, a controlling reaction can enhance the likelihood that the victim experiences further trauma and decrease the likelihood of help-seeking.

Another negative reaction frequently encountered in disclosures to friends or family members are *egocentric* reactions. These reactions may stem from deep love for the victim, but if they are not controlled, they can increase the emotional pain and pressure that the victim is already feeling. Items measuring egocentric reactions on the SRQ include, "Expressed so much anger at the perpetrator that you had to calm him/her down" and "Has been so upset that he/she needed reassurance from you."

Disclosing a sexual assault is an emotional experience for a survivor. If disclosure is made shortly after the assault, the victim may still be processing their own emotions and is likely seeking support. If the individual receiving the disclosure reacts in an egocentric fashion with an excessively emotional reaction, the victim may be forced to spend their limited emotional resources on calming the other person down, rather than attending to their own emotional needs. The person receiving the disclosure may be extremely upset, but if their sadness or anger or some combination thereof forces a refocus of attention from the victim's needs to calming the person who is receiving the disclosure, that reaction becomes a burden to the victim, and is classified as a negative reaction. A qualitative study of disclosure among LGBTQ victims of sexual assault showed that some victims of sexual assault decided not to disclose (i.e., were silenced) because they did not want to upset a loved one by disclosing the assault (Schulze, Koon-Magnin, & Bryan, 2019). This theme was also present in Ahrens' 2006 study of rape victims who reported being silenced. Egocentric reactions are examples of "unsupportive acknowledgment" because they focus on the needs of the person receiving the disclosure rather than the victim who is reaching out for support.

A final type of negative reaction is called *distraction*. This can take a variety of forms, including advising victims to keep their assault a secret, thus enhancing the sense of shame surrounding the sexual assault. However, it may also take more apparently benign forms, such as encouraging victims to put the experience behind them and focus on the future or urging them to distract themselves with family or work or hobbies. These two latter forms of distraction are often employed by well-intentioned loved ones who sincerely think that a distraction will help the victim "move on" from the assault and feel better. However, this can send the message to the victim that they are overreacting or that the assault was not that big of a deal. This can lead the victim to feel confused, question their experience, and decide not to seek help-services. Because of its minimizing effect, distraction is a form of "unsupportive acknowledgment."

There are two types of reactions to news of a sexual assault that are considered positive social reactions: emotional support/belief and tangible aid/ information support. *Emotional support/belief* is any type of reaction that comforts, reassures, or validates the victim. A few sample items from the SRQ that demonstrate emotional support/belief include, "Showed understanding of your experience," "Comforted you by telling you it would it would be all right or by holding you," and "Listened to your feelings." These types of reactions can communicate to the victim that they are loved and respected, that their experience was clearly traumatic, and that the individual receiving the disclosure is there for them during this difficult time. Knowing that they do not have to deal with their traumatic situation alone and that there is someone who will support them may serve as a protective factor against victims experiencing depression, anxiety, and self-blame. It also does not decrease the risk of help-seeking, as a negative reaction likely would.

A final positive social reaction identified by Ullman is *tangible aid/ information support*, such as helping victims secure medical care, legal assistance, or counseling. If the individual who learns about an assault makes clear to the victim that they are there to help them locate and make use of whatever services they would like to seek, that person is providing tangible aid/information support. If the individual offers to accompany and be a moral support to the victim during the process, they are also providing emotional support/belief. These positive reactions may help promote a path toward healing by validating the victim, assuring them that they will have support moving forward, and encouraging them to make use of relevant resources that are available for them.

It should be noted that most survivors who disclose a sexual assault do not experience just one of these types of reactions. The survivor may experience multiple types of reactions in a single disclosure experience. For example, a romantic partner may express an egocentric reaction by threatening to harm the perpetrator, engage in victim blaming by asking how the victim let this happen, and take control by making decisions for the victim and saying they can never tell anyone else about the assault. Or the survivor may confront different types of reactions from the different individuals to whom they disclose their experience. For example, a trusted friend may provide only emotional support/belief, a rape crisis advocate may provide emotional support/belief as well as tangible aid/information support, and an investigator might behave in a way that makes the victim feel that they are being blamed for the incident.

The type of reaction received by a victim is extremely impactful with regard to their future healing. Dozens of scientific studies have demonstrated that negative reactions lead to harmful outcomes for the victim, most notably a meta-analysis on the impact of social reactions on mental health outcomes (Dworkin et al., 2019). This analysis of 51 studies revealed that if a victim feels controlled, like they are treated differently, or that the person they have disclosed to is attempting to distract them, it can increase the risk that victims will experience pathologies including substance use, posttraumatic stress disorder (PTSD), depression, anxiety, and general distress. The authors emphasized that when a victim reaches out to a loved one seeking support, they likely anticipate that they will receive that support. If instead they are dismissed or not treated with compassion and respect, they are said to have experienced an "expectancy violation":

> There was evidence that certain negative social reactions may be more harmful than others. Although victim blame is often regarded as a particularly harmful form of social reaction to violence disclosure, this analysis suggests that other reactions that might be well-intentioned—like controlling survivors, treating them differently, distracting them, or otherwise unsupportively acknowledging them—may actually be especially important to avoid. This is somewhat surprising, as victim blame theoretically represents an expectancy violation. However, it is perhaps possible that the messages communicated by more egregiously negative social reactions (e.g., that the victimization is the survivor's fault) may be easier for survivors to avoid internalizing than those communicated by more subtly negative or well-intentioned social reactions (e.g., that distraction is a preferred method of coping). (Dworkin et al., 2019, p. 11)

The experience of receiving a positive social reaction does not, on its own, protect the victim from further suffering. In fact, this meta-analysis of 51 studies found positive association between receiving tangible aid/information support and experiencing negative mental health outcomes (Dworkin et al., 2019). The authors speculate that this finding represents a selection effect such that individuals who were struggling most at the time of disclosure (e.g., were already displaying symptoms of depression) were most likely to receive responses that emphasized specific resources and recommendations for follow-up. This interpretation demonstrates the difference between receiving a positive reaction and *experiencing* it as a positive reaction. If a victim reports that they *perceived* the positive reaction as positive, there may be a small protective impact. "That is, survivors who perceived the social reactions they received in a more positive light at one time point tended to have somewhat less psychopathology at that same time point and the next time point" (Dworkin et al., 2019, p. 11). To summarize, a negative reaction following a disclosure can be extremely harmful whereas a positive reaction following a disclosure, if it is perceived positively by the victim, has a small protective effect against several types of negative mental health consequences.

FURTHER READING

Ahrens, Courtney E. "Being silenced: The impact of negative social reactions on the disclosure of rape." *American Journal of Community Psychology* 38, no. 3–4 (2006): 263–274.

Dworkin, Emily R., Charlotte D. Brill, and Sarah E. Ullman. "Social reactions to disclosure of interpersonal violence and psychopathology: A systematic review and meta-analysis." *Clinical Psychology Review* 72 (2019): 101750.

Filipas, Henrietta H., and Sarah E. Ullman. "Social reactions to sexual assault victims from various support sources." *Violence and Victims* 16, no. 6 (2001): 673.

Griffin, Vanessa Woodward, Ericka Wentz, and Emily Meinert. "Explaining the why in #WhyIDidntReport: An examination of common barriers to formal disclosure of sexual assault in college students." *Journal of Interpersonal Violence* (2021): 08862605211016343.

Schulze, Corina, Sarah Koon-Magnin, and Valerie Bryan. *Gender Identity, Sexual Orientation, and Sexual Assault: Challenging the Myths.* Lynne Rienner Publishers, 2019.

Ullman, Sarah E. "Psychometric characteristics of the Social Reactions Questionnaire: A measure of reactions to sexual assault victims." *Psychology of Women Quarterly* 24, no. 3 (2000): 257–271.

Q18. ARE MOST VICTIMS OF SEXUAL ASSAULT PHYSICALLY INJURED?

Answer: Approximately half of all female sexual assault victims report minor physical injuries (e.g., bruises, scratches) following the assault. Only a small percentage of sexual assault victims have physical injuries that require medical attention (e.g., a stab wound, internal bleeding). However, the literature on trauma and physical health outcomes clearly demonstrates that experiencing a traumatic event such as sexual assault during one's lifetime increases the likelihood of developing numerous negative physical health problems, including diabetes, heart disease, and asthma.

The Facts: Many victims of sexual assault do not report their assaults to any medical professionals or law enforcement. As a result, injuries suffered during the attack are never documented in any official reports. However, victimization surveys capture assaults regardless of whether they were formally reported to such agencies. These surveys typically ask respondents who disclose a sexual assault about what injuries, if any, were sustained during the assault.

One 2013 report focused on 17 years of data collected in the National Crime Victimization Survey (NCVS) evaluated the frequency of experiencing physical injury during a sexual assault (Planty, Langton, Krebs, Berzofsky, & Smiley-McDonald, 2013). The findings were presented across three time periods: 1994–1998, 1999–2004, and 2005–2010. The researchers found in each of these periods, 42–47 percent of respondents who reported a sexual assault reported that they experienced no physical injury as a result of the assault. Conversely, 53–58 percent of respondents who reported a sexual assault reported that they did experience a physical injury as a result of the sexual assault. Of those who did experience an injury, most did not seek treatment (59–74 percent across the three time periods sought no treatment). Fewer than half of respondents who reported being injured during a sexual assault sought treatment for the injury (26–41 percent across the three time periods), typically in a medical facility such as an emergency department or doctor's office.

The NCVS does not provide specific information about the nature of the injuries sustained. However, it does provide information about the presence of weapons in the commission of a crime. Across all three time periods, respondents reported that a weapon was used in 6–11 percent of cases (Planty et al., 2013). This means that in the vast majority of sexual assaults recorded between 1994 and 2010, no weapon was used as part of the attack.

Another important resource is the National Violence Against Women Survey (NVAWS). Although it was released in 2000, making it more than twenty years old, it is of value to this conversation because it was the last report to provide national estimates of the frequency and *nature* of injury due to sexual assault. Overall, 31.5 percent of women and 16.1 percent of men in this sample who were victims of rape reported a physical injury (Tjaden & Thoennes, 2000). Among those rape victims who reported an injury, the most common type of was a "scratch, bruise, (or) welt" (72.6 percent); no other type of injury was reported by more than 15 percent of the respondents (Tjaden & Thoennes, 2000). Injuries reported by 5–15 percent of the survey respondents included "broken bone, dislocated joints" (14.1 percent), "head, spinal cord injury" (6.6 percent), "laceration, knife wounds" (6.2 percent), "internal injury" (5.8 percent), or "sore muscle, sprain, strain" (5.8 percent).

Of those women who reported an injury during their rape, the survey found that 64.4 percent did not receive medical care. The 35.6 percent of those women who reported an injury during their rape and did receive medical care were most likely to do so in a hospital (81.9 percent) or doctor's office (54.8 percent). Less common sources of medical care included care administered in an ambulance or by a paramedic (19 percent), dental care (16.9 percent), or physical therapy (16.7 percent; Tjaden & Thoennes, 2000). To summarize, approximately 11 percent of the women who reported a rape in the NVAWS sought medical care for an injury. This is somewhat lower than the updated estimates provided by the 2013 NCVS in which just over half of all female sexual assault victims experienced some injury (range of 53–58 percent across the three time periods) and approximately one-third of those respondents sought medical aid (range of 26–41 percent across the three time periods).

The NVAWS demonstrated that injuries from sexual assault were more likely in certain circumstances: when the assault was completed (compared to attempted); when it took place in either the victim or perpetrator's residence; when the assailant was an intimate partner; when the perpetrator was intoxicated; or when the victim was not intoxicated. The two largest predictors of a sexual assault resulting in injury to the victim were if the perpetrator threatened to harm the victim or if the perpetrator had a weapon.

Smaller studies of community or undergraduate samples from individual college campuses (i.e., not nationally representative samples) have also been used to assess the likelihood of experiencing an injury during a sexual assault. A meta-analysis of nearly 200 such studies was conducted in 2017 to assess the impact of different characteristics of sexual assault on mental health outcomes (Dworkin, Menon, Bystrynski, & Allen, 2017). Overall, these 195 studies, which were published across a 40-year period, indicated that 26 percent of sexual assault victims reported a physical injury. Furthermore, the report states that "it appears that assault characteristics, like stranger perpetrators, weapon use, and resulting physical injury, are associated with higher risk for psychopathology" (Dworkin et al., 2017, p. 77). In other words, even if most victims of sexual assault are not physically injured, those who are injured face a greater likelihood of experiencing negative consequences such as depression, anxiety, suicidality, or substance abuse.

Although victimization reports are a useful tool for assessing the prevalence of sexual assault and the likelihood of sustaining an injury during the assault, they are not the only source of data relating to this topic. Another approach to documenting the nature and frequency of injuries during assault is to study the forensic evaluations of victims who come in for a sexual assault nurse examiner (SANE) exam (see Q32 for more information on SANE). Researchers warn, however, that there is likely a selection bias in such samples, as a victim may be more likely to seek medical services if they have experienced bodily injury during the assault. Sexual assault forensic exams generally include documentation of both bodily injury (e.g., scrapes, bruises, and more serious wounds) as well as anal or genital injury. Assessments of genital injury focus on injuries referenced collectively by the abbreviation TEARS (Tears, Ecchymoses, Abrasions, Redness, Swelling):

> Tears are defined as any breaks in tissue integrity, including fissures, cracks, lacerations, cuts, gashes, or rips. Ecchymoses are defined as skin or mucous membrane discolorations, known as "bruising" or "black and blue" areas because of the damage of small blood vessels beneath the skin or mucous membrane surface. Abrasions are defined as skin excoriations caused by the removal of the epidermal layer and with a defined edge. Redness is erythemous skin that is abnormally inflamed because of irritation or injury without a defined edge or border. Swelling is edematous or transient engorgement of tissues. (Sommers, 2007, p. 276)

A 2003 study of adult female patients (defined as patients not treated as pediatric, aged 15 or older) found that 41 percent had no documented injuries following a sexual assault (Sugar, Fine, & Eckert, 2003). Another 52 percent of patients had injury to their bodies, most commonly "bruises and abrasions" (Sugar et al., 2003, p. 73). Five percent of patients in this study required admission for medical services. This study also found that certain factors were associated with an increase in the likelihood of bodily injury: reporting within 24 hours, the perpetrator being an intimate partner (as compared to an acquaintance); the perpetrator being a stranger (as compared to an acquaintance); oral or anal penetration being involved in the assault; a weapon being used during the assault; and the assault taking place outside (Sugar et al., 2003). Overall, 20 percent of the patients in this sample had injury to their genital or anal areas. This risk was highest among those who reported within 24 hours, had no prior sexual history, and reported that the sexual assault involved anal penetration (Sugar et al., 2003).

Although it was conducted in Australia and thus may not be generalizable to a United States context, similar findings were reported in a study of adult male patients who received sexual assault forensic exams (Zilkens et al., 2017). In total, 58 percent of these patients reported some general bodily injury (with "mild" injury documented among 46.4 percent of men who received a physical exam). The risk of bodily injury was higher among men who reported that the assault involved "blunt force," multiple assailants, or "deprivation of liberty" (for example, being bound with a rope). A smaller subset of the sample reported anal injury (14.3 percent) or genital injury (6.5 percent) and a total of two men were documented as having an oral injury (Zilkens et al., 2017). Because of social stigma associated with male victimization, it is possible that male victims are more likely to seek a medical exam only if there is physical injury, whereas a female victim may be more likely to seek an exam regardless of whether they sustained physical injury in the assault (e.g., for pregnancy and prophylaxis against infection).

Another factor that has been studied with regard to physical injury is the impact of victim resistance to an assault. Such resistance can take a variety of forms, including attempting to run away, fight off an assailant, or scream to attract attention from a bystander. Recent research suggests that resistance on the part of a targeted victim during an attempted assault—particularly physical resistance—increases the target's risk of suffering physical injury (Wong & Balemba, 2016). These findings were based on a meta-analysis of six studies—but the 2016 report could not determine whether the victim's resistance led the offender to inflict injury or whether the offender inflicted injuries that sparked resistance by the victim.

In order to protect potential victims and prevent sexual assault, self-defense programs have been established in numerous communities across the United States. Some scholars have argued against teaching self-defense strategies as a form of rape prevention, contending that it places the onus on the victim to defend themselves from being victimized rather than the perpetrator from being violent (Ullman, 2020). Other experts reject this viewpoint, and some point out that research has found that survivors of sexual assault may find self-defense training beneficial as a tool to improve their confidence and sense of safety. In a theoretical discussion of self-defense as a rape prevention strategy, researcher Sarah E. Ullman concluded, "rape resistance and self-defense training should be a part of a broader array of prevention programs aimed at reducing rape and its consequences. While all women do not have to embrace and/or take advantage of it, it should be available for those who want and need it" (Ullman, 2020, p. 14).

Although physical injury is often documented or discussed at the time of the assault, a growing line of scholarship suggests that this is an incomplete consideration of the issue. Rather, research on the long-term impact of traumatic experiences indicates that a traumatic event that takes place at one time, particularly in childhood, may have outcomes on physical health much later in life. Psychologists have identified a set of adverse childhood events (ACEs) that are associated with an increase in the development of numerous mental and physical health problems well into adulthood, include diabetes, heart disease, and asthma (Gilbert et al., 2015). Experiencing a single traumatic event—regardless of when it took place during one's life course or whether the victim showed signs of PTSD in the aftermath of the assault—may be associated with an increase in heart disease (Sumner et al., 2015).

Lifetime traumatic events (LTEs) have also been "associated with adverse downstream effects on physical health, independent of PTSD and other mental disorders. Although the associations are modest they have public health implications due to the high prevalence of traumatic events and the range of common physical conditions affected" (Scott et al., 2013, p. 1). Given the large number of people who have experienced sexual trauma, as well as the frequency with which they are diagnosed with health issues found to be related to traumatic experience, it is difficult to estimate the true physical impact that a sexual assault may have on its victim.

To summarize, most victims of sexual assault do not experience severe physical injuries immediately following the assault. Although serious physical injuries are not typical in cases of sexual assault, they are possible, particularly when the perpetrator uses a weapon. Recent research demonstrates that there are long-term physical health impacts for those who experience traumatic events, including sexual assault (Smith et al., 2018).

FURTHER READING

Dworkin, Emily R., Suvarna V. Menon, Jonathan Bystrynski, and Nicole E. Allen. "Sexual assault victimization and psychopathology: A review and meta-analysis." *Clinical Psychology Review* 56 (2017): 65–81.

Gilbert, Leah K., Matthew J. Breiding, Melissa T. Merrick, William W. Thompson, Derek C. Ford, Satvinder S. Dhingra, and Sharyn E. Parks. "Childhood adversity and adult chronic disease: an update from ten states and the District of Columbia, 2010." *American Journal of Preventive Medicine* 48, no. 3 (2015): 345–349.

Planty, Michael, Lynn Langton, Christopher Krebs, Marcus Berzofsky, and Hope Smiley-McDonald. *Female Victims of Sexual Violence, 1994–2010.* *Washington, DC*: U.S. Department of Justice, Office of Justice Programs, Bureau of Justice Statistics, 2013.

Scott, Kate M., Karestan C. Koenen, Sergio Aguilar-Gaxiola, Jordi Alonso, Matthias C. Angermeyer, Corina Benjet, Ronny Bruffaerts, et al. "Associations between lifetime traumatic events and subsequent chronic physical conditions: A cross-national, cross-sectional study." *PloS One* 8, no. 11 (2013): e80573.

Smith, Sharon G., Xinjian Zhang, Kathleen C. Basile, Melissa T. Merrick, Jing Wang, Marcie-jo Kresnow, and Jieru Chen. *The National Intimate Partner and Sexual Violence Survey: 2015 Data Brief–Updated Release.* National Center for Injury Prevention and Control, 2018.

Sommers, Marilyn Sawyer. "Defining patterns of genital injury from sexual assault: a review." *Trauma, Violence & Abuse* 8, no. 3 (2007): 270.

Sugar, Naomi F., David N. Fine, and Linda O. Eckert. "Physical injury after sexual assault: findings of a large case series." *American Journal of Obstetrics and Gynecology* 190, no. 1 (2004): 71–76.

Sumner, Jennifer A., Laura D. Kubzansky, Mitchell SV Elkind, Andrea L. Roberts, Jessica Agnew-Blais, Qixuan Chen, Magdalena Cerdá, et al. "Trauma exposure and posttraumatic stress disorder symptoms predict onset of cardiovascular events in women." *Circulation* 132, no. 4 (2015): 251–259.

Tjaden, Patricia, and Nancy Thoennes. "Prevalence and consequences of male-to-female and female-to-male intimate partner violence as measured by the National Violence Against Women Survey." *Violence against Women* 6, no. 2 (2000): 142–161.

Ullman, Sarah E. "Rape resistance: A critical piece of all women's empowerment and holistic rape prevention." *Journal of Aggression, Maltreatment & Trauma* (2020): 1–21.

Wong, Jennifer S., and Samantha Balemba. "Resisting during sexual assault: A meta-analysis of the effects on injury." *Aggression and Violent Behavior* 28 (2016): 1–11.

Zilkens, Renate R., Debbie A. Smith, S. Aqif Mukhtar, James B. Semmens, Maureen A. Phillips, and Maire C. Kelly. "Male sexual assault: Physical injury and vulnerability in 103 presentations." *Journal of Forensic and Legal Medicine* 58 (2018): 145–151.

Q19. IS VICTIM BLAMING A PROBLEM IN THE UNITED STATES?

Answer: Yes, victim blaming is a pervasive problem in the United States. Because it is so common and widespread, it impacts victims in multiple ways, particularly in terms of their mental health and recovery following a sexual assault.

The Facts: Victim blaming exists at many levels with impacts on many aspects of sexual assault, including disclosure (Q17), victim mental health (Q16), secondary victimization (Q17), and case attrition (Q27). Common examples of victim blaming focus on the way that an individual was dressed or some aspect of their behavior (e.g., being out at a certain time of night, drinking alcohol). Rather than focusing on the perpetrator's behavior (i.e., breaking the law and committing a violent crime against another person), victim blaming either implies or explicitly suggests that survivors of sexual attacks are to blame for their own assault. Victim blaming is more commonplace in cases in which the victim and assailant knew each other. Stated another way, victims who are attacked by strangers are, on average, less likely to be blamed for their assaults (Persson & Dhingra, 2020). Furthermore, not all people are equally likely to blame victims. Multiple studies have found that men hold victim-blaming attitudes toward sexual assault survivors at higher rates than do women (Grubb & Turner, 2012; Persson & Dhingra, 2020; Suarez & Gadalla, 2010).

Attributing blame to victims of sexual assault is problematic for several reasons. First, victim blaming has a strong and significant impact on a victim's mental health and decision making (e.g., whether to disclose, whether to seek medical assistance) following an assault. If a victim experiences victim blaming after disclosing a sexual assault, it can lead to secondary victimization and silencing (Q17). One teen victim described her first attempt at disclosing a sexual assault to her then-boyfriend:

> I was sort of easing into it. I didn't say anything like, 'I was sexually assaulted.' And I didn't even really say anything in detail, but just with that brief hinting and overview. He asked me not to talk about it. He said, 'I would prefer if you didn't go into it. And it would

probably be better if you didn't tell anyone because it sort of makes you come off as really pathetic.' (Schulze, Koon-Magnin, & Bryan, 2019, p. 80)

It took more than a year after this demeaning, judgmental, and callous response from her boyfriend before she was able to muster the courage to disclose her experience to another person.

Second, a bystander who witnesses predatory behavior but holds victim-blaming attitudes may be less likely to intervene to help the targeted person (Pugh, Ningard, Vander Ven, & Butler, 2016). In a qualitative study of attitudes and beliefs of undergraduate women, researchers found that

> in the presence of potentially risky situations, evaluating the victim was more important and more relevant than evaluating the situation as a whole . . . If the potential victim was not a friend, the respondent would need to evaluate whether she was worthy of help, and this evaluation was more dependent on the personal characteristics of the potential victim rather than the characteristics of the situation . . . For most respondents, a potential victim's perceived promiscuity seemed to stimulate a negative judgment of her morality, thus placing her in the blame-worthy category. (Pugh et al., 2016, p. 414)

Researchers believe that higher rates of victim-blaming attitudes within a community may indirectly increase incidence of sexual assault in that community.

Third, if embedded in the culture of an agency (e.g., law enforcement, a district attorney's office) or held by key members of an agency (e.g., detectives, prosecutors), victim-blaming attitudes can have a significant impact on case outcomes. There is a large body of literature on the impact of victim-blaming attitudes on the treatment of sexual assault by law enforcement. Generally, it suggests that victim blaming among police officers promotes secondary victimization (further harming the victim through insensitive or judgmental treatment) and increases case attrition (failure to progress through the criminal justice system, see Q28).

In a qualitative study of adolescent female victims of sexual assault who reported their assaults to police, the 65 percent who reported feeling blamed, judged, or disbelieved by police typically said that law enforcement engaged in one of three behaviors: "Questioning her story or making comments to suggest that her story is inaccurate or untrue," "Questioning or commenting on the victim's behavior around the time of the assault," or "Questioning or commenting on the victim's behavior outside the context of the assault" (Greeson, Campbell, & Fehler-Cabral, 2016, p. 108). Each of these behaviors sends the message to the victim that the assault was somehow their fault, and experiencing these comments enhances the risk of secondary victimization. Being met with doubt or skepticism by law enforcement also decreases the likelihood that a case will progress through the criminal justice system. If a law enforcement officer does not believe that a crime took place, they are unlikely to devote significant law enforcement resources (i.e., time, forensic analysis) to investigating it.

Fourth, multiple studies have documented that that victim blaming negatively impacts jury decision making. Researchers often provide survey participants with a variety of hypothetical scenarios and ask them to rate items such as the degree of culpability that should be attributed to the victim and to the perpetrator (van der Bruggen & Grubb, 2014). These studies are known as "mock juror" studies or vignette studies because the participants are evaluating a written description of a hypothetical scenario and not actively involved in an actual court proceeding. However, these studies are relatively consistent in their findings that victim blaming is particularly pronounced among male respondents and when the victim is depicted as a gay male (van der Bruggen & Grubb, 2014).

In an innovative study conducted in London, England, researchers sat in on eight rape trials. They found that the defense regularly brought up myths promoting victim blaming and that these myths were rarely corrected by either the prosecutor or the judge (Temkin, Gray, & Barrett, 2018).

Finally, victim blaming minimizes the role and culpability of the offender who committed the crime. Placing the onus to avoid being victimized on the victim implies that offending is inevitable and cannot be controlled.

These are not all of the potential impacts of victim blaming, but it should be clear at this point that this phenomenon can be far-reaching and significant in many aspects of the aftermath of sexual assault. The nature and source of the victim blaming reaction may influence the victim's recovery following a sexual assault and the likelihood of a case leading to an arrest or conviction.

FURTHER READING

Greeson, Megan R., Rebecca Campbell, and Giannina Fehler-Cabral. "'Nobody deserves this': Adolescent sexual assault victims' perceptions of disbelief and victim blame from police." *Journal of Community Psychology* 44, no. 1 (2016): 90–110.

Grubb, Amy, and Emily Turner. "Attribution of blame in rape cases: A review of the impact of rape myth acceptance, gender role conformity and substance use on victim blaming." *Aggression and Violent Behavior* 17, no. 5 (2012): 443–452.

Persson, Sofia, and Katie Dhingra. "Attributions of blame in stranger and acquaintance rape: A multilevel meta-analysis and systematic review." *Trauma, Violence, & Abuse* (2020): 1524838020977146.

Pugh, Brandie, Holly Ningard, Thomas Vander Ven, and Leah Butler. "Victim ambiguity: Bystander intervention and sexual assault in the college drinking scene." *Deviant Behavior* 37, no. 4 (2016): 401–418.

Schulze, Corina, Sarah Koon-Magnin, and Valerie Bryan. *Gender Identity, Sexual Orientation, and Sexual Assault: Challenging the Myths.* Lynne Rienner Publishers, 2019.

Suarez, Eliana, and Tahany M. Gadalla. "Stop blaming the victim: A meta-analysis on rape myths." *Journal of Interpersonal Violence* 25, no. 11 (2010): 2010–2035.

Temkin, Jennifer, Jacqueline M. Gray, and Jastine Barrett. "Different functions of rape myth use in court: Findings from a trial observation study." *Feminist Criminology* 13, no. 2 (2018): 205–226.

Van der Bruggen, Madeleine, and Amy Grubb. "A review of the literature relating to rape victim blaming: An analysis of the impact of observer and victim characteristics on attribution of blame in rape cases." *Aggression and Violent Behavior* 19, no. 5 (2014): 523–531.

Q20. DO RAPE MYTHS IMPACT SEXUAL ASSAULT SURVIVORS?

Answer: Yes, rape myths impact sexual assault survivors because their belief is so widespread and has remained persistent over time. In addition to impacting how victims perceive their own assaults, rape myths also influence how and whether they disclose their impact to loved ones. In addition, they diminish the likelihood that the victim will report their assault to law enforcement or seek other resources (e.g., medical assistance, counseling). While early rape myth questionnaires or surveys focused exclusively on female victims of male perpetrators, more recent research has expanded to study myths about sexual assault against male or transgender victims perpetrated by assailants of any gender.

The Facts: The term "rape myth" was coined by scholar Martha Burt in 1980 to describe "prejudicial, stereotyped, or false beliefs about rape,

rape victims, and rapists (which serve to create) a climate hostile to rape victims" (Burt, 1980, p. 217). Hundreds of studies since then have analyzed the core content of existing rape myths, refined measurement techniques for assessing belief in rape myths, and identifying unique rape myths that apply to specific demographic groups or communities.

Rape myths may take many forms, but they generally serve one of three purposes: (1) to blame the victim for the assault, (2) to remove or excuse the perpetrator's responsibility for the assault, or (3) to trivialize the seriousness of the assault. Examples of each type of rape myth are discussed below. The Illinois Rape Myth Acceptance Scale (IRMAS), first introduced in 1999, was the standard measure for assessing the content of and support for rape myths for over a decade (Payne, Lonsway, & Fitzgerald, 1999). It was then updated to reflect more modern language. The examples provided here are from the updated version of the rape myth acceptance scale (McMahon & Farmer, 2011).

Rape myths that blame the victim for the assault are particularly harmful (see Q19). These myths tend to focus on any action that the victim took prior to the assault that could have allegedly "contributed to" or "precipitated" the assault. Sample statements on existing rape myth scales include, "When girls go to parties wearing slutty clothes, they are asking for trouble" and "If a girl goes to a room alone with a guy at a party, it is her own fault if she is raped" (McMahon & Farmer, 2011). Myths that send these victim-blaming messages shame the victim and decrease the likelihood that the victim will report the assault to police or seek help services, because the victim is ashamed and may believe that they "got what they asked for" or what they "deserved." Victim blaming beliefs are extremely harmful in terms of the victim's ability to heal and their overall mental health following a sexual assault. They also make it harder to stop men who commit rape and other acts of sexual violence or assault. Not only does victim blaming make prosecuting offenders more difficult, it can also give perpetrators confidence that they can continue to assault women without suffering any consequences or accepting any responsibility for their actions.

Other types of rape myths remove blame from the perpetrator by excusing their criminal behavior as unintentional or somehow unavoidable. For example, "Rape happens when a guy's sex drive gets out of control" or "If a guy is drunk, he might rape someone unintentionally" (McMahon & Farmer, 2011). Rape myths like this benefit perpetrators who are able to shirk responsibility, not have their behavior questioned, and avoid negative repercussions. It can also create a sense of guilt or confusion for a victim who is left to wonder, if the perpetrator is not to blame for this assault, who is? Again, the implication may be that the victim is at fault.

Finally, rape myths that trivialize a sexual assault are problematic because they send the message that a victim may be confused about what happened or is overreacting to something that was not actually that serious. Examples of this type of rape myth include, "If the accused 'rapist' doesn't have a weapon, you really can't call it a rape" or "When girls are raped, it's often because the way they said 'no' was unclear" (McMahon & Farmer, 2011). If a victim internalizes this belief and begins to question their own experiences and feelings, it is far less likely that the victim will seek assistance following an assault or report that assault to police., because they may not want to be seen as overreacting to something that falls short of a criminal offense.

The key item to keep in mind about rape myths is that they are, in fact, myths. They contradict the legal definitions of rape and the empirical scholarship on sexual assault. For example, it is not required in criminal definitions of sexual assault that a weapon be used. Many assailants overpower or otherwise incapacitate their victims and complete a sexual assault without use of a weapon. Those assaults are crimes, subject to the very same penalties as assaults committed at gun or knife point. As another example, a great deal of literature on motivations for rape indicate that many offenders are motivated by the desire to overpower or exert control over a victim, thus undermining the myth that rape is primarily the result of an overactive sex drive. After all, there are plenty of ways for a person with a strong sex drive to pursue sexual gratification that do not involve victimizing nonconsenting others. Exploring the underlying assumptions of rape myths and how they impact victims of sexual assault is very important for understanding the experiences of sexual assault survivors to ensure that outreach and response services are accessible and welcoming to those who need them.

The first decade of scholarship on rape myths focused only on myths depicting female victims of male perpetrators. However, in the 1990s, researchers began to identify and test myths relating to sexual assault against males. A team of researchers created statements that captured three types of myths: (1) men cannot be raped (see Q7), (2) if a man is raped, it is his own fault, and (3) rape is not that traumatic for men (Struckman-Johnson & Struckman-Johnson, 1992). The myths indicating that men cannot be raped function similarly to the myths relating to female sexual assault: they trivialize the assault by suggesting it is impossible and thus did not happen. The statements measuring this type of myth included, "It is impossible for a man to rape a man" (in which greater agreement indicates more support for the myth that men cannot be raped by other men) and

"Even a big, strong man can be raped by another man" (in which lower agreement indicates more support for the myth that strong men cannot be raped by other men).

Myths relating to blaming male victims operate in the same way as myths blaming female victims: they suggest that the victim brought the assault upon themselves and thus got what they asked for or deserved. Sample statements include, "Most men who are raped by a woman are somewhat to blame for not escaping or fighting off the woman" and "Most men who are raped by a woman are somewhat to blame for not being more careful." Finally, Struckman-Johnson and Struckman-Johnson (1992) measured myths relating to the traumatic impact of a sexual assault on a man. For example, "Most men who are raped by a man do not need counseling after the incident." Statements capturing this type of myth operate in the same way that myths relating to trivializing the assault operate for female victims. It sends the message that the victim is overreacting to the assault, making a big deal out of nothing, and should be over it by now. Each of these forms of rape myths is harmful to male victims and likely contribute to their lower rates of reporting sexual assault to the police and other help services (Davies, 2002; Davies & Rogers, 2006).

In 2019, a rape myth instrument called the Identity-Inclusive Sexual Assault Myths Scale (IISAMS) was introduced, with measures representing victims of diverse gender identities and sexual orientations (Schulze, Koon-Magnin, & Bryan, 2019). The IISAMS was built by asking members of the LGBTQ community to look at and reflect on the modified IRMAS to see whether key aspects of the LGBTQ experience were missing. Any myths that the study participants mentioned hearing were included in a pilot study of the IISAMS, which elicited higher levels of agreement among participants than the IRMAS (Schulze et al., 2019).

Some rape myth statements on the IISAMS explicitly relate to sexual orientation, such as the false assertion that "Because they never turn down sex, bisexuals can't be raped." Of course, this is a myth, because anyone of any sexual orientation can decline to consent to a sexual encounter, but this was a sentiment that LGBTQ interview participants had heard expressed and thus was included in development of the survey instrument. Because it is a recent development, the IISAMS also introduces more modern examples of victim blame that are not measured in existing rape myth instrumentation, such as the use of dating apps to meet a potential romantic partner. Two such statements include, "Men who rely on bars and clubs to find 'hook-ups' are more likely to be accused of rape" and "If a woman agrees to meet someone through a hook-up app, she should not be surprised if the person assumes that she wants to have sex." Although further research is needed, the pilot study of the IISAMS along with the existing male rape myth scale and IRMAS suggest that the most strongly believed myths are those relating to male rape, followed by IISAMS (myths relating primarily to the LGBTQ community), and finally IRMAS. This hierarchy of belief may reflect the fact that the IRMAS is the best-known rape myth instrument and has been the focus of many programs aimed at dispelling rape myths and improving responses to sexual assault victims.

Multiple studies have been conducted to see how belief in rape myths relate to other types of attitudes and beliefs. Generally, men are more likely than women to subscribe to rape myths. They are more likely to believe or express support for victim blaming, excuse the behavior of perpetrators, and trivialize or undermine an experience of sexual assault (Angelone, Cantor, Marcantonio, & Joppa, 2020; Suarez & Gadalla, 2010). A meta-analysis of 37 studies also demonstrated that people who support rape myth attitudes are also more likely to hold racist and sexist attitudes and harbor hostility toward women (Suarez & Gadalla, 2010). As the authors concluded, "the large effect sizes observed of racism, classism, sexism, ageism, religious intolerance, and racial identity support a structural perspective of rape myths as a complex sociocultural issue" (Suarez & Gadalla, 2010, p. 2027). A 2021 study supported these results, demonstrating a particularly important relationship between rape myth acceptance and sexism (Angelone et al., 2020). Prior literature indicates a complicated interworking of different types of attitudes and beliefs that may interact to have significant impacts on victims during the traumatic aftermath of a sexual assault.

As a final note, it should be stated that victims of sexual assault are not immune to holding rape myth attitudes. If a person is raised in a society in which such beliefs are prevalent, they are likely to internalize them to some degree. If that individual is then sexually assaulted it does not follow that they will suddenly stop believing myths and falsehoods that they may have believed for years and heard expressed by people they love, respect, and/or trust. This internal conflict adds to the struggle in determining whether to disclose, report, or otherwise seek help following a sexual assault. It also increases the risk of negative mental health consequences (as discussed in Q16).

To summarize, rape myths are common and widespread in the United States. They are problematic in their impact on victims, who feel blamed for the assaults against them. They are also problematic because they minimize the culpability of the assailant, decreasing the likelihood that they are held accountable for their crimes.

FURTHER READING

Angelone, D. J., Nicole Cantor, Tiffany Marcantonio, and Meredith Joppa. "Does sexism mediate the gender and rape myth acceptance relationship?" *Violence against Women* (2020): 1077801220913632.

Burt, Martha R. "Cultural myths and supports for rape." *Journal of Personality and Social Psychology* 38, no. 2 (1980): 217.

Davies, Michelle. "Male sexual assault victims: A selective review of the literature and implications for support services." *Aggression and Violent Behavior* 7, no. 3 (2002): 203–214.

Davies, Michelle, and Paul Rogers. "Perceptions of male victims in depicted sexual assaults: A review of the literature." *Aggression and Violent Behavior* 11, no. 4 (2006): 367–377.

McMahon, Sarah, and G. Lawrence Farmer. "An updated measure for assessing subtle rape myths." *Social Work Research* 35, no. 2 (2011): 71–81.

Payne, Diana L., Kimberly A. Lonsway, and Louise F. Fitzgerald. "Rape myth acceptance: Exploration of its structure and its measurement using the Illinois rape myth acceptance scale." *Journal of Research in Personality* 33, no. 1 (1999): 27–68.

Schulze, Corina, Sarah Koon-Magnin, and Valerie Bryan. *Gender Identity, Sexual Orientation, and Sexual Assault: Challenging the Myths.* Lynne Rienner Publishers, 2019.

Struckman-Johnson, Cindy, and David Struckman-Johnson. "Acceptance of male rape myths among college men and women." *Sex Roles* 27, no. 3–4 (1992): 85–100.

Suarez, Eliana, and Tahany M. Gadalla. "Stop blaming the victim: A meta-analysis on rape myths." *Journal of Interpersonal Violence* 25, no. 11 (2010): 2010–2035.

Q21. HAS THE ME TOO MOVEMENT HAD AN EFFECT ON SEXUAL ASSAULT SURVIVORS?

Answer: The fact that it is now a commonly known term demonstrates that almost certainly, the Me Too movement has had an impact on past, present, and future survivors of sexual assault. The Me Too movement has brought attention to the problem of sexual assault, provided an accessible community for survivors seeking support, and prompted dialogue about sexual harassment and sexual assault in multiple arenas, most notably in the entertainment industry. However, given its recent emergence and difficulties in measurement of exposure to the movement, research on its specific impacts remains preliminary.

The Facts: The Me Too movement has become well known throughout the United States since 2017; however, it is more than a social media
hashtag. In fact, the advocacy organization behind the Me Too movement
was founded more than a decade before the phrase went viral.

The Me Too movement began in 2006 when Black activist Tarana Burke
used the term to draw attention to the pervasiveness of sexual harassment
and assault, particularly within communities of color. The movement did
not explode into public discourse, however, until 2017, when actress Alyssa
Milano tweeted "#MeToo" in response to a discussion of sexual harassment. The hashtag quickly began "trending" on Twitter and was tweeted
more than 12 million times in just 24 hours (Hoffman, 2021). The fact that
the Me Too movement was actually founded by a Black activist but did not
gain widespread public attention until it was repeated by a White actress
has been a significant topic of debate (see Palmer, Fissel, Hoxmeier, & Williams [2021] for a discussion of representation in the Me Too movement).

On the "History and Inception" page of the Me Too movement's website
(metoomvmt.org) the development of the Me Too movement is described
in this way:

> In those early years, we developed our vision to bring resources, sup-
> port, and pathways to healing where none existed before. And we got
> to work building a community of advocates determined to interrupt
> sexual violence wherever it happens. In 2017, the #metoo hashtag
> went viral and woke up the world to the magnitude of the problem of
> sexual violence. Within a six-month span, our message reached a
> global community of survivors. Suddenly there were millions of peo-
> ple from all walks of life saying "me too."

Essentially, the movement aims to create a safe space for survivors of sexual
assault—in particular those from marginalized communities—to reach out
to others and find support without judgment. The organization also aims
to promote accountability for perpetrators by drawing attention to occurrences of sexual harassment or assault. After the #MeToo hashtag went
viral and became a part of the lexicon, conversations around sexual assault
became accessible to social media users all over the world, creating an
online community.

Researchers have begun to explore this community and its impact, but
at this point, their findings are preliminary and the full impact of this
movement on sexual assault survivors remains to be seen. A special issue of
the *American Journal of Criminal Justice*, published in 2021, was devoted to
assessing the impact of the Me Too movement and several of the featured

studies are relevant to this discussion. A study of 626 undergraduates' participation in the Me Too movement looked at three forms of participation: "(1) signing an online petition in support of the #MeToo movement; (2) posting the #MeToo movement on personal social media platforms; and (3) attending a protest in support of the #MeToo" (Hoffman, 2021, p. 7). Analyses showed that female and LGBTQ students were more likely to report participation in Me Too than male and heterosexual students, respectively. Students who were members of fraternities or sororities or a sports team were less likely to participate than students who were not involved in these organizations or sports teams (Hoffman, 2021). These findings are in line with prior work on sexual assault attitudes and support for victims. Although this study did not find significant differences in Me Too involvement based on respondent race, there is reason to believe that it may have an impact.

A qualitative study explored the influence of media (and particularly social media) coverage of sexual assault to determine where participating respondents get their information on sexual assault, how accurately they understand the dynamics of sexual assault, and whether they are inclined to believe or disbelieve disclosures of sexual assault (Acquaviva, O'Neal, & Clevenger, 2020). These lines of inquiry reflect concerns about findings that media depictions of sexual assault are often inaccurate and promote victim blaming myths about the nature of sexual assault (Aroustamian, 2020).

Specifically, the study sought to examine how media exposure impacted understanding of sexual assault among undergraduate students, graduate students, and recent college graduates (within the previous 2 years). When asked how they learned what they know about sexual assault, more than 60 percent of the sample reported that they had learned about sexual assault through the media (64.7 percent), through personal connections (64.7 percent), or through a school environment such as a college course (61.76 percent). Almost all participants (91.2 percent) could name a perpetrator involved in a current or recent scandal relating to sexual assault, with the most frequently cited name being Harvey Weinstein. Following a reference to any specific perpetrator, participants were asked for their impressions of that case. Most participants (70.6 percent) suggested that they believed the accusations but a sizable minority (29.4 percent) indicated that they did not (Acquaviva et al., 2020).

Another research study found that the efforts of Me Too activists to use social media to educate Americans about the realities of sexual assault and harassment may be having an impact. Overall, the study demonstrated a decline in participants' expression of doubt toward claims of sexual assault even 6 months after the peak of activity around Me Too. These findings suggest that the Me Too movement may have increased belief in sexual assault survivors' accounts of victimization. However, a study of more than 4,500 tweets containing the term "#MeToo" revealed a significant subset of those tweets contained content hostile toward the Me Too movement. Specifically:

> Our analysis of #metoo tweets revealed that negative and ambivalent attitudes toward the #MeToo Movement were conveyed through six themes. Tweeters displayed the following themes: (1) invalidating the accusations made as part of the #MeToo Movement; (2) insisting, and likely believing, that accusations made were false; (3) claiming that there were alternative motives for those accusations; (4) showing a concern for the harm that accusations, not necessarily false, may cause those accused; (5) exhibiting concerns about the effects of the #MeToo Movement on male power, privilege, and status; and (6) questioning the integrity of the #MeToo Movement as a whole. (Nutbeam & Mereish, 2021, pp. 6–7)

Further subthemes emerged within these analyses, revealing additional sources of criticism or doubt based on expressions of racism and sexism, or relating to revenge, politics, and famous people being accused of sexual assault (Nutbeam & Mereish, 2021). In addition to measuring the impact of Me Too on individual's level of knowledge and attitudes toward sexual assault, researchers have assessed potential impacts on behavior.

Using tweets and Reddit posts, researchers conducted a qualitative analysis to identify themes relating to Me Too (Alaggia & Wang, 2020). After analysis, the authors identified the following six themes in the social media postings: "1) Social media and popular press as prompting disclosures; 2) Internal barriers impacting disclosures of sexual abuse and/or sexual assault disclosures; 3) Family factors and mixed responses to disclosures; 4) Mixed response from friends/peers to disclosures; 5) Responses from professionals; 6) Unaware it was sexual abuse/assault" (Alaggia & Wang, 2020, p. 103). The most prevalent theme, that media (and social media) coverage of MeToo had prompted the individual to make a disclosure, indicated a substantial impact of this movement on survivors of sexual assault. Some of the tweets/posts analyzed indicated that the individual had never previously disclosed the assault, or had not done so in many years. Other key themes discussed in these tweets/posts demonstrate the difficult dynamics associated with sexual assault disclosure (Q17), including reasons people chose not to disclose. Another prominent point of discussion was the variety of responses (many negative) received by victims who had come forward with disclosures.

Some scholars, practitioners, and activists have expressed concern about the impact of Me Too. Particularly, they fear that it may be triggering for survivors of sexual assault because the coverage and discussion of sexual assault has become so heavy on so many platforms that the subject is nearly unavoidable (Swanson & Szymanski, 2020). Furthermore, many of the activists interviewed reported feeling burnt out or overwhelmed by their repeated exposure to disclosures of sexual assault (Swanson & Szymanski, 2020).

In a study of college students who were surveyed during a 3-year period that included the rise of awareness of the Me Too movement, researchers saw an increase in labeling sexual assault encounters as such (Jaffe, Cero, & DiLillo, 2021). The authors speculate that this trend may reflect a more accurate awareness of what constitutes sexual assault, allowing more survey respondents to recognize and apply the label to their own past experiences. Furthermore, reports of a more specific occurrence of sexual assault—sexual assault on an airplane flight—emerged following the spread of the "MeToo" movement. At this point, "it is unknown if sexual misconduct (on airplanes) is increasing, or if people are reporting incidents more than they have in the past" (Lucas, 2021, p. 1). However, the increase (whether in occurrences or in public awareness of these offenses) has led to responses from both the federal government and the airline industry including the introduction of new bills, recommendations of best practices from the National In-Flight Sexual Misconduct Task Force, and research on such incidents as experienced by flight attendants (Lucas, 2021).

Because it is relatively new and difficult for researchers to precisely measure, the impact of the Me Too movement on sexual assault survivors is still being explored. In the words of scholars, "Both the #metoo movement and research investigating its impact is relatively recent and the effects of such efforts remain unclear" (Acquaviva et al., 2020, p. 22).

FURTHER READING

Acquaviva, Brittany L., Eryn Nicole O'Neal, and Shelly L. Clevenger. "Sexual assault awareness in the #Metoo era: Student perceptions of victim believability and cases in the media." *American Journal of Criminal Justice* (2020): 1–27.

Alaggia, Ramona, and Susan Wang. "'I never told anyone until the# metoo movement': What can we learn from sexual abuse and sexual assault disclosures made through social media?" *Child Abuse & Neglect* 103 (2020): 104312.

Aroustamian, Camille. "Time's up: Recognising sexual violence as a public policy issue: A qualitative content analysis of sexual violence cases and the media." *Aggression and Violent Behavior* 50 (2020): 101341.

Daigle, Leah E. "Research on sexual violence in the #MeToo era: Prevention and innovative methodologies." *American Journal of Criminal Justice* (2021): 1–4.

Hoffman, Chrystina Y. "Factors associated with #Metoo involvement among college students." *American Journal of Criminal Justice* (2020): 1–17.

Jaffe, Anna E., Ian Cero, and David DiLillo. "The #Metoo movement and perceptions of sexual assault: College students' recognition of sexual assault experiences over time." *Psychology of Violence* 11, no. 2 (2021): 209–218.

Lucas, Kweilin T. "In-flight sexual victimization in the #Metoo era: a content analysis of media reports." *American Journal of Criminal Justice* 46, no. 1 (2021): 130–148.

me too. "History and Inception." (2020). https://metoomvmt.org/get-to -know-us/history-inception/. Accessed 8 Feb 2021.

Nutbeam, Meena, and Ethan H. Mereish. "Negative attitudes and beliefs toward the #MeToo movement on Twitter." *Journal of Interpersonal Violence* (2021): 08862605211001470.

Palmer, Jane E., Erica R. Fissel, Jill Hoxmeier, and Erin Williams. "# MeToo for whom? Sexual assault disclosures before and after #MeToo." *American Journal of Criminal Justice* 46, no. 1 (2021): 68–106.

Strauss Swanson, Charlotte, and Dawn M. Szymanski. "From pain to power: An exploration of activism, the #Metoo movement, and healing from sexual assault trauma." *Journal of Counseling Psychology* 67, no. 6 (2020): 653–668.

Szekeres, Hanna, Eric Shuman, and Tamar Saguy. "Views of sexual assault following #MeToo: The role of gender and individual differences." *Personality and Individual Differences* 166 (2020): 110203.

5

Government and Criminal Justice Responses to Sexual Assault Victims

Given the number of people who are impacted by sexual violence and the suffering that so often follows, the government and criminal justice system have developed legislation and programs aimed at better serving victims. One major piece of legislation, the Violence Against Women Act, which was originally passed in 1994, has provided millions of dollars in funding to serve victims of sexual assault. Key features and impacts of this legislation will be discussed in Q22 ("Has the Violence Against Women Act [VAWA] helped victims of sexual assault?").

However, researchers and advocates for victims of sexual assault have identified significant shortcomings in the American justice system's response to these types of crimes. In the early 2000s, thousands of untested rape kits were discovered in evidence rooms in cities across the United States. The discovery of this massive backlog of kits was a devastating blow for sexual assault victims and advocates. In response to this discovery, the federal government has invested millions of dollars in testing these old kits and improving processes to ensure that a backlog does not occur again in the future. These issues will be discussed in depth in Q23 ("Are steps being taken to address the 'rape kit backlog'?").

Many sexual assault victims do not knowingly encounter the impacts of these large federal programs. Rather, they interact with the criminal justice system, particularly with law enforcement and prosecutors, on a smaller scale within their own communities. A variety of victim-centered and trauma-informed policies and procedures have been or can be implemented by these agencies to improve victim response services, as discussed in Q24 ("Are there steps that law enforcement can take to better respond to sexual assaults?") and Q25 ("Are there steps that prosecutors can take to better respond to sexual assaults?"). For example, many jurisdictions have implemented collaborative inter-agency teams known as Sexual Assault Response Teams (SARTs) to improve the response to sexual assault victims. The organization and efficacy of these groups is summarized in Q26 ("Are sexual assault response teams [SARTs] an effective method of addressing the problem of sexual assault?"). Overall, this chapter will give readers a sense of what a sexual assault victim may experience in their interactions with the criminal justice system if they report their experience to authorities.

Q22. HAS THE VIOLENCE AGAINST WOMEN ACT (VAWA) HELPED VICTIMS OF SEXUAL ASSAULT?

Answer: Probably, although more likely in terms of improved response than in sexual assault prevention. The Violence Against Women Act (VAWA) is a federal law that provides resources to criminal justice practitioners as well as public and private agencies who work to respond to domestic violence or sexual assault. By addressing sexual and domestic violence at a national level and not treating such crimes as personal events to be handled privately, passage of this act represented a significant change in the social response to these crimes in the United States (Gover & Moore, 2020). However, it is very difficult to measure the effectiveness of this policy because of differences in implementation across jurisdictions and other factors.

The Facts: VAWA was first passed by the United States Congress in 1994 as part of the Violent Crime Control Act. According to the Congressional Research Service, "The Violence Against Women Act of 1994 (1) enhanced investigations and prosecutions of sex offenses and (2) provided for a number of grant programs to address the issue of violence against women from a variety of angles including law enforcement, public and private entities and service providers, and victims of crime" (Seghetti & Bjelopera, 2012, p. 2).

Since VAWA's initial passage, researchers have identified key changes in the ways that law enforcement agencies investigate and respond to reports of sexual and domestic violence, including "1) law enforcement response to victims, 2) law enforcement response to offenders, and 3) law enforcement agency operations" (Jennings, Power, & Perez, 2020, p. 4). With regard to victims, stakeholders including criminal justice practitioners, scholars, and activists have focused substantial attention on understanding and increasing reporting practices; that is why survivors of sexual assault may contact (or decline to contact) law enforcement following the assault. As discussed elsewhere (Q11), most victims do not report their assaults to law enforcement. Improved criminal justice response (both in terms of victim satisfaction and holding offenders accountable) requires contact with those victims, so considerable effort has focused on increasing rates of reporting.

To this end, VAWA encourages practices that would promote a sense of victim safety to come forward and report their assault (e.g., adopting victim-supportive attitudes in place of victim-blaming attitudes; Q19). It also seeks to remove barriers that may prevent victims from seeking services or reporting (e.g., victims are not charged for a sexual assault forensic exam; Jennings et al., 2020). Many law enforcement agencies also regularly engage with professional victim advocates (Q31) some of whom work directly for the department and others who are employed by a community agency and partner with the police. In many jurisdictions, VAWA resources have been used to establish units specifically devoted to the investigation of sexual offenses, which enhances victim satisfaction with the experience of reporting. Even if agencies do not have sufficient resources to implement specialized units, the increased availability of and funding for training has provided law enforcement with an opportunity to examine their attitudes toward victims and identify strategies to avoid secondary victimization, the harmful outcome in which sexual assault survivors are retraumatized by those they interact with following the assault (Jennings et al., 2020).

The Office of Violence Against Women was established in 1995 within the Department of Justice. This office now oversees VAWA funding for multiple grant programs, including, "Grants to Enhance Culturally Specific Services for Victims of Sexual Assault, Domestic Violence, Dating Violence and Stalking Program," "Grants for Outreach and Services to Underserved Populations Program," "Improving Criminal Justice Responses to Sexual Assault Domestic Violence, Dating Violence, and Stalking Grant Program," "Training and Services to End Violence Against Women with Disabilities Grant Program," "Tribal Sexual Assault Services Program," and "STOP (Services, Training, Officers, and Prosecutors) Formula Grant Program." These programs and the many others funded by VAWA have awarded more than $8 billion to state, local, and tribal criminal justice agencies, nonprofit victim service agencies, and research institutions (Gover & Moore, 2020). A major goal is to fund victim services at the state and local level, allowing practitioners within the specific jurisdictions to propose appropriate and feasible projects for their sites.

VAWA was reauthorized by Congress in 2000, 2005, and 2013. Each reauthorization has included new provisions. For example, in 2000, the original law's focus on domestic violence was expanded to a broader definition of intimate partner violence, including dating violence. The 2005 reauthorization explicitly recognized protections for immigrants who were being trafficked or otherwise victimized. In 2013, the reauthorization required that service providers who received VAWA funding not discriminate against anyone based on their sexual orientation. Also included in the 2013 reauthorization was an emphasis on eliminating the rape kit backlog (see Q23). As of mid-2021, the most recent reauthorization (2013) has expired. A new reauthorization passed the U.S. House of Representatives in both 2019 and 2021, but has not been taken up for a vote in the U.S. Senate.

Therefore, with this background in mind, has VAWA helped victims of sexual assault? In a statement encouraging the reauthorization of VAWA in 2018, the American Psychological Association stated that, "VAWA has vastly improved our nation's response to domestic and sexual violence" (APA, 2018). This conclusion was supported by a study of the number of rapes and sexual assaults in 1996–2002, the years following the initial implementation of VAWA. The study indicated that these crimes decreased even after controlling for the general decrease in crime during that time period and criminal justice-related funding from other sources (Boba & Lilley, 2009). The authors attributed this decline to three factors: (1) effective identification and incapacitation of the offenders responsible for these crimes, (2) improved practices within the criminal justice system leading to a stronger deterrent effect, and (3) increased victim reporting and victim help-seeking as a result of the new programs leading to more cases coming to the attention of the criminal justice system so that offenders could be identified and punished (Boba & Lilley, 2009).

A 2020 evaluation of VAWA concluded that "while no entity has conducted a large-scale, rigorous multisite evaluation of VAWA programs to date, the Act has led to great strides in positive program outputs, DOJ's National Institute of Justice establishing a violence against women research program, and the Federal government funding hundreds of individual program evaluations" (Gover & Moore, 2020). Specifically:

> Every 6 months, OVW's discretionary grant programs serve approximately 125,000 victims and the formula grant programs serve more than 400,000 victims each year. OVW provides more than 2 million housing and shelter bed nights to victims and children each year. OVW grants provide legal assistance to 28,000 victims every 6 months.

OVW funded technical assistance providers train almost 12,000 nurses who provide medical forensic care. Every year through its civil legal assistance programs, OVW practitioners assist victims in securing more than 200,000 protection orders, and OVW funds over 200 prosecutors' and over 300 law enforcement officers' salaries. These funds enable jurisdictions to create and implement specialized law enforcement units, prosecution units, and dedicated courts. (Gover & Moore, 2020, p. 14)

Victimology research is generally challenging because it is hard to access victims and recruit them to participate in research without further traumatizing them. The variation in policies across jurisdictions also makes it very difficult to systematically evaluate the overall impact of VAWA on rates of sexual assault (Gover & Moore, 2020). However, as demonstrated in the list of services discussed above, there are many examples of VAWA funding being used to tangibly support and improve responses to sexual assault.

Finally, there is an entity known as the VAWA Measuring Effectiveness Initiative (VAWA MEI) that helps the Office on Violence against Women (OVW) by analyzing and providing regular summary reports of OVW data from different grant programs and initiatives. The VAWA MEI project is part of the Justice Policy Program at the Cutler Institute for Health and Social Policy, Muskie School of Public Service, University of Southern Maine. The specific projects reported to this organization and the reports featured on their website and submitted to Congress can also help interested readers evaluate the effectiveness of various programs that have been implemented with support from VAWA funding.

Overall, VAWA is too far-reaching and multifaceted with various applications and implementations of funded programs throughout the United States to meaningfully study its direct impact as a single piece of legislation. However, given the sheer number of programs and positions it funds in communities serving millions of survivors of sexual assault, it is reasonable to assume that VAWA has helped sexual assault survivors in their efforts to recover and bring their attackers to justice.

FURTHER READING

American Psychological Association. *The Violence Against Women Act.* Public Interest Government Relations Office, 2018.

Boba, Rachel, and David Lilley. "Violence Against Women Act (VAWA) funding: A nationwide assessment of effects on rape and assault." *Violence Against Women* 15, no. 2 (2009): 168–185.

Gover, Angela R., and Angela M. Moore. "The 1994 Violence Against Women Act: A historic response to gender violence." *Violence Against Women* (2020): 1077801220949705.

Jennings, Wesley G., Ráchael A. Powers, and Nicholas M. Perez. "A review of the effects of the Violence Against Women Act on law enforcement." *Violence Against Women* (2020): 1077801220949694.

Moore, Angela, and Angela Gover. "Guest editors' introduction: Violence against women—Reflecting on 25 years of the Violence Against Women Act and directions for the future." *Violence Against Women* (2020): 1077801220949693.

Parmley, Angela M. Moore. "Violence against women research post VAWA: Where have we been, where are we going?" *Violence Against Women* 10, no. 12 (2004): 1417–1430.

Seghetti, Lisa M., and Jerome P. Bjelopera. "The violence against women act: Overview, legislation, and federal funding." *Congressional Research Service* 10 (2012): 1–35.

Q23. ARE STEPS BEING TAKEN TO ADDRESS THE "RAPE KIT BACKLOG"?

Answer: Yes. In the early 2000s, it became evident that multiple jurisdictions across the United States had thousands of sexual assault forensic kits (often referred to as "rape kits") sitting in police evidence rooms and warehouse shelves across the nation. These kits had either never been submitted for forensic testing or had been submitted but were never tested. It is estimated that there were more than 200,000 such kits across the country, a phenomenon often referred to as the "rape kit backlog." Intense media coverage of this discovery, as well as systematic evaluation by researchers, spurred a national movement to test these kits. The Bureau of Justice Assistance provided substantial grants to some of the communities with a substantial number of such kits to have them tested. In addition to helping test the backlog of evidence by reducing the number of unsubmitted or untested kits, these initiatives allowed researchers to empirically investigate how the backlog developed and provide policy recommendations to minimize the potential of this problem recurring in the future.

The Facts: As discussed in Q15, a "rape kit" or SAK (sexual assault kit) is a collection of forensic evidence collected from a victim of sexual assault in the hours or days immediately following the assault. The exam generally takes several hours to complete and includes such invasive procedures as an internal and external examination of the anus and genitals, fingernail scrapings, hair plucking (which may include head hair, body hair, and/or pubic hair), and photographic documentation of injury (including genital injury). Although it is an unpleasant and likely painful process for the sexual assault survivor, many choose to submit to a sexual assault forensic exam to preserve forensic evidence of the assault they experienced (Campbell, Feeney, Fehler-Cabral, Shaw, & Horsford, 2017).

The physical evidence collected as part of a forensic examination can be extremely useful to law enforcement and the prosecution if a case moves forward in the criminal justice system. Given the potential evidentiary value of these kits, many Americans expressed surprise and anger when two of the nation's largest jurisdictions—New York and Los Angeles—reported that between them, they had more than 28,000 completed kits that had never been properly processed (Campbell et al., 2017). Shortly thereafter, a report by Human Rights Watch "determined that only 1,474 of the 7,494 completed rape kits booked into evidence in Illinois from 1995 to 2009 could be confirmed as tested." In other words, during that time span, only one out of five rape kits taken into evidence by authorities in Illinois ever underwent testing (Campbell et al., 2017, p. 367). A 2012 report by the National Institute of Justice stated that agency "staff, researchers and investigative journalists have uncovered the fact that backlogged and untested sexual assault kits (SAKs) are a major problem facing forensic crime laboratories and law enforcement agencies throughout the United States" (Peterson, Johnson, Herz, Graziano, & Oehler, 2012, p. i).

The Joyful Heart Foundation, founded by actress and activist Mariska Hargitay to combat child abuse, sexual assault, and domestic violence, subsequently worked to track the backlog across jurisdictions and maintain a website (endthebacklog.org) detailing efforts to document and test these unsubmitted kits. Media coverage of the backlog found in various cities, along with advocacy work to contextualize and publicize the findings, brought the issue significant attention and prompted a wave of testing of previously unsubmitted or untested SAKs.

After the backlog of SAKs was discovered, jurisdictions essentially had four options as to how to proceed:

(i) test no SAKs in the backlog, (ii) test all SAKs in the backlog with no prioritization, (iii) test all SAKs in the backlog with prioritization (e.g., process all stranger SAKs within the statute of limitations before processing any SAKs beyond the statute of limitations or any nonstranger SAKs), and (iv) processing only some of the SAKs (e.g., only the stranger SAKs within the statute of limitations). (Wang & Wein, 2018, p. 1110)

Electing not to test any kits in the backlog is problematic for many reasons and was not an option that advocates, scholars, or practitioners generally supported. Testing all kits (known as the "forklift approach") was possible for some jurisdictions. For example, both New York and Los Angeles, among the earliest jurisdictions to identify thousands of untested SAKs in their possessions, have both cleared their backlogs and implemented policies to ensure that no similar situation recurs in the future (Fucci, 2015). But even jurisdictions committed to testing all of the SAKs in their backlog needed to develop a method of prioritizing which cases to submit first. Typical considerations included whether the case was within the statute of limitations (i.e., within the time frame in which it could still be legally prosecuted), whether the suspected offender was alive, and whether the victim was still alive. However, some jurisdictions chose to test only some of the previously unsubmitted or untested SAKs.

A major argument for testing all kits, even in cases where the timeline for prosecution of the crime has lapsed, was to add profiles to the Combined DNA Index System (CODIS), a national database of DNA profiles associated with crime (Campbell, Pierce, Sharma, Feeney, & Fehler-Cabral, 2019). In one jurisdiction that chose to test all backlogged SAKs,

> 59% of all tested SAKs yielded a DNA profile eligible for upload into CODIS, 39% of all tested SAKs yielded a DNA hit, and almost 1000 new DNA profiles had been added to CODIS for potentially solving future crimes. . . . Serial sex offenders were frequently identified in the process. Over a quarter of the defendants identified through the testing and investigating of these previously unsubmitted SAKs were linked to more than one victim. (Lovell, Luminais, Flannery, Bell, & Kyker, 2018, p. 113)

Although some jurisdictions prioritized stranger cases (attacks carried out by someone who was a stranger to the victim) over nonstranger cases, research indicates high value in testing SAKs in both of these instances.

Perhaps the most obvious outcome of testing the SAKs is the increased likelihood that some results could provide justice for victims of sexual assault. Although a SAK cannot definitively "prove" whether a rape took place (Q15), it can provide very useful information. For example, if DNA of another individual is found on the victim's body it indicates that there was physical contact between the victim and the person whose DNA profile was detected. Depending on the type of DNA specimen (e.g., saliva, semen) found and where it was located, the victim's account of the assault can be corroborated, as such findings make it very difficult for the assailant to deny that any contact occurred. If the victim knows the accused assailant's name, law enforcement can collect a reference sample for comparison and test whether the DNA belongs to the accused assailant. If the perpetrator was a stranger or is otherwise unknown to the victim (i.e., if the victim was unconscious during the assault), DNA evidence may be particularly useful in helping to identify a suspect.

Once the specimen collected in the SAK is tested, it is uploaded to CODIS. DNA profiles can be entered into CODIS in one of two ways: associated with an offender or associated with a crime scene. DNA profiles that are collected from offenders upon arrest for another crime are saved in the system's Offender Index along with identifying information about the offender. However, there are also DNA profiles that are found at crime scenes but are not linked to any specific offender (i.e., because the crime is not solved and the offender is not identified). These profiles are stored in CODIS' Forensic Index. As more offender profiles are added to the system, it increases the likelihood of returning a "forensic hit"—a match between an offender profile and unknown DNA found at a crime scene that has been stored in the Forensic Index. With this in mind, it is also evident that testing all DNA evidence collected as part of a SAK is of value beyond the individual case, in that it supports the development of the CODIS database. As stated by Rebecca Campbell, a leading scholar in this field, "rape kit testing has tremendous utility to the criminal justice system, so the failure to test SAKs routinely and consistently is a serious concern" (Campbell et al., 2017, p. 367).

Campbell et al. (2016) assessed for differences in the likelihood of receiving a DNA "hit" for SAKs associated with cases in which the offender was known and SAKs associated with cases in which the offender was unknown (i.e., a stranger). They found that there was no significant difference in the likelihood of a testing "hit," underscoring the importance of submitting SAKs for testing even when the assailant's identity is known. Other researchers agree that "non-stranger SAKs should also be submitted for testing, as they are equally likely to yield a DNA hit—thereby providing corroborating accounts of the sexual assault, confirming the identity of the offender, and even helping solve other crimes when the crimes are linked via DNA" (Lovell et al., 2018, p. 114).

Growing research demonstrates the value of analyzing forensic evidence regardless of whether the case has a known suspect (Campbell, Pierce, Sharma, Feeney, & Fehler-Cabral, 2016; Lovell et al., 2018). If the DNA present in the kit does not match any offender or crime in the CODIS database, it at least continues to add profiles to the CODIS database. However, it may also provide a match to another crime or a known offender in the CODIS database. According to recent scholarship, "a stranger offender commits on average almost three times as many additional DNA crimes as a nonstranger offender. Moreover, for a stranger offender, the likelihood is much higher than for a nonstranger offender that these additional crimes are in the backlog" (Wang & Wein, 2018, p. 1115). If there are time or resource constraints on reducing a rape kit testing backlog, some scholars suggest that it is reasonable to prioritize stranger assault cases over known-offender cases. For example, "If we are to 'weight' the utility of a CODIS hit, it seems likely that a hit producing a potential suspect where there was no suspect beforehand *must* have greater weight than a hit in a case where a suspect has already been developed" (Strom & Hickman, 2016, p. 597). These scholars emphasize that there is value in testing all kits, but recognize that practical constraints sometimes require that analyses of evidence for some cases are prioritized whereas analyses for other cases are delayed. A recent cost-benefit analysis indicated that testing a single SAK costs, on average, $1,641 (Wang & Wein, 2018). However, this report and others estimate that a single sexual assault costs hundreds of thousands of dollars (e.g., victim costs, lost productivity, criminal justice personnel, court costs) (DeLisi et al., 2010). Thus, the authors conclude that testing all kits that are currently backlogged would, on the whole, be a cost-efficient option—contradicting the approach that many jurisdictions have taken of selecting just certain kits to test rather than testing all of them in an attempt to "save money."

Beyond these clear benefits of SAK testing, researchers have argued that testing SAKs is also important for identifying potential serial assailants and to increase the likelihood of discovering wrongful convictions. Given all these potential benefits, the failure to submit and forensically test all SAKs has profound implications. "When SAKs are not analyzed for DNA evidence, sexual offenders are not identified and apprehended, which poses a significant threat to public safety," noted Campbell. "For rape survivors, the failure to test the kit is a breach of trust as they consented to the medical forensic exam with the understanding that the kit would be analyzed and acted upon by the criminal justice system" (Campbell et al., 2017, p. 367). Finally, SAK testing failures and delays can be devastating for the wrongly convicted, because "the evidence that could clear their names is sitting on shelves in police property storage facilities" (Campbell et al., 2017, p. 367).

Given these obvious and compelling benefits to testing SAKs, researchers sought to determine what led to the development of this backlog impacting thousands of victims across so many jurisdictions. A review of evidence collected in property crimes, homicides, and sexual assault cases in a national sample of more than 3,000 law enforcement agencies over a 5-year period found that DNA evidence existed but was not submitted for testing in a substantial number of cases. All told, investigators identified 27,595 rape cases across the United States in which a rape kit had not been sent for forensic testing, despite reporting DNA evidence present in a nontrivial subset of these cases. The most likely reason for not analyzing DNA evidence when it was available, cited by 44 percent of agencies, was because there was no known suspect (Strom & Hickman, 2010). Prior to the development of CODIS, police were only able to test DNA evidence when they had a suspect's DNA to compare it to. Now that CODIS exists, however, testing DNA presents the opportunity to identify a suspect in a specific case even if none is known to law enforcement at the time. However, some law enforcement officers or agencies still adhered to a practice in which they only submitted rape kits for testing when there was a suspect sample for comparison. Because this study used a national sample, researchers were able to consider characteristics of the jurisdictions themselves. They found backlogged DNA evidence in both large jurisdictions (59 percent of sexual assault cases with untested DNA evidence) and small jurisdictions (28 percent of sexual assault cases with untested DNA evidence) (Strom & Hickman, 2010). It was also not limited to DNA evidence representing just one type of crime, but included sexual assaults, homicides, and property crimes.

Research showed that not all of the SAKs were stored and shelved without DNA testing for the same reasons. For example, some SAKs that were not originally tested were collected before the DNA technology available today existed. These cases may still contribute to the backlog and many jurisdictions are now moving to test them with the most current technology (Lovell et al., 2018). Other SAKs were tested using existing technology at the time they were collected, but could be retested now with more advanced techniques that would increase the likelihood of identifying a DNA match. Although they were once submitted and tested, these cases may also be counted in the backlog, because they could now be retested for a more complete evidentiary treatment. However, the majority of scholarship has focused on those cases in which a SAK was collected and never submitted for testing.

Law enforcement personnel play a critical gatekeeping role in this process because if they do not submit the evidence for testing, it will not be tested. The medical professionals who collect the SAKs provide them to law enforcement with the victim's permission and then it is up to the police, who are in charge of the SAK during the chain of custody at this point, to send it to a forensic lab for testing.

Scholars have identified three major reasons why law enforcement agencies operating during the time the backlog developed declined to forward a SAK for testing. First, if the assailant was unknown to the victim and no reference sample of DNA could be submitted for potential confirmation identification, some law enforcement officers saw no additional value of testing any DNA from the SAK. That is, "law enforcement personnel may not be submitting rape kits for forensic analysis because they do not perceive that DNA testing is necessary or helpful to their task of investigating a reported crime" (Campbell et al., 2017, p. 369). Second, some practitioners cited resource constraints (i.e., insufficient funding for forensic testing, substantial delays in receiving forensic results due to high volume of cases being sent for testing) as a reason for not submitting a SAK for testing (Campbell et al., 2017; Campbell & Fehler-Cabral, 2018). Finally, if law enforcement did not believe that a victim was telling the truth about the assault or they felt like the case was weak, they were unlikely to submit the SAK for testing (Campbell & Fehler-Cabral, 2018).

While it makes intuitive sense that an investigator would not want to pour more resources into a case that they believe is unlikely to go to trial, that is a problematic approach because the risks and consequences of error are so high. As discussed elsewhere (Q14), the frequency of false complaints is extremely low. It is much more likely that the victim is telling the truth about the assault and, if they submitted to the invasive and painful forensic exam, that they are invested in helping to prove the case. Furthermore, if a case is weak, the evidence contained in the kit could be of value in strengthening the case.

Research suggests that many of the discretionary decisions made not to test a SAK reflected victim-blaming myths (see Q19) that undermined the victim's account of the attack. "Taken together, the results of this study suggest that this "new" problem of untested rape kits is actually a rather old problem: untested SAKs have been accumulating in police storage facilities for decades because the criminal justice system has not dedicated sufficient resources to combat sexual violence, which is due in no small part to entrenched gender, race, and class biases about rape and credibility of rape victims" (Campbell & Fehler-Cabral, 2018, p. 98).

A second important line of scholarship relating to the backlog of SAKs has focused on the development and implementation of new policies within communities to avoid any future recurrence of a backlog. The city of Mobile, Alabama, started The Promise Initiative, "a comprehensive trauma-informed sexual assault response plan to transform police culture surrounding sexual assault" (Lathan, Langhinrichsen-Rohling, Duncan, & Stefurak, 2019, p. 1734). Researchers and criminal justice practitioners worked together to design and institute new trauma-informed policies in the Mobile Police Department, including mandatory testing of all SAKs. This new policy demonstrates law enforcement's commitment to avoiding another SAK backlog in the future (Lathan et al., 2019). City leaders in Detroit, Michigan, also took steps to improve future responses to investigating sexual assault, particularly with regard to SAKs. Qualitative interviews with members of the Detroit SAK Collaborative, the people responsible for responding to Detroit's backlog, led researchers to make seven key recommendations that incorporate the needs of wider stakeholders within the community as well as victims of sexual assault seeking justice (Campbell & Fehler-Cabral, 2020). These recommendations included "identify a champion of the cause to create and sustain interorganizational collaboration," "designate a senior executive as project coordinator for oversight and management," and "involve both front-line staff and high-level executives to streamline decision making." There must be buy-in from leadership, someone to keep the members of all agencies motivated and moving forward, and someone to handle various the logistics necessary to address such a complex problem. The study also urged recognition of each of the multiple agencies involved in the response, so that stakeholders "take time to build knowledge and respect within the multidisciplinary team" and "utilize multiple strategies for managing conflict and group participation." Finally, the recommendations emphasize the long-term nature of the problem of backlogged SAKs: "develop a sustainable staffing plan to balance workloads" and "prepare for change because change is constant." Recognizing that there will be turnover in staff and changes in important variables such as "funding, resources, and community support" (Campbell & Fehler-Cabral, 2020, p. 168) is critical. Without adequate participation and organization, a change in one position, a lapse in federal funding, or negative media coverage may derail a community's efforts to test their SAKs. Thus, having a realistic sense of the challenges associated with such a task and committed personnel in various agencies is essential.

With regard to current rape kit backlogs, the above practices are critical to victim healing and recovery and may also increase the faith of victims of sexual assault in the criminal justice process. However, some untested SAKs date back decades. In some cases where SAKs finally undergo testing, law enforcement or prosecutors may find themselves in the position of contacting victims who believed their cases to be closed, thus possibly reopening emotional wounds and memories from years and years in the past. Communities seeking to test backlogged SAKs thus must be very thoughtful and intentional about their victim notification procedures so as not to further traumatize the individual to whom they are reaching out.

Victim advocates may play a particularly important role in the notification process and in follow-up with the victims.

In short, the backlog of sexual assault forensic exams in the United States was a substantial problem impacting hundreds of thousands of cases. Furthermore, the impacts of the backlog are significant because they show deliberate indifference to potential evidence and failure to fully investigate a serious violent crime. This failure obviously harms the victim who underwent the exam with the full expectation that the evidence would be tested. It also undermines public safety efforts by not contributing to CODIS, data from which can be valuable in identifying serial offenders. Finally, wrongfully convicted individuals have been identified and exonerated following the DNA analysis of evidence related to the crime for which they were convicted. Failure to test all kits limits the likelihood that such a discovery would occur. Over the last decade, significant resources have been devoted to bringing the backlog up to date, particularly in some jurisdictions throughout the United States (notable examples include Detroit, Michigan; Houston, Texas; and Cuyahoga County, Ohio). Lessons learned from these jurisdictions may inform other locations as they work to test previously unsubmitted or untested SAKs. Key considerations for these locations should include promoting sustainable multidisciplinary collaborations and employing victim-centered policies and approaches (Pinchevsky, 2018).

FURTHER READING

Campbell, Rebecca, and Giannina Fehler-Cabral. "Why police 'couldn't or wouldn't' submit sexual assault kits for forensic DNA testing: A focal concerns theory analysis of untested rape kits." *Law & Society Review* 52, no. 1 (2018): 73–105.

Campbell, Rebecca, and Giannina Fehler-Cabral. "The best way out is always through: Addressing the problem of untested sexual assault kits (SAKs) through multidisciplinary collaboration." *Victims & Offenders* 15, no. 2 (2020): 159–173.

Campbell, Rebecca, Hannah Feeney, Giannina Fehler-Cabral, Jessica Shaw, and Sheena Horsford. "The national problem of untested sexual assault kits (SAKs): Scope, causes, and future directions for research, policy, and practice." *Trauma, Violence, & Abuse* 18, no. 4 (2017): 363–376.

Campbell, Rebecca, Steven J. Pierce, Dhruv B. Sharma, Hannah Feeney, and Giannina Fehler-Cabral. "Should rape kit testing be prioritized by victim–offender relationship? Empirical comparison of forensic testing outcomes for stranger and nonstranger sexual assaults." *Criminology & Public Policy* 15, no. 2 (2016): 555–583.

Campbell, Rebecca, Steven J. Pierce, Dhruv B. Sharma, Hannah Feeney, and Giannina Fehler-Cabral. "Developing empirically informed policies for sexual assault kit DNA testing: Is it too late to test kits beyond the statute of limitations?" *Criminal Justice Policy Review* 30, no. 1 (2019): 3–27.

DeLisi, Matt, Anna Kosloski, Molly Sween, Emily Hachmeister, Matt Moore, and Alan Drury. "Murder by numbers: Monetary costs imposed by a sample of homicide offenders." *The Journal of Forensic Psychiatry & Psychology* 21, no. 4 (2010): 501–513.

Fucci, Glenne Ellen. "No law and no order: local, state and federal government responses to the United States rape kit backlog crisis." *Cardozo Public Law, Policy and Ethics Journal* 14, no. 1 (Fall 2015): 193–228.

Lathan, Emma, Jennifer Langhinrichsen-Rohling, Jessica Duncan, and James "Tres" Stefurak. "The Promise Initiative: Promoting a trauma-informed police response to sexual assault in a mid-size Southern community." *Journal of Community Psychology* 47, no. 7 (2019): 1733–1749.

Lovell, Rachel, Misty Luminais, Daniel J. Flannery, Richard Bell, and Brett Kyker. "Describing the process and quantifying the outcomes of the Cuyahoga County sexual assault kit initiative." *Journal of Criminal Justice* 57 (2018): 106–115.

Lovell, Rachel, Laura Overman, Duoduo Huang, and Daniel J. Flannery. "The bureaucratic burden of identifying your rapist and remaining 'cooperative': What the sexual assault kit initiative tells us about sexual assault case attrition and outcomes." *American Journal of Criminal Justice* (2020): 1–26.

Peterson, Joseph, Donald Johnson, Denise Herz, Lisa Graziano, and Taly Oehler. "Sexual assault kit backlog study." The National Institute of Justice, 2012.

Spohn, Cassia. "Sexual assault case processing: The more things change, the more they stay the same." *International Journal for Crime, Justice and Social Democracy* 9(1) (2020): 86–94. https://doi.org/10.5204/ijcjsd.v9i1.1454

Strom, Kevin J., and Matthew J. Hickman. "Unanalyzed evidence in law-enforcement agencies: A national examination of forensic processing in police departments." *Criminology and Public Policy* 9, no. 2 (2010): 381–404.

Strom, Kevin J., and Matthew J. Hickman. "Untested sexual assault kits: Searching for an empirical foundation to guide forensic case processing decisions," *Criminology and Public Policy* 15, no. 2 (May 2016): 593–[ii].

Pinchevsky, Gillian M. "Criminal justice considerations for unsubmitted and untested sexual assault kits: A review of the literature and suggestions for moving forward." *Criminal Justice Policy Review* 29, no. 9 (2018): 925–945.

Wang, Can, and Lawrence M. Wein. "Analyzing approaches to the backlog of untested sexual assault kits in the USA." *Journal of Forensic Sciences* 63, no. 4 (2018): 1110–1121.

Q24. ARE THERE STEPS THAT LAW ENFORCEMENT CAN TAKE TO BETTER RESPOND TO SEXUAL ASSAULTS?

Answer: Absolutely. Decades of research on the troubled relationship between law enforcement and sexual assault victims have led to clear recommendations for improvement. As a result, many victim-centered and trauma-oriented reforms have been implemented in jurisdictions throughout the country to try and strengthen the relationship between law enforcement and the victims they are tasked with serving.

The Facts: Numerous books and academic articles have been published outlining criticisms of law enforcement's handling of sexual assault victims and cases. Attention to these criticisms has led researchers, activists, and criminal justice practitioners to examine existing practices and identify areas for improvement. The early identification of the phenomenon of secondary victimization (i.e., insensitive response to victims of sexual assault that worsens their already traumatic experience), for example, led to the development of recommendations for fundamental changes to improve the victim's experience within the criminal justice system. The simple shift of framing law enforcement's interaction with the victim of crime as "an interview" in which they are gathering information rather than "an interrogation" where they are trying to gauge the victim's honesty can substantially alter the nature of that interaction, with clear benefits to the victim.

A major 2013 study titled "Policing and Prosecuting Sexual Assault: Inside the Criminal Justice System" led to the development of a number of improvements in law enforcement practice. These reforms, argued the study's authors, would "reduce case attrition, hold those who commit crimes accountable, and improve the treatment of victims who report their crimes to law enforcement agencies" (Spohn & Tellis, 2013, p. 229). This study and its resulting recommendations are outlined below.

The study, which was part of a project funded by the National Institute of Justice, granted researchers substantial access to 5 years' worth of sexual assault case files from both the county and city of Los Angeles, California. The study also included extensive interviews with 52 members of the Los Angeles Police Department (LAPD), 24 members of the Los Angeles Sheriff's Department (LASD), and 30 county prosecutors (Spohn & Tellis, 2013). The qualitative data gained in these interviews were used to generate a list of policy reform recommendations for law enforcement agencies.

First, researchers emphasized the importance of establishing and maintaining special units dedicated to the investigation of sex crimes. Of course, not all law enforcement agencies have sufficient number of employees to develop a special unit, but the study's authors asserted that even if a department or agency only gives specialized training to a single detective, it improves the odds that it will be able to ensure an appropriate response to a sexual assault victim.

Even in large jurisdictions, however, the mere existence of a specialized unit is not enough to ensure its success. Department leadership needs to be supportive of the unit and view it as a valuable component of the jurisdiction's response to sexual assault. Furthermore, the members of the unit must feel the same way.

During the interviews conducted for the 2013 study, participant after participant indicated that investigating sex crimes is not the same as investigating other types of crimes. Unlike homicide, the victims are alive. Unlike theft or vandalism, it is the victim's body that is a crime scene. Moreover, the traumatic impact of sexual assault on the victim is far more severe than most other types of crime (with the exception of homicide or attempted homicide) and the risk of secondary victimization is high (Q16). Thus, only detectives who are genuinely invested in catching sex offenders and sensitive to the issues facing sexual assault victims during this challenging time should be considered for the unit. If someone is placed in a sex crimes unit who does not want to be there it may do more harm than good, because a victim will likely sense this and suffer an increased risk of secondary victimization.

Second, the study's authors emphasized that it is critical for all members of law enforcement who interact with victims of sexual assault to receive training on sexual assault cases. Even if the jurisdiction has a sex crimes unit, it is still possible that the victim's first interaction will be with a patrol officer because they are often the first responders to the scene. If a patrol officer is untrained and does a poor job of documenting statements or evidence in their initial report, it can hurt the investigation down the line, leading to case attrition (Q27). If the first responding officer alienates the victim by being dismissive or judgmental, it can decrease the likelihood that the victim will be willing to cooperate with the police moving forward. The authors emphasized that one training session is insufficient and that training should be a recurring event. These annual training programs ensure that the officers do not forget what they have learned and provide opportunities for them to learn the most recent and complete information possible.

For example, the literature on the neurobiology of trauma as it relates to sexual assault victimization has expanded significantly since the early 2010s. By receiving ongoing training, law enforcement personnel tasked with responding to victims of sexual assault gain a better understanding of why many victims do not report their assaults right away or why the narrative account of the assault may evolve in the first 48 hours following the assault (Q12). There are important scientific explanations for these phenomena, but without training, someone may mistakenly attribute disjointed or shifting accounts to dishonesty rather than mental or emotional turmoil. More recent studies demonstrate that effective training of law enforcement officers significantly improves their attitudes toward sexual assault victims (Campbell, Lapsey, & Wells, 2020) and understanding of how trauma may manifest in a recent victim of crime (Campbell et al., 2020; Franklin, Garza, Goodson, & Bouffard, 2020). A history of specialized training relating to sexual assault has been shown to prepare officers to better respond to sexual assault cases (Garza & Franklin, 2021).

Third, the authors of the 2013 study argued that "to be effective, law enforcement must engage the victim as an ally in the investigation" (Spohn and Tellis, 2013). They noted that the victim can strengthen the investigation by helping to locate potential evidence, for example, by sharing messages sent by the suspect via social media. It may also help with evidence generation by working with law enforcement to make a "pretext phone call." This investigative strategy can be used when the alleged assailant is someone the victim knows and the victim calls on a recorded line to try and get the assailant to apologize, admit guilt, or provide some other form of incriminating statement that can be used as evidence against them. In order for this approach to be used, the victim must be an active part of the process and engaged with law enforcement. Although it was not explicitly mentioned by the authors as a part of this recommendation, treating the victim as an ally during the investigation would also likely promote further victim cooperation by reducing the likelihood that the victim feels like their case is unimportant or is not being taken seriously.

Fourth, based on their findings, the authors suggest that law enforcement receive training specifically on the use of exceptional clearances.

This specific method for reclassifying a case from active investigation (discussed in Q13) is often misused (Spohn & Tellis, 2013). An exceptional clearance is only supposed to be used in very specific circumstances (e.g., if law enforcement have identified the offender but that person is deceased and therefore cannot be arrested). When these clearances are applied in cases that are not truly "exceptional" and when probable cause does exist for an arrest, it may lead to cases being closed before all investigative steps are exhausted. If exceptional clearances were better understood and implemented uniformly across jurisdictions, it would give people a clearer sense of how sexual assault cases are actually resolved.

Finally, the authors recommended that all departments have clear written policies, procedures, and expectations for law enforcement officers who are responsible for investigating sex crimes. This is a relatively simple recommendation and could be implemented regardless of the size, location, or other unique features of the department. There are resources to aid in the development of such policies, the implementation of which would demonstrate law enforcement's commitment to providing a strong response to cases of sexual assault. One such resource is the "Enhancing Law Enforcement Response to Victims" program sponsored by the Office of Victims Services and available from the International Association of Chiefs of Police (IACP).

FURTHER READING

Campbell, Bradley A., David S. Lapsey, and William Wells. "An evaluation of Kentucky's sexual assault investigator training: Results from a randomized three-group experiment." *Journal of Experimental Criminology* 16, no. 4 (2020): 625–647.

Franklin, Cortney A., Alondra D. Garza, Amanda Goodson, and Leana Allen Bouffard. "Police perceptions of crime victim behaviors: A trend analysis exploring mandatory training and knowledge of sexual and domestic violence survivors' trauma responses." *Crime & Delinquency* 66, no. 8 (2020): 1055–1086.

Garza, Alondra D., and Cortney A. Franklin. "The effect of rape myth endorsement on police response to sexual assault survivors." *Violence against Women* 27, no. 3–4 (2021): 552–573.

Spohn, Cassia, and Katharine Tellis. *Policing and Prosecuting Sexual Assault: Inside the Criminal Justice System.* Lynne Rienner Publishers, 2013.

Rich, Karen. "Trauma informed police responses to rape victims." *Journal of Aggression, Maltreatment & Trauma* 28, no. 4 (2019): 463–480.

Q25. ARE THERE STEPS THAT PROSECUTORS CAN TAKE TO BETTER RESPOND TO SEXUAL ASSAULTS?

Answer: Yes, some specific practices for prosecutors have been identified that can improve victim interactions with the court system. As the primary gatekeeper to the court system, prosecutors are the actors responsible for implementing most of these changes.

The Facts: After an offender is identified and arrested, the case is handed over to the district attorney's office where a prosecutor will decide whether to pursue charges against the suspect. In most criminal cases, the prosecution is handled in a "horizontal" format such that each phase of the court proceedings is handled by a different prosecutor. That is, one prosecutor is responsible for determining the appropriate crimes with which to charge the offender, another prosecutor is in charge of presenting potential charges to the grand jury, another prosecutor represents the state at arraignments, and so on. However, in cases that involve particularly traumatic events, including murder and sexual assault, many jurisdictions have implemented what is known as "vertical prosecution." In these specific cases, the same prosecutor is in charge of the case from start to finish and will work with the victim from the initial interview through the sentencing hearing. This is believed to be a more trauma-informed approach to prosecuting sexual assaults because it reduces the number of new contacts that the victim has to make during the course of the criminal justice process and reduces the number of times that they must recount the narrative of the assault, although the impact of vertical prosecution is not yet empirically determined (Spohn, 2021). Regardless of whether the case is handled horizontally or vertically, the prosecutor will play a central role in determining whether the case moves forward. Criminal justice scholars sometimes refer to prosecutors as the "gatekeepers" of the criminal justice system (Spohn, Beichner, & Davis-Frenzel, 2001), because they have sole discretion over whether and which charges are filed in their jurisdictions. No one can appeal a prosecutor's decision not to file charges or force a prosecutor to pursue a certain charge or sentencing recommendation. Thus, understanding their role is key to understanding the criminal justice process. Prior literature indicates that prosecutors make decisions based on a series of "focal concerns," a few pieces of data that impact the ultimate decision, such as severity of the crime, level of harm caused to the victim, strength of evidence (Spohn et al., 2001), and whether the victim is viewed as credible (Beichner & Spohn, 2005). As discussed in Q24, a major study out of Los Angeles conducted by Cassia Spohn and Katherine Tellis led to the development of a set of specific policy recommendations for prosecutors in sexual assault cases (Spohn & Tellis, 2013, p. 231). Five of these recommendations, based on both quantitative analysis of case outcomes and qualitative interviews, are discussed below.

First, the authors urged prosecutors to file criminal charges more often in sexual assault cases. According to the American Bar Association, "A prosecutor should seek or file criminal charges only if the prosecutor reasonably believes that the charges are supported by probable cause, that admissible evidence will be sufficient to support conviction beyond a reasonable doubt, and that the decision to charge is in the interests of justice" (3–4.2a, Criminal Justice Standards for the Prosecution Function). If the case that is initially brought to the prosecutor for review does not meet the standard just outlined, they can ask law enforcement to investigate more fully rather than decline to file charges (Spohn & Tellis, 2013).

In their investigation of police and prosecutor's practices in Los Angeles, Spohn and Tellis also found that many law enforcement officers would bring the notes of their initial investigation to the prosecutor to see whether it was enough to file charges. When the prosecutor said "no" (which was the result in most cases), the detective then closed the investigation with the rationale that the prosecutor had declined to file charges in the case. This is not an appropriate use of a prearrest evaluation. Rather, if the prosecutor declines to file charges at the prearrest evaluation, law enforcement should resume investigating and attempt to gather more evidence until all avenues have been exhausted. Only after that point, if a prosecutor still declines to file charges, should a case be set aside or closed. If this practice was implemented, it would mean that prosecutors should not make a judgment as to whether an arrest should be made until a thorough investigation is complete. Thus, law enforcement would not be able to clear a case until it had been thoroughly investigated.

Third, in line with a trauma-informed approach, Spohn and Tellis recommended that prosecutors "establish a formal process in conjunction with law enforcement for the interview with the victim so that one interview occurs with representatives from both law enforcement and the prosecutor's office present. This will reduce trauma for victims and make it less likely that inconsistencies in the words victims use to describe the assault to law enforcement officials and prosecutors will result in the rejection of charges" (Spohn & Tellis, 2013, p. 230). The two benefits of conducting a joint victim interview (with both law and enforcement and the prosecutor present) are significant. First, combining these interviews means that the victim will have to recount their story one less time, field questions about the traumatic and personal event one less time, and risk secondary victimization one less time, thus reducing the risk of further trauma. Second, because both agencies will be represented at the same meeting and will hear each question being asked, both will be privy to the same information. This decreases the risk of new or distinct information coming up during two separate interviews, which some investigators may mistakenly interpret as dishonesty on the part of the victim (see Q12).

Fourth, the authors argue that prosecutors need training on interview techniques with people who have suffered trauma. Many cases that are reported to police do not move to a prosecution phase, decreasing the frequency of contact between victims and prosecutors. However, it is clear that prosecutors play a critical role in case processing and thus are in a position to impact the victim through secondary victimization, further trauma as a result of judgmental, minimizing behavior, or victim-blaming treatment.

For example, if law enforcement investigates a sexual assault case and identifies a suspect, makes an arrest, and passes the case to the prosecutor, only to have the prosecutor declines to file charges, that may constitute a severe emotional blow to the victim. This relates to the fifth recommendation that Spohn and Tellis make, which is that if prosecutors decline to move forward with charges in a case, they should make every effort to fully explain should their decision to the victim. This would give the victim the opportunity to ask questions about the process. It may also give the prosecutor the opportunity to explain that just because a sexual assault can't be proven in court, it doesn't mean that law enforcement doesn't believe the victim. If this is one such case, the prosecutor can commend the victim's bravery in coming forward and emphasize the fact that because they came forward and the assailant now has an arrest record, any future cases involving the perpetrator may be stronger. Of course, that scenario does not provide the victim with justice, but it at least provides some transparency within the system and acknowledges the victim's experience.

As an additional recommendation, Spohn and Tellis recommended careful analysis of the most frequently rejected legal cases "to inform training protocols for investigations, evidence collection, and successful prosecution" (Spohn & Tellis, 2013, p. 230). Adopting such a practice would promote conversations to help identify potential similarities in cases that do not move forward and give criminal justice stakeholders the opportunity to discuss areas of improvement that may help address those types of cases. For example, they could strategize about the use of specific practices early on in the process such as pretextual phone calls or reaching out to the friend or family member to whom the victim first disclosed their experience (known as an "outcry witness"). Or perhaps the group may identify trends in grand jury or jury decisions that may lead them to consider introducing expert testimony on a particular issue. These types of changes may be simple to implement and have a significant impact on ultimate case disposition, but are far more likely to be identified and implemented if a jurisdiction engages in a systematic review of cases.

FURTHER READING

Beichner, Dawn, and Cassia Spohn. "Prosecutorial charging decisions in sexual assault cases: Examining the impact of a specialized prosecution unit." *Criminal Justice Policy Review* 16, no. 4 (2005): 461–498.

Spohn, Cassia. "Specialized units and vertical prosecution approaches." In *The Oxford Handbook of Prosecutors and Prosecution*, edited by Ronald F. Wright, Kay L. Levine, & Russell M. Gold, 259. Oxford University Press, 2021.

Spohn, Cassia, Dawn Beichner, and Erika Davis-Frenzel. "Prosecutorial justifications for sexual assault case rejection: Guarding the 'gateway to justice.'" *Social Problems* 48, no. 2 (2001): 206–235.

Spohn, Cassia, and Katharine Tellis. *Policing and Prosecuting Sexual Assault: Inside the Criminal Justice System.* Lynne Rienner Publishers, 2013.

Q26. ARE SEXUAL ASSAULT RESPONSE TEAMS (SARTS) AN EFFECTIVE METHOD OF ADDRESSING THE PROBLEM OF SEXUAL ASSAULT?

Answer: Sexual assault response teams (SARTs) are interdisciplinary multiagency collaborative groups that seek to increase reporting, improve victims' experiences as they navigate the criminal justice system, and promote public safety by holding offenders accountable and providing education on sexual assault prevention. SARTs are perceived by key stakeholders as valuable tools in responding to sexual assault. However, the data are limited as to whether the presence of a SART impacts criminal justice outcomes (e.g., higher rates of reporting, arrests, or convictions).

The Facts: Before addressing this question fully, it is important to understand what a SART is and what these groups intend to achieve. The criminal justice system is large and complex and may be intimidating or overwhelming to those who are unfamiliar with it, particularly in a time of increased vulnerability like just after a traumatic event. For example, following a sexual assault, a victim may go to the hospital for a forensic examination (often called a "rape kit"; see Q15) and share the story of their sexual assault with the sexual assault nurse examiner (SANE) or other medical professional who is conducting the exam. The victim may also call 911 to report the assault to law enforcement, at which point a patrol officer will respond to the scene and interview the victim about the facts of the assault (again requiring the victim to provide a narrative account of the assault). After the case is assigned to a detective, that detective will contact the victim to begin an investigation and the victim will be asked to recount the details of the assault to the detective who will be assigned to their case (requiring the victim to provide their third account). If suffi-cient evidence is available to identify and arrest a suspect, the case may be referred to a prosecutor who will decide whether to file charges. However, this decision is often informed by a meeting with the victim in which the prosecutor asks about facts of the case, forcing the victim to provide yet another account of the assault. Most jurisdictions also have trained rape crisis advocates who are available to the victim throughout this entire process, from the time of the initial presentation at the hospital or con-tact with law enforcement through the final disposition of the case—and even after as the victim needs further support (see Q31 for a discussion of rape crisis advocates). Although the victim will likely have contact with representatives from each of these agencies (medical, law enforcement, prosecution, advocate), these agencies usually have no mandate or require-ment to have close contact with each other. If each agency works to build its own file, seeking information from the victim and reporting back to the victim as the investigation progresses, the victim can easily become overwhelmed. They are forced to repeat their account of their experience over and over again, each time introducing the possibility of experienc-ing secondary victimization and potentially exhausting their engagement with the process. Introducing an interagency collaborative group of those individuals who are most likely to interact with sexual assault victims in the area, a group known as a sexual assault response team (SART), is a key innovation in improving responses to sexual assault. These multia-gency, multidisciplinary groups generally include representatives from law enforcement, prosecutors, SANEs, and rape crisis advocates. Other mem-bers of a SART in some communities also include mental health profes-sionals, academics, and forensic scientists.

SARTs first appeared in the 1970s and are now present in hundreds of jurisdictions throughout the United States. The Department of Justice provides guidelines for how to create, organize, and run a SART, but different jurisdictions have implemented these guidelines differently based on their own unique characteristics. SARTs are community specific and generally work within a single county, although some SARTs serve multiple counties (Greeson Campbell, & Bybee, 2015). According to national guidelines, the two primary goals of SARTs are, "to improve the quality of victims' experiences of seeking help (i.e., making systems more accessible and responsive to survivors) and to increase offender accountability by increasing reporting and conviction rates of sexual assault cases in the criminal justice system" (Greeson & Campbell, 2015). Another goal of some SARTs is to enhance public awareness of the problem of sexual assault and provide knowledge that can help to prevent or reduce sexual assault (Greeson & Campbell, 2015).

SARTs typically have a single individual who serves as a leader or coordinator. The groups meet on a regular basis (monthly or quarterly) and may engage in many activities during these meetings. A common activity is case review, in which a specific sexual assault investigation is presented to the group and then discussed to determine the appropriate next steps for handling this case. Other common activities include guest speakers or cross-agency trainings to keep all members of the SART informed and up-to-date on research and policy developments impacting sexual assault response. There may be steps and processes within each agency that could be improved upon and would benefit from a review conducted by other professionals familiar with responding to sexual assault. To this end, many SARTs engage in policy development and evaluation together.

In a major national study of SARTs, members expressed confidence that SART benefited sexual assault victims in their communities (Greeson et al., 2015). This study used phone interviews with members of 127 SARTs throughout the United States to assess SART structures and perceptions of effectiveness. Moreover, when asked whether the existence of a SART in the community improved "victims' help-seeking experiences," "victims' participation in the criminal justice system," "police processing of sexual assault cases," and "prosecution of sexual assault cases," representatives of SARTs that had been in existence for longer periods of time perceived their organizations as more effective in all of these areas than SARTs that were newer (Greeson et al., 2015).

Much of the published work on SARTs attempts to better understand the interactions between agencies and members that may pose obstacles to collaboration (Moylan & Lindhurst, 2015). In the first review of scientific literature on SARTs, the authors identified five challenges to developing and maintaining a successful SART: (1) barriers to coordinating efforts across multiple organizations, (2) getting buy-in from all relevant organizations, (3) members joining the SART who have competing or conflicting goals, (4) confusion or disagreement over who is responsible for each role on a SART, and (5) agencies having access to different information that may be protected from other SART members due to confidentiality concerns (Greeson & Campbell, 2013). These challenges have been studied with regard to how they impact the SART members' experiences on the team, but it remains unclear whether or how these challenges ultimately impact SART goals in such areas as victim experience, perpetrator accountability, and prevention education.

In fact, the actual impact of a SART on victim outcomes and perpetrator accountability is unclear at this point. A few jurisdictions have implemented studies to assess whether the introduction of a SART had an impact on case outcomes (e.g., number of arrests, convictions), but the studies have been largely inconclusive. For example, a study of cases in Rhode Island concluded that "the program has demonstrated positive effects in that there is demand among sexual assault victims for SART services . . . At this stage in the development of the SART program there is, however, no clear effect on the legal outcome of cases" (Wilson & Klein, 2005). However, despite the fact that the SART did not statistically significantly increase the likelihood of a case moving farther through the criminal justice system, the authors caution that their sample was small enough that significant effects may not have been detectable.

A three-site study of the effect of SARTs and SANEs (see Q32) found that the presence of these programs increased the likelihood of a perpetrator being arrested, charged, and convicted (Nugent-Borakove et al., 2006). However, the authors note that other variables have stronger effects on the likelihood of arrest and conviction than the presence of a SART or SANE program. Furthermore, this study used a comparison of cases in which the victim had both an exam from a SANE and had their case handled by a SART, in contrast to victims who had neither a SANE exam or a SART. Thus, it is not possible to detect to what degree these impacts were due to the SART and to what degree they were due to the additional evidence obtained by a SANE exam.

Overall, however, there is reason to believe that SARTs benefit victims of sexual assault and help improve treatment of sexual assault survivors within the community. The stakeholders who form these groups are generally motivated (Mathews & Hulton, 2020) and perceive that their efforts are effective and worthwhile (e.g., Greeson et al., 2015).

FURTHER READING

Greeson, Megan R., and Rebecca Campbell. "Sexual Assault Response Teams (SARTs): An empirical review of their effectiveness and challenges to successful implementation." *Trauma, Violence, & Abuse* 14, no. 2 (2013): 83–95.

Greeson, Megan R., and Rebecca Campbell. "Coordinated community efforts to respond to sexual assault: A national study of sexual assault response team implementation." *Journal of Interpersonal Violence* 30, no. 14 (2015): 2470–2487.

Greeson, Megan, Rebecca Campbell, and Deborah Bybee. "Sexual assault Response Team (SART) Functioning and Effectiveness: Findings from the national SART project." (2015). https://www.nsvrc.org/sites/default/files/publication_researchbrief_sexual-assault-response-team-functioning-effectiveness.pdf

Mathews, Phyllis Adams, and Linda Hulton. "Interprofessional collaboration practice: Are you doing it well? Individual perceptions within Sexual Assault Response Team (SART)." *Journal of Interprofessional Education & Practice* 19 (2020): 100326.

Moylan, C. A., and T. Lindhorst. "Catching flies with honey: The management of conflict in sexual assault response Teams." *Journal of Interpersonal Violence* 30, no. 11 (2005): 1945–1964.

Nugent-Borakove, M. Elaine, P. Fanflik, David Troutman, Nicole Johnson, A. Burgess, and A. O'Connor. *Testing the Efficacy of the SANE/SART Programs.* American Prosecutors Research Institute, 2006.

Wilson, Doug, and Andrew Klein. *An Evaluation of the Rhode Island Sexual Assault Response Team (SART).* BOTEC Analysis Corporation, 2005.

6

❖❖❖

Government and Criminal Justice Responses to Sexual Offenders

The material covered to this point, particularly in Chapters 3 and 5, has established that there are many problems with how sexual assault victims are treated in the criminal justice system, particularly with regard to secondary victimization. As will be discussed in Q27 ("Do most sex offenses result in prison time for the offender?"), case attrition is another serious problem in the criminal justice system. Case attrition—arrests that ultimately fail to produce convictions—may traumatize victims of sexual assault by failing to hold most sex offenders accountable for their crimes. However, the remaining questions in this chapter will also discuss substantial problems with how sex offenders are handled by the criminal justice system. Q28 ("Do most *convicted* sex offenders serve time in jail or prison?") demonstrates that the small percentage of sex offenders who *are* convicted are generally treated harshly in the criminal justice system, even following their period of incarceration. Upon release, federal and state laws require sex offenders submit to registration and community notification, as well as additional constraints such as residency restrictions or GPS monitoring. In the most severe cases (i.e., repeat violent offending, crimes against children), sex offenders may be civilly committed or chemically castrated upon release from the department of corrections. While these initiatives may be appropriate for some offenders, contrary to popular knowledge, much research shows that most sex offenders are not serial offenders, as will be discussed in Q29 ("Do all sex offenders reoffend?"). That research calls into question many of the public safety initiatives that have been put into place to protect society, such as sex offender registries, as will be discussed in Q30 ("Are sex offender registries effective public safety tools?"). Overall, this chapter will introduce some of the major issues associated with the criminal justice system's attempt to control sex offenders. There are offices and agencies designated for this purpose (e.g., within the Department of Justice, the Office of Sex Offender Sentencing, Monitoring, Apprehending, Registering, and Tracking; SMART) but the scientific evidence suggests that there are still significant problems.

Q27. DO MOST SEX OFFENSES RESULT IN PRISON TIME FOR THE OFFENDER?

Answer: No. If the question was, "Do most *convicted* sex offenders go to prison?" the answer would be, "yes." But because the question refers to all sex offenders, the answer is "no." Most rapes are never brought to the attention of law enforcement (see Q11), which means that those rapists are not investigated, identified, or arrested. Of those cases that are reported to law enforcement, few lead to an arrest (generally around 10 percent). Of those that do lead to an arrest, only some will result in charges being filed by the prosecutor and even fewer result in convictions. This phenomenon, known as case attrition, means that most sex offenders do not go to prison.

The Facts: The American criminal justice system is sometimes compared to a funnel. Although millions of crimes are committed each year in the United States, only a small portion are processed all the way through the criminal justice system and end up with a sentence being imposed. The wide top of the funnel represents the many cases that could potentially move through the criminal justice system, but with each additional step in the process, the funnel narrows as more and more cases drop away. When a case is no longer moving through the criminal justice process, which can happen for many different reasons, that is what criminal justice scholars call, "case attrition." The case has fallen out of the criminal justice funnel.

As discussed in Q11, far less than half of all sexual assaults are reported to the police. However, case attrition among those sexual assault cases that do come to the attention of law enforcement is a significant problem. Of those crimes that are reported, most will be investigated and some of those investigations will lead to an arrest. However, there will be cases in which the investigation does not lead to identification of a suspect, or in which police do not have sufficient evidence (i.e., probable cause) to arrest a suspect. Those instances constitute further case attrition. If there is probable cause to make an arrest and the file is passed to the district attorney, the prosecutor may decide not to file charges. In another case, the prosecutor may decide to file charges but a grand jury of citizens choose not to indict the offender. In another case, the prosecutor may file charges and a grand jury may indict the offender, but the jury responsible for rendering a verdict at trial (known as a petit jury) finds the defendant not guilty. By the time the funnel has narrowed to those crimes that result in an offender being found guilty, the percentage of original cases that remain is in the single digits.

Two major studies of sexual assault case attrition provide more specific data on these trends: the work of Spohn and Tellis (2013) and the work of Morabito and colleagues (2019). Researchers conducted a study of all cases of sexual assault against adults in the county of Los Angeles, California, across a 5-year period (2005–2009), which totaled more than 7,000 cases across the two jurisdictions: LA Police Department (LAPD) and LA Sheriff's Dept (LASD). The researchers analyzed case files for all sexual assaults against adults during the 5-year study period and then looked at the ultimate outcomes for these cases. As shown in Table 27.1, among the cases reported to LAPD, a total of 616 arrests were made, representing just 12.24 percent of sexual assault cases reported to LAPD during that period. Of these, prosecutors filed charges in 486 cases (9.66 percent of the total number of sexual assaults reported), the defendant was convicted in 390 cases (7.75 percent of total reported cases), and the defendant received a prison sentence in 232 cases (4.61 percent of reported cases). Ultimately, out of 5,031 rapes reported to LAPD during the 5-year period being studied, 232 offenders were incarcerated. Even if the attrition rate was calculated using the extremely generous sampling frame of only those who are arrested, still fewer than 40 percent (37.66 percent) of offenders were incarcerated. The result only rose above 50 percent when the number of defendants sentenced to prison were divided into the number of defendants convicted (232/390 = 59.5 percent).

The rates of arrest, conviction, and incarceration were slightly higher among cases under the LA Sherriff's Office's jurisdiction (see Table 27.1). Of the 2,269 cases that were reported to the LASD during the 5-year study period, 770 resulted in arrest (nearly 34 percent of reported cases). Ultimately, charges were filed against 405 people (17.8 percent of reported cases), 317 defendants were found guilty (13.97 percent of reported cases) and 179 (7.89 percent of reported cases), were sent to prison. To summarize, 179 sex offenders were sent to prison for the 2,269 sexual assaults reported to LASD during the 5-year study period, which represents just 23.2 percent of those who were arrested (substantially lower than LAPD's rate). Again,

Table 27.1. Case attrition

	Spohn & Tellis (2013) LAPD Cases = 5,031		Spohn & Tellis (2013) LASD Cases = 2,269		Morabito et al. (2019) Cases from 6 sites = 3,269	
Arrest Made - Total	n = 616	12.24%	n = 770	33.94%	n = 544	18.8%
Charges Filed	n = 486	9.66%	n = 405	17.80%	n = 363	11.1%
Defendant Convicted	n = 390	7.75%	n = 317	13.97%	n = 189	5.8%
Sentenced to Probation	n = 145	2.88%	n = 111	4.89%		
Sentenced to Prison	n = 232	4.61%	n = 179	7.89%		

Note: Percentages calculated as n by estimated total number of reported sexual assaults

the likelihood of going to prison only passed 50 percent when the number of defendants sentenced to prison was divided by the number of defendants convicted (179/317 = 56.5 percent).

The findings of Cassia Spohn and Katherine Tellis' 2013 work suggest that case attrition is a serious problem. However, these data reflect a snapshot of time (2005–2009) in just one county (Los Angeles, California). Scholars put more faith in research that has been replicated, particularly if it can be replicated under different conditions. A federally funded study by Melissa S. Morabito, Linda Meyer Williams, and April Patavina used six sites throughout the United States to see whether the findings reported by Spohn and Tellis were present elsewhere. The 2019 Morabito–Williams–Patavina study included small, medium, and large jurisdictions and analyzed case outcomes for 3,269 sexual assault cases that were reported in these locations between 2008 and 2010. Of those cases, 544 resulted in arrest (almost 19 percent of reported cases), 363 resulted in charges being filed (11.1 percent of reported cases) and a defendant was found guilty or pled guilty in 189 cases (5.8 percent of reported cases). These results, which came from multiple other parts of the country, are fairly consistent with Spohn and Tellis' findings. The findings are also consistent with work by scholar Rebecca Campbell on case attrition in the Midwest. Another study of data stretching from 1999 to 2014 in a large Midwestern jurisdiction analyzed more than 23,000 sexual assault cases reported during this time period (Venema, Lorenz, & Sweda, 2019). Overall, the majority of cases were suspended (42.5 percent) or cleared by exceptional means (24.8 percent), a category that should be reserved for use only in a very specific set of circumstances, as discussed in Q13. A total of 13.2 percent were cleared by arrest and 3.5 percent remained open (Venema et al., 2019).

Notably, the data presented thus far were calculated by dividing the number of arrests, convictions, incarcerations, or case clearances, respectively, into the total number cases reported to law enforcement. But the actual number of sexual assaults (and thus, the likely number of sexual offenders) in these jurisdictions was much higher because research clearly demonstrates that most sexual assaults are never reported to law enforcement. Researchers are able to more accurately estimate the total rate of sexual assault victimization through the use of victim surveys (see Q2, Q4) in which participants are asked about any assault that took place, regardless of whether it was reported to police. The rates of sexual assault disclosure in victimization surveys is far higher than the number of cases that are reported to law enforcement. According to national data around the time that Spohn & Tellis collected their data, the rate of reporting of sexual assaults was 36 percent (Planty, Langton, Krebs, Berzofsky, & Smiley-McDonald, 2013), indicating that only 36 out of every 100 sexual assaults that took place were reported to law enforcement. If these figures were recalculated with the number of arrests, convictions, and incarceration sentences, divided into the likely more accurate estimate of the true number of sexual assault cases taking place in the jurisdiction the rate of attrition would be even more staggering. For example, if the 5,031 cases reported to LAPD represents only 36 percent of the sexual assaults that took place in LA during that 5-year period, that would mean there were approximately 8,944 cases that went unreported during that time for a total of 13,975 sexual assaults. If we then divide the number of arrests made by LAPD (n = 616) by 13,975, only 4.4 percent of assaults in LAPD jurisdiction resulted in an arrest. Following the same approach, fewer than 3 percent of sexual assaults resulted in a conviction (390 arrests out of 13,975 sexual assaults), and in only 1.66 percent of cases (232 incarceration sentences out of 13,975 sexual assaults) did an offender go to prison.

FURTHER READING

Morabito, Melissa S., Linda Meyer Williams, and April Pattavina. *Decision Making in Sexual Assault Cases: Replication Research on Sexual Violence Case Attrition in the U.S.* Office of Justice Programs' National Criminal Justice Reference Service, 2019.

Planty, Michael, Lynn Langton, Christopher Krebs, Marcus Berzofsky, and Hope Smiley-McDonald. *Female victims of sexual violence, 1994–2010.* U.S. Department of Justice, Office of Justice Programs, Bureau of Justice Statistics, 2013.

Spohn, Cassia, and Katharine Tellis. *Policing and Prosecuting Sexual Assault: Inside the Criminal Justice System.* Lynne Rienner Publishers, 2013.

Venema, Rachel M., Katherine Lorenz, and Nicole Sweda. "Unfounded, cleared, or cleared by exceptional means: Sexual assault case outcomes from 1999 to 2014." *Journal of Interpersonal Violence* (2019): 0886260519876718.

Q28. DO MOST CONVICTED SEX OFFENDERS SERVE TIME IN JAIL OR PRISON?

Answer: Yes. Convicted sex offenders typically face incarceration sentences as well as a variety of other public safety initiatives that they may be subject to upon release from the correctional system. Sex offender registries, perhaps the best-known public safety initiative aimed at reducing sexual offending, are present in every state and will be discussed in depth in Q30. Other initiatives that are present in some jurisdictions but not others include residency restrictions, civil commitment, and surgical or chemical castration. The goals and impacts of these policies are discussed below.

The Facts: Once convicted of a felony sexual offense like rape or sexual assault, the offender will typically be subject to a period of incarceration in a prison. A study by the Bureau of Justice Statistics (BJS) examined the likelihood of incarceration based on crime type in the 75 largest counties in the United States (Cohen & Kyckelhahn, 2010). This study revealed that 80 percent of offenders convicted of rape were sentenced to a period of incarceration. By comparison, 100 percent of offenders convicted of murder, 86 percent of offenders convicted of robbery, and 76 percent of offenders convicted of other violent crimes were sentenced to a period of incarceration (Cohen & Kyckelhahn, 2010). A 2018 report of the incarcerated population in the United States (both at the state and federal level) found that at the end of 2017, "an estimated (13%) of sentenced state prisoners were serving time for . . . rape or sexual assault (167,000)" (Carson, 2020). Individuals convicted of a penetrative sexual violation typically receive prison sentences. Federal sentencing guidelines also recommend prison sentences for offenders convicted of Criminal Sexual Abuse, the terminology the federal statutes use for sexual assault (see Q2). Based on the seriousness of the offense (for example, sentences are often longer if the victim was a child, a weapon was used, or serious bodily injury was inflicted on the victim) and the offender's prior criminal record, a life in prison sentence may be imposed (approximately 4 percent of the time; Cohen & Kyckelhahn, 2010). Far more often, however, the offender will serve a period of incarceration and then be released from prison. In the BJS study, 34 percent of offenders convicted of rape were sentenced to less than 4 years in prison, 33 percent were sentenced to 4–10 years, and 33 percent were sentenced to a period of more than 10 years.

For many types of crimes, release from prison represents the end of correctional supervision. However, with regard to sex offending, there are a variety of additional forms of supervision and control that follow the offender after release from prison. The best-known and most widespread policies, registries and community notification, are discussed in depth in Q30. Some jurisdictions across the United States also have other laws that impact hundreds of thousands of sex offenders who have been released from prison. These laws, which include residency restrictions, civil commitments, and surgical or chemical castrations, are defended as necessary to ensure that the public is safe from the released offender.

The first policy restricting where a released sex offender could live was passed in Florida in 1995. Since then, residency restrictions have diffused across communities and become widespread throughout the United States (Levenson & Zgoba, 2014). Although they differ from state to state (and sometimes even within states), a typical residency restriction prohibits anyone who has been convicted of a sex offense from living near places that attract groups of children, such as schools, day care centers, libraries, parks, or playgrounds. The required distance is usually in the range of 1,000 to 2,500 feet (approximately half a mile).

Since schools, parks, playgrounds, and other places that attract children are prominent and commonplace in many residential locations, there are some communities in which there are very few housing options available to convicted sex offenders. forcing them to become homeless or to live in clusters, often in areas that lack sufficient resources to adequately track these offenders, introducing an additional burden to law enforcement in those communities and potentially additional risk to children in these areas (Zgoba, 2011). The rationale for imposing residency restrictions on released sex offenders is that if they are not allowed to live near places where children gather, it will protect children in the community from becoming potential victims of opportunity. However, these laws are applied to all sex offenders, regardless of whether they have committed an offense against a child, which has led to scholarly criticism (Huebner et al., 2014). In addition, being forced to reside far from these areas may not deter an offender who is motivated to sexually abuse a child from traveling the short distance necessary to seek out a victim.

Research examining the residences of convicted sex offenders living in places without residency restrictions suggests that living close to a school does not make it any more or less likely that a registered sex offender will commit a sexual crime (Zgoba, 2011; Mustaine, 2014). Another concern expressed by scholars in this field is that residency restrictions promote "stranger-danger" fears and the false belief that children are most likely to be sexually abused or assaulted by a stranger. In fact, in more than 90 percent of reported cases, children are assaulted by known others— family members, friends, babysitters, teachers, coaches, and others with whom they have regular contact (Snyder, 2000). With this in mind, some scholars argue that the resources being poured into residency restrictions could have a more substantial impact on rates of sex offending if they were redirected to evidence-based educational programs and prevention efforts.

Another approach that is available in nearly half of states and within the federal system is the civil commitment of sex offenders after they have completed their period of criminal incarceration (Harris, 2014) The government has two mechanisms for controlling a person: criminal and civil. Criminal proceedings and incarceration following conviction for a criminal offense are the traditional route for managing a convicted offender. However, starting with Washington in 1990, some states reintroduced civil commitment statutes allowing the government to exert civil authority over an individual even after their period of criminal confinement was complete and they had been released. The basic idea behind these policies, which had existed as laws to protect the public against "sexual psychopaths" in the early twentieth century before mostly fading away by the 1960s, is that if a sex offender is believed to be such a threat to public safety that they cannot be safely released into society even after completing their prison sentence, the state may exercise its civil authority and keep the offender institutionalized in a mental health facility until they no longer pose a threat.

The United States Supreme Court has upheld this practice as constitutional, because the interest in public safety outweighs the individual offenders' liberty, so long as the state can demonstrate that the individual poses a danger to society due a "mental abnormality" or that the offender is unable to control their actions. During the period of civil commitment, the offender must be granted access to psychological treatment, although the nature and quality of that treatment may vary from state to state. If the offender is deemed to no longer pose a threat, they may be released from the institution. Until then, they are committed to state control indefinitely. As of 2020, there are over 6,000 civilly committed sex offenders in the United States (Hoppe, Meyer, De Orio, Vogler, & Armstrong, 2020).

Another approach that some states use to control or reduce sexual offending by men convicted of sexual crimes is chemical castration, a process in which the subject is required to take drugs that reduce their levels of testosterone, a chemical closely associated with sex drive. The primary assumption underlying this practice is that the sexual offenses that the man committed were motivated by sexual arousal, and that reducing his ability to become aroused would in turn reduce the risk of him sexually assaulting someone (Scott & del Busto, 2014). Requiring offenders to take drugs that reduce their levels of testosterone is believed to reduce the frequency of sexual urges and make it less likely that the offender will experience sexual arousal. The effects of these drug treatments are temporary; the reduced arousal may take effect in about two weeks, and if the offender stops taking the drug, his testosterone level and ability to become sexually aroused eventually returns to its state prior to starting the prescription. There also are a variety of side effects that these drugs may introduce (Scott & del Busto, 2014). However, a judge can require an offender to take the medications despite these side effects.

Another type of drug used for chemical castration is a selective serotonin reuptake inhibitor, commonly known as an SSRI. These drugs are regularly proscribed for people dealing with depression, anxiety, or obsessive-compulsive disorder. Because some sex offenders are motivated by diagnosable paraphilias that involve repetitive and compulsive thoughts, SSRIs may be able to help this type of offender control their thoughts and compulsions. A more dramatic approach, allowed in only five states (California, Florida, Iowa, Louisiana, and Texas) and only at the request of the offender, is surgical castration. This procedure, in which the offender's testicles are removed, is permanent, irreversible, and cannot be court mandated. If an offender decides that the only way to control his sexual offending is to remove his testicles (where most, but not all of the body's testosterone is produced), the offender may elect to have his testicles removed. Both chemical and surgical castration remain controversial and are not in place in as many states as residency restrictions and civil commitment, but they are used in enough jurisdictions (including the highly populous states of California and Florida) and impact enough offenders to warrant discussion.

There are two additional items of note with regard to the topic of punishing convicted sex offenders. First, the United States Supreme Court has ruled the use of capital punishment for sexual offenders to be unconstitutional. In *Coker v. Georgia* (1978), the Supreme Court ruled that imposing the death penalty on an offender convicted of rape of an adult was a cruel and unusual punishment. The state of Louisiana challenged this ruling in the 2008 case of *Kennedy v. Louisiana*, which concerned an offender who had raped a child. Again, the Supreme Court ruled that a penalty of death was cruel and unusual, a disproportionate response to a sexual crime. Thus, the death penalty is not a punishment that can be imposed on sex offenders.

Second, it is worth noting that there are some cases in which a judge decides against an incarceration sentence or provides a very short one; not all states have sentencing guidelines. In those states, the judge can impose whatever sentence they see fit. In states with sentencing guidelines, they are only advisory (not compulsory) and a judge can go outside of them if they deem it appropriate. They usually do have to provide a written justification, but it is within their discretion as long as there is no mandatory statutory requirement in place

In some instances, these judicial decisions showing exceptional leniency toward convicted rapists have attracted outrage. Such was the case of Stanford University swimmer Brock Turner in California in 2015. The presiding judge sentenced Turner to just 6 months in jail and 3 years of probation following convictions on several sexual assault charges, including three felonies. The public outcry against such lenient sentences is often strong; the judge in Turner's case was recalled by California voters after he imposed this sentence.

FURTHER READING

Carson, E. Ann. *Prisoners in 2018*. Bureau of Justice Statistics, U.S. Dept of Justice, Office of Justice Programs, and United States of America, 2020.

Cohen, Thomas H., and Tracey Kyckelhahn. *Felony Defendants in Large Urban Counties, 2006*. Bureau of Justice Statistics, U.S. Dept of Justice, Office of Justice Programs, 2010.

Harris, Andrew J. "The civil commitment of sexual predators: A policy review." In *Sex Offender Laws: Failed Policies, New Directions* (2nd ed.), edited by Richard G. Wright, 339. Springer: 2014.

Hoppe, Trevor, Ilan H. Meyer, Scott De Orio, Stefan Vogler, and Megan Armstrong. "Civil commitment of people convicted of sex offenses in the United States." UCLA School of Law Williams Institute (2020).

Huebner, Beth M., Kimberly R. Kras, Jason Rydberg, Timothy S. Bynum, Eric Grommon, and Breanne Pleggenkuhle. "The effect and implications of sex offender residence restrictions: Evidence from a two-state evaluation." *Criminology & Public Policy* 13, no. 1 (2014): 139–168.

Levenson, Jill S., and Kristen M. Zgoba. "Sex offender residence restrictions: The law of unintended consequences." In *Sex Offender Laws: Failed Policies, New Directions* (2nd ed.), edited by Richard G. Wright, 180–189. Springer: 2014.

Mustaine, Elizabeth Ehrardt. "Sex offender residency restrictions: Successful integration or exclusion." *Criminology & Public Policy* 13 (2014): 169.

Scott, Charles, and Elena del Busto. "Chemical and surgical castration." In *Sex Offender Laws: Failed Policies, New Directions* (2nd ed.), edited by Richard G. Wright, 190–218. Springer: 2014.

Snyder, Howard N. *Sexual Assault of Young Children as Reported to Law Enforcement: Victim, Incident, and Offender Characteristics: A Statistical Report Using Data from the National Incident-Based Reporting System.* U.S. Department of Justice, Office of Justice Programs, Bureau of Justice Statistics, 2000.

Zgoba, Kristen M. "Residence restriction buffer zones and the banishment of sex offenders: Have we gone one step too far?" *Criminology & Public Policy* 10 (2011): 391.

Q29. DO ALL SEX OFFENDERS REOFFEND?

Answer: No, not all sex offenders reoffend—commit criminal sexual acts—after they are released from prison. But measuring the reoffending patterns of sex offenders is exceptionally complicated. There are no widely agreed-upon standards and definitions for measuring recidivism (when an ex-convict reoffends). Studies have taken an assortment of different positions on appropriate length of time for follow-up, the type of offenses to include (e.g., all offenses, all violent offenses, only sexual offenses), and the measure of reoffending (e.g., official record of rearrest, official record of reconviction, offender's self-report). These issues are explored below.

The Facts: "Recidivism" is the term used by criminal justice scholars and professionals when a convicted offender commits a new crime. However, there is not a definitive standard for how to measure the concept of recidivism. Many scholars differentiate between types of recidivism (e.g., rearrested for the same type of offense or a new type of offense), and some scholars only include a re-offense if the offender was convicted (instead of only arrested, which requires a lower standard of proof). The lengths of time that offenders are followed to measure potential recidivism is inconsistent across studies as well. There is general agreement that the period of measurement begins after an offender is released from prison, but some short recidivism studies follow the offenders for just a few months, while at the other extreme, there are studies that follow the offenders for 20 or more years. The risk of an offender recidivating is generally highest upon release (particularly the first 6 months) and declines over time. A 2018 study suggests that after 10–15 years without recidivism, a convicted sex offender who has been released from prison is no more likely to commit a new sex crime than an average person with no offense history (Hanson, Harris, Letourneau, Helmus, & Thornton, 2018).

Two large early studies are frequently referred to in this debate: a 3-year study by the Bureau of Justice Statistics (BJS; Langan, Smith, & Durose, 2003) and a meta-analysis by Hanson and Morton-Bourgon (2005). In addition, a new BJS study on recidivism rates among people convicted of sex offenses was published in 2019 (Alper & Durose, 2019). The methods and findings of each of these three studies are discussed in turn. The first BJS study in 2003 tracked all offenders released from prison in 15 states during the year of 1994 and for 3 years postrelease (Langan, Smith, & Durose, 2003). This group included 9,691 sex offenders and 262,420 offenders convicted of other crimes. This study indicated that the general population of offenders (68 percent) were more likely than sex offenders (43 percent) to be rearrested, and the new arrest was more likely to be a felony among the general population of offenders than among sex offenders. Sex offenders were more likely to be arrested for a new sex crime (5.3 percent) than the general population of offenders (1.3 percent), but the rate among both groups was low. In 2005, Karl Hanson and Kelly Morton-Bourgon published a meta-analysis of 82 studies of sex offender recidivism. It tracked a total of 29,450 sex offenders across studies for an average of 5 years after release. They found that the general recidivism rate was 36.2 percent, the violent recidivism rate was 14.3 percent, and the sexual recidivism rate was 13.7 percent.

A 2019 BJS study tracking offenders over a 9-year follow-up period generally led to the same conclusions (Alper & Durose, 2019). The study followed 67,966 offenders released from prison in 30 states in the year 2005 for a period of 9 years after release. Overall, the rate of rearrest was lower for sex offenders (67 percent) than offenders incarcerated for nonsexual offenses (84 percent). However, sex offenders (7.7 percent) were more likely than the general population of offenders (2.3 percent) to be arrested for a new sexual offense. However, because a higher portion of the sample was comprised of offenders released after serving time for a nonsexual offense, this group was actually responsible for a larger percentage of new rapes and sexual assaults than were the released sex offenders. That is, of all new rapes and sexual assault arrests within this group of more than 67,000 offenders, 84 percent of the arrests were of offenders who were released from prison after an incarceration sentence for something other than a sex crime. The remaining 16 percent of arrests for new rapes or sexual assaults were arrests of sex offenders.

Among both groups, the risk of recidivism was highest in the first year (29.0 percent of sex offenders, 43.2 percent of general offenders) and declined to a low in year 9 (16.1 percent of sex offenders, 24.8 percent of general offenders). For all offenders, the most common type of crime leading to rearrest during this period was a public order crime such as disorderly conduct, failure to abide by the conditions of parole, or driving under the influence (DUI). In fact, public order crimes accounted for 23.4 percent of all arrests of sex offenders in year 1 of this study (Alper & Durose, 2019). The next highest category of crime was 6.6 percent of sex offenders arrested in year 1 for a violent crime. In short, even when followed up for a period of 9 years, most sex offenders who were rearrested were taken into custody for something other than a sexual offense.

Taken together, these three studies all suggest that many released sex offenders do come into contact with the criminal justice system again. However, they are less likely to recidivate than the general population of offenders. If they are arrested for a new crime, it is more likely to be a nonsexual offense than a sexual offense. However, released sex offenders are disproportionately more likely to be arrested for a new sex offense than the general population of offenders.

Furthermore, there are some concerns regarding researchers' ability to accurately measure recidivism. Data clearly indicate that, compared to other types of crimes, sex offenses are underreported (see Q11). Thus, it may be that the new crimes being committed are not coming to the attention of law enforcement and are therefore not recorded in recidivism statistics. On the other hand, some have argued that released sex offenders are under such strict scrutiny that their crimes may be discovered by law enforcement at higher rates.

Measuring recidivism postrelease for a criminal conviction, however, does not provide a complete or accurate picture of offending patterns. "It is believed that a substantial portion of sex offenders' criminal activity is not detected therefore raising doubts about the criminal career picture provided by official indicators of offending" (Mathesius & Lussier, 2014, p. 134). With this consideration in mind, some researchers have focused on the concept of "cost avoidance"—the ability of sex offenders to commit multiple offenses before being caught.

Measuring these offenses is extremely difficult and generally relies on the honesty of convicted offenders to provide retrospective histories of their offending patterns prior to arrest and incarceration. In a study of 384 incarcerated men sentenced for a first sexual offense, researchers questioned the participants about all of the prior sexual offenses that they had committed—not just those known to the criminal justice system (Mathesius & Lussier, 2014). The study found that the offenders were convicted of their first sexual offense at the average age of 39.6 years. The age at which the offenders, on average, reported *committing* their first sexual offense was 32.1 years. The 7.5-year gap between the first offense and first conviction, which the author's term "cost avoidance," is not reflected in official records of offending or recidivism. Despite being incarcerated for the first time, the offenders in this study reported an average of 2.4 victims and a median of 10 "criminal events" (note: the median is reported here because averages are more easily skewed by a single high response, as was present in these data, whereas medians are not).

These findings suggest that a lot of offending (and reoffending) is not measured completely or accurately by looking at official statistics, as most recidivism studies do. In a publication by the Office of Sex Offender Sentencing, Monitoring, Apprehending, Registering, & Tracking (SMART) on the topic of recidivism, the author notes that,

> Research has clearly shown that many sex offenses are never reported to authorities, and several studies have shown that the likelihood that a sexual assault will be reported to law enforcement decreases with the victim's age. In addition, only a subset of sex offenses that are reported to law enforcement result in the arrest of the perpetrator. Given these dynamics, there is widespread recognition that the officially recorded recidivism rates of sexual offenders are a diluted measure of reoffending. (Przybylski, 2015, p. 1)

Clearly, there are limitations to the accurate measure of recidivism among perpetrators of sex crimes.

FURTHER READING

Alper, M., and M. Durose. *Recidivism of Sex Offenders Released from State Prison: A 9-Year Follow-Up (2005-14)(NCJ 251773).* Bureau of Justice Statistics, U.S. Department of Justice, 2019.

Hanson, R. Karl, Andrew J. R. Harris, Elizabeth Letourneau, L. Maaike Helmus, and David Thornton. "Reductions in risk based on time offense-free in the community: Once a sexual offender, not always a sexual offender." *Psychology, Public Policy, and Law* 24, no. 1 (2018): 48.

Hanson, R. Karl, and Kelly E. Morton-Bourgon. "The characteristics of persistent sexual offenders: A meta-analysis of recidivism studies." *Journal of Consulting and Clinical Psychology* 73, no. 6 (2005): 1154.

Langan, Patrick A., Erica L. Smith, and Matthew R. Durose. *Recidivism of Sex Offenders Released from Prison in 1994.* U.S. Department of Justice, Office of Justice Programs, Bureau of Justice Statistics, 2003.

Mathesius, Jeffrey, and Patrick Lussier. "The successful onset of sex offending: Determining the correlates of actual and official onset of sex offending." *Journal of Criminal Justice* 42, no. 2 (2014): 134–144.

Przybylski, Roger. "Recidivism of adult sexual offenders." *United States Department of Justice. Office of Justice Programs Office of Sex Offender Sentencing, Monitoring, Apprehending, Registering, and Tracking, SOMAPI Research Brief* (2015): 1–6.

Q30. ARE SEX OFFENDER REGISTRIES EFFECTIVE PUBLIC SAFETY TOOLS?

Answer: Most scientific evidence does not support the claim that sex offender registries keep society safer by reducing overall rates of sexual offending or recidivism rates of offenders, although there are some exceptions. Many scholars who study sex offender registries are highly critical of these devices. They contend that registries were never designed to keep society safe, because they are not evidence-based and contradict what researchers know about trends in sexual offending. These scholars suggest that registries were implemented primarily as an emotional reaction to a particularly heinous crime, and that they are maintained as a moral statement that society will not tolerate sexual offending.

The Facts: Before discussing the research findings related to sex offender registries, it is useful to provide some background on precisely what these registries and their corresponding public notification policies entail. Following particularly egregious sexual attacks against children in the late 1980s and early 1990s, sex offender registries and community notification statutes began to spread across the United States (Terry & Ackerman, 2014). The federal Jacob Wetterling Crimes Against Children and Sexually Violent Predators Act (1994) required law enforcement agencies to create and maintain a list of known sex offenders within their jurisdictions. A 1996 amendment to this federal legislation known as Megan's Law required that these lists ("registries") be available to the community so that residents could take safety precautions to protect themselves and their children. The approaches that jurisdictions took to provide "community notification" varied substantially, with inconsistencies both within and between states (Terry & Ackerman, 2014).

In 2006, the Adam Walsh Act was passed into law. It replaced the prior legislation, providing the most extensive federal legislation to control sex offenders in United States history. A major piece of the Adam Walsh Act is the Sex Offender Registration and Notification Act (SORNA), which provides clear guidance on what information must be included on a registry and how community notification should work (Evans, Lytle, & Sample, 2015).

Under SORNA, every state must maintain a searchable website with entries on all registered sex offenders in the state. An entry on a public registry must contain at least the following information: the offender's name; a recent photograph; a physical description; current offense (i.e., the one for which the offender is required to appear on the registry); any past sex offense convictions; a description of the offender's vehicle including its license plate number; the offender's home address; and the addresses of any employers or educational institutions that the offender works for or attends. These requirements increased consistency in community notification across the United States (Evans, Lytle, & Sample, 2015).

A significant change brought in by SORNA was the introduction of a tier system ranging from I (least serious registered sex offenders) to III (highest risk registered sex offenders) based on the conviction offense. The tier system implicitly recognizes that not all sex offenders pose an equal risk to society in terms of their likelihood of recidivating (see Q29) or threatening public safety. Tier 1 offenders are perpetrators thought to pose the least threat of recidivism. Tier 1 offenders must remain on the registry for at least 15 years (it is possible to appeal for a 5-year reduction) and must report to their registration location (e.g., a sheriff's office or department of corrections facility) in person once a year to ensure that their information remains up to date. Tier II offenders, who are believed to pose a higher threat than Tier I offenders, must remain on the registry for at least 25 years, with no possibility of reducing that time. Tier II offenders must report to their registration location in person every 6 months. The highest risk offenders, Tier III offenders, must remain on the sex offender registry for the rest of their natural life, with no exceptions, and must report to their registration location in person every 3 months.

Other key elements of SORNA include: clear timeline for registration (before leaving a correctional facility or, if not incarcerated, within 3 days); establishing failure to register as a federal offense so that sex offenders who fail to register can be punished by up to 10 years in prison; requiring that DNA be on file for all registered sex offenders in the jurisdiction; and the application of most sex offender regulations to juvenile offenders as well as adults.

A major criticism of sex offender registries is that they focus on preventing stranger attacks, which account for only a small percentage of all sexual assaults. Crimes against children, in particular, are committed by a known assailant (e.g., family member, babysitter, teacher) upwards of 90 percent of the time (Snyder, 2000). Emphasizing registries as the primary approach for reducing or controlling sex offenders may create a false sense of security for people who think that their risk of victimization can be controlled by simply avoiding people or addresses listed on the registry. This may lead to complacency in environments in which risks actually do arise and cause parents or other caregivers to overlook warning signs of abuse because no registered sex offenders are present. Compared to sex offender registries, teaching people how to recognize and respond to warning signs of sexual abuse is far less expensive and does not incorrectly emphasize the least common type of assaults—those committed by strangers.

These laws also suffer from a few logistical limitations. Moreover, many sex offenders who should be on a registry remain unaccounted for a variety of reasons, including slippage into homelessness or fleeing the jurisdiction. One study found that there may be inaccuracies in as many as half of registry entries (Levenson & Cotter, 2006). Even if every offender who should be on the registry was included, and even if every entry was perfectly accurate, most people do not utilize this resource (Makin, Walker, & Story, 2018). One 2018 report found that across five studies, only roughly one-third of respondents sought information from their community sex offender registries (Makin et al., 2018, p. 298).

Furthermore, scholars have documented a variety of collateral consequences that pose challenges to registered sex offenders and their ability to reenter society after completing their sentence and leaving prison. These challenges include instances of vigilante justice (including being targeted for physical violence), harassment of the offender or their family members, trouble gaining or maintaining employment, and difficulty obtaining stable housing (Tewksbury, 2005). These negative outcomes associated with community notification "also raise the possibility that notification laws make returning to criminal behavior more attractive to registered sex offenders by subjecting them to public ridicule and social isolation"

(Prescott & Rockoff, 2011). A deterrence-based approach to crime control leads to the expectation that sex offender registration and notification policies should reduce the rates of sexual offending. In fact,

> The majority of (studies focused on the incidence of new sex crimes) have failed to find significant effects at either the aggregate level, or when measuring sexual re-offense among known offenders. Other studies have detected modest effects, suggesting that registration and notification may be associated with offense reduction under certain conditions, for instance, when public notification is reserved for those at highest risk to reoffend as determined by a validated risk assessment instruments. (Harris, Levenson, Lobanov-Rostovsky, & Walfield, 2018)

In other words, these researchers suggest that notification may serve a protective function if reserved for those offenders who have been identified as high-risk offenders. However, it may be problematic when applied to all sex offenders, including those at low risk of reoffending. Although most studies do not find that registries significantly deter offending, however, it does not necessarily mean that they have no impact (Bierie, 2016). The rate of sexual offending in society is low and law enforcement does not become aware of most crimes that do take place, artificially reducing the recorded numbers of offenses and further limiting the chance of finding that registries have a significant effect on recidivism among sex offenders. Some large studies of the impact of registry and notification policies have found significant reductions in offending after a SORNA policy was implemented (Prescott & Rockoff, 2011). However, the research is far from definitive and, given the high financial cost of registries, critics say that they should have more robust and consistent evidence of their impact.

The Congressional Budget Office estimated that implementing the provisions of the Adam Walsh Act of 2006 would cost the federal government $1.5 billion. It is unclear how much the policy has cost the states, but estimates are in the millions of dollars annually in most states (Justice Policy Institute, 2008). Because of the high cost of implementing all of the requirements of the Adam Walsh Act, many states have decided to accept financial penalties from the federal government for nonimplementation, reasoning that the penalties are smaller than the financial loss of implementing a policy with questionable effectiveness (Bierie, 2016).

Despite these problems, scholarship on perceptions of sex offender registries suggests that they are an extremely popular policy with the general public (Levenson, Brannon, Fortney, & Baker, 2007; Koon-Magnin, 2015).

The high level of public support for sex offender registries and notification policies may reflect a desire to express collective intolerance for sexual offending more than belief in an evidence-based policy.

FURTHER READING

Bierie, David M. "The utility of sex offender registration: a research note." *Journal of Sexual Aggression* 22, no. 2 (2016): 263–273.

Evans, Mary K., Robert Lytle, and Lisa L. Sample. "Sex offender registration and community notification." *Sex Offender Laws: Rhetoric and Reality* (2014): 142–164.

Harris, Andrew J., Jill S. Levenson, Christopher Lobanov-Rostovsky, and Scott M. Walfield. "Law enforcement perspectives on sex offender registration and notification: Effectiveness, challenges, and policy priorities." *Criminal Justice Policy Review* 29, no. 4 (2018): 391–420.

Justice Policy Institute. *What Will It Cost States to Comply with the Sex Offender Registration and Notification Act?* National Juvenile Justice Network, 2008.

Koon-Magnin, Sarah. "Perceptions of and support for sex offender policies: Testing Levenson, Brannon, Fortney, and Baker's findings." *Journal of Criminal Justice* 43, no. 1 (2015): 80–88.

Levenson, Jill S., Yolanda N. Brannon, Timothy Fortney, and Juanita Baker. "Public perceptions about sex offenders and community protection policies." *Analyses of Social Issues and Public Policy* 7, no. 1 (2007): 137–161.

Levenson, Jill S., and Leo P. Cotter. "The effect of Megan's Law on sex offender reintegration." *Journal of Contemporary Criminal Justice* 21, no. 1 (2005): 49–66.

Makin, David A., Andrea M. Walker, and Samantha C. Story. "Are we interested? A trend analysis of sex offender internet registries." *Criminal Justice Studies* 31, no. 3 (2018): 297–309.

Prescott, J. J., and Jonah E. Rockoff. "Do sex offender registration and notification laws affect criminal behavior?" *The Journal of Law and Economics* 54, no. 1 (2011): 161–206.

Terry, K., and A. R. Ackerman. "A brief history of sex offender registration." In *Sex Offender Laws: Failed Policies, New Directions* (2nd ed.), edited by Richard G. Wright, 65–98. Springer: 2014.

Tewksbury, Richard. "Collateral consequences of sex offender registration." *Journal of Contemporary Criminal Justice* 21, no. 1 (2005): 67–81.

7

❖

Prevention and Response Services
Outside of the Criminal Justice System

Sexual assault is a serious social problem. As established in Chapters 1 and 2, a substantial portion of the population of the United States has experienced a sexual assault. And those who have not personally experienced a sexual assault themselves almost certainly know a victim of sexual assault. A problem this widespread, impacting so many people, cannot be addressed solely by the criminal justice system. Meanwhile, numerous prevention and response services have developed outside of the criminal justice system to help reduce the rates of assault and to improve outcomes for sexual assault survivors. There are professional advocates known as rape crisis advocates whose only agenda is to promote the best interests and healing of the survivor, discussed in Q31 ("Are there professionals outside of the criminal justice system who can help victims following a sexual assault?"). There are now medical professionals who are specially trained in responding to sexual assault, whose role will be discussed in Q32 ("Do SANE programs improve outcomes for sexual assault victims?").

Scholars continue to provide useful models of "trauma-informed" practices that, if employed, should reduce the risk of secondary victimization and promote a supportive, helpful environment for survivors of sexual assault, discussed in Q33 ("Do trauma-informed practices help victims of sexual assault?"). Because of their obligations under Title IX, institutions of higher education have implemented detailed policies, new professional roles, and substantial programming efforts to help reduce sexual violence on college campuses, discussed in Q34 ("Does Title IX apply to sexual misconduct at institutions of higher education?"). Moreover, sexual assault is a complicated social problem impacting people of all social backgrounds and influencing numerous aspects of an individual's life. Thus, a comprehensive response to sexual assault will require prevention and response services outside of the criminal justice system. Discussion of the four questions covered in this section provides a broad overview of the types of services that exist to support and respond to sexual assault survivors outside of the criminal justice system.

Q31. ARE THERE PROFESSIONALS OUTSIDE OF THE CRIMINAL JUSTICE SYSTEM WHO CAN HELP VICTIMS FOLLOWING A SEXUAL ASSAULT?

Answer: Absolutely. Two of the most influential responders following a sexual assault fall outside of the criminal justice system's purview: sexual assault nurse examiners (SANEs) and rape crisis advocates. Numerous campus, community, and national groups also offer help lines and educational programming. One of the most prominent of these organizations is the Rape, Abuse & Incest National Network (RAINN). Finally, thousands of mental health professionals respond to and support patients who are survivors of sexual assault.

The Facts: If a victim seeks medical attention following a sexual assault, they may be responded to by a SANE. These specially trained nurses typically have other full-time responsibilities within the hospital or medical facility, but are called upon if a sexual assault survivor arrives at the hospital to receive treatment. To become a certified SANE requires 40 hours of classroom training and 40 hours of clinical training in addition to prior nursing education through classroom and clinical experience, passing a certification exam, demonstrating knowledge of the most up to date information on sexual assault and how to properly conduct a sexual assault forensic exam (discussed in Q15). Not all hospitals have SANEs available, in which case the medical response and sexual assault forensic exam is provided by an emergency room doctor or other medical professional. The development and support of SANE programs, however, are widely seen as an indication of that medical facility's commitment to providing high-quality specialized care to sexual assault survivors. The impact and efficacy of SANE programs are discussed fully in Q32.

Another key responder is a rape crisis advocate. The advocate serves two primary roles: (1) ensure survivors receive the support services available to them, and (2) protect survivors from further traumatization during the disclosure or reporting experience known as secondary victimization (Q17; Campbell, 2006). These specially trained individuals sometimes hold professional staff positions at hospitals and other health care facilities, but many serve as volunteers. The position of rape crisis advocate developed in the 1970s and is now present in every state, with advocates available in thousands of cities and towns throughout the United States. Rape crisis advocates are typically housed within rape crisis centers and work to support the victim in whatever ways they need following a sexual assault.

Many victims who do not ever contact the criminal justice system (see Q11) do sometimes reach out for other forms of social support, like that provided by a rape crisis advocate. An advocate can serve many functions to these survivors, including being a listening ear and a shoulder to cry on or helping to reduce any feelings of self-blame experienced by the victim. Many rape crisis centers offer both in-person counseling appointments and over-the-phone support to victims, so that no matter how or when the victim feels the need to reach out—whether it is the day of their assault or years later—there is someone there to listen to their story and provide support. If a victim pursues medical care, the advocate will often go to the hospital with them to assist in whatever way is needed. This may be as simple as getting the person a beverage or helping them find a safe ride home, or as involved as sitting with the victim while they call and inform their parents or significant other about the assault. Advocates are typically available to those individuals as well, in recognition of the fact that family and friends of victim's are also impacted by sexual assault (although indirectly) and may be working through difficult feelings of their own. Law enforcement agencies in most communities collaborate with rape crisis advocates and allow the advocates to be present during victim interviews. In these instances, the advocate can serve as a buffer against the possibility of secondary victimization by requesting interview breaks for the victim and helping to rephrase or reframe questions that may sound accusatory. If a case progresses through the criminal justice system, advocates may even attend court hearings with the victim and work to orient them to the complexities of the criminal court system.

One of the most widely cited studies on rape crisis advocates compared the experiences of sexual assault survivors who had an advocate present at the hospital and in interactions with law enforcement with the experiences of survivors who did not secure an advocate (Campbell, 2006). The study found that victims who had an advocate present at the hospital during a rape kit exam were more likely to receive additional services and less likely to experience negative interactions with medical personnel. Similar findings were reported in interactions with law enforcement. Victims who had a rape crisis advocate present during the interview were less likely to report negative interactions with law enforcement and more likely to have a police report taken following their assault. Overall, survivors who were accompanied by an advocate reported less distress in the medical experience and in interactions with law enforcement compared to survivors who did not have an advocate present. These findings led the study author to conclude that, "Rape victim advocates appear to provide numerous benefits and can prevent serious negative consequences for rape survivors" (Campbell, 2006, p. 44). Because rape crisis advocates are not generally employed by or directly associated with the criminal justice system, they are in a unique position to observe, provide assessments, and make recommendations regarding the interactions between the victim and the criminal justice system. A study of 47 advocates operating in four states leveraged that position to better understand the victim–criminal justice system relationship. "Rape victim advocates may provide a more accurate assessment of the revictimization of victims by the police and medical systems because they are not experiencing the emotional trauma that may make victims reluctant to speak to researchers" (Maier, 2008, p. 802). More recent research on the role of advocates has focused primarily on the advocates and their own mental health functioning (Dworkin, Sorrell, & Allen, 2016; Houston-Kolnik, Odahl-Ruan, & Greeson, 2017). Because of their frequent exposure to vulnerable individuals in upsetting circumstances, emotionally difficult narrative accounts, and potential danger, it is possible for rape crisis advocates to experience trauma of their own, known as secondary traumatic stress.

Another support system for survivors of sexual assault are prevention programs (often run by institutions of higher education) aimed at teaching young adults how to recognize and intervene against predatory behavior. This approach, known as bystander intervention, is intended to disrupt potential sexual assaults before they can occur by increasing the awareness of others who may be in the vicinity of potential danger. Numerous colleges and universities across the country have developed and implemented programs and trainings to teach their students how to serve as effective bystanders. However, at this time, the actual effectiveness of the programs on reducing sexual assault remains unclear. According to a 2016 review of the literature on these programs, "results indicate that bystander programs are promising from the standpoint of increasing young adults' willingness to intervene and confidence in their ability to intervene when they witness dating or sexual violence, however, the utilization of actual bystander behaviors was less straightforward" (Storer, Casey, & Herrenkohl, 2016, p. 256). In other words, the training sessions and programs did teach students how to recognize and intervene in the case of potential sexual assault, but researchers cannot definitively conclude whether the knowledge gained resulted in behavior that prevented a sexual assault.

Finally, there is a robust digital support system online for victims of sexual assault. Perhaps the best known, and certainly the largest public resource promoting work against sexual violence is RAINN. In addition to housing the National Sexual Assault Hotline (800-656-HOPE), the organization's website includes a variety of materials aimed at multiple audiences (e.g., survivors of sexual assault, parents, students) to provide critical information about how to recognize and respond to sexual assault.

The organization website includes educational information and resources on topics including warning signs of sexual violence, advice for parents who suspect their child is being abused, and state-by-state laws defining sexual assault (see Figure 31.1).

Figure 31.1. Rape, Abuse & Incest National Network (RAINN)

Victim Services

The victim services experts at RAINN take a victim-centered, trauma-informed approach to developing programs and services that support survivors of sexual violence and their loved ones. As the country's leading provider of sexual assault services, we have developed programs to help survivors in all stages of recovery.

- RAINN created and operates the National Sexual Assault Hotline, accessible 24/7 by phone (800.656.HOPE) and online (online.rainn.org). We work closely with more than 1,000 local sexual assault service providers to offer confidential support services to survivors regardless of where they are in their recovery. Our telephone and online hotlines have helped more than 3.5 million survivors. Learn more about local service providers.
- We operate the DoD Safe Helpline for members of the Department of Defense community who have been affected by sexual assault.
- We offer innovative technology and services for partners in the field, including organizations, universities, and government agencies.
- We also provide training services for companies and organizations, as well as staff and volunteers at more than 1,000 local sexual assault service provider partners.
- We work with volunteers across the country to make a difference in the lives of survivors. Learn more here.

Figure 31.1. (Continued)

Public Education

RAINN's communications experts raise the visibility of sexual violence and advance the public's understanding of the crime. We work with the media, entertainment industry, and colleges across the country to provide accurate information about sexual violence prevention, prosecution, and recovery.

- RAINN is recognized as the go-to source for media seeking expert commentary and research on sexual violence news and stories and also curates news content highlighting RAINN's work in the field and the work of our partners.
- We collaborate with the entertainment industry to ensure that shows and films reflect the reality of the crime.
- We maintain an active social media presence, reacting to current events and ensuring that people who need support can find it through the National Sexual Assault Hotline.
- We operate the Speakers Bureau, a network of more than 3,500 survivors who volunteer to share their stories with local communities and the media.
- We work with students to raise visibility for the issues of sexual violence prevention and recovery on campus.

Public Policy

RAINN's policy team works at the federal and state level to improve the criminal justice system, prevent sexual assault, and ensure justice for survivors.

- We help create and advocate for laws and regulations that make communities safer and support survivors.
- We work closely with the Departments of Justice, Education, and Health & Human Services to improve the federal response to sexual violence.
- We lead the national effort to end the rape kit backlog, while collaborating with allies to promote state action through the Rape Kit Action Project.
- We maintain the Laws in Your State database, the most up-to-date source of information for students, lawmakers, and others seeking to understand sexual violence laws across the nation (with special thanks to our partner, Hogan Lovells).

Consulting Services

RAINN's consulting and subject matter experts work with clients across the public, private, and nonprofit sectors to develop targeted, effective sexual violence education and response programs. RAINN's services prepare organizations to effectively provide education about sexual violence and to respond to incidents in a way that facilitates healing and promotes safe and healthy communities. To do this, we offer a variety of specialized consulting services to meet each organization's unique needs, including hotline services, consulting, program assessments, and education and training.

Figure 31.1. (Continued)

- We have demonstrated expertise in assisting a variety of organizations, including federal partners, institutions of higher education, hospitality and amusement organizations, and other businesses.
- We offer both the technology infrastructure and the victim service expertise to provide quality, anonymous, and confidential crisis intervention services via telephone or online hotline in English and Spanish.
- We provide tailored consulting to help organizations that are at any point in the process—whether this is the first conversation an organization has had on the topic or there have been policies in place for years.
- We conduct victim-centered, trauma-informed education and response program assessments based on leading research, regulatory guidance, and state and federal laws to evaluate program strengths and weaknesses.
- We are a leader in providing comprehensive sexual violence education and trainings for professionals and volunteers nationwide, providing content that engages, educates, and prepares adult learners to support and help survivors of sexual assault.

Source: RAINN, 2021. Reprinted with permission. https://www.rainn.org/programs-and-expertise

To summarize, there are a variety of professionals independent of the criminal justice system who respond to victims of sexual assault. Survivors are particularly likely to encounter sexual assault nurse examiners or rape crisis advocates. There may also be community or campus-based programs where the survivor is located. Finally, there are numerous online resources available to victims of sexual assault, including a national emergency hotline hosted by RAINN.

FURTHER READING

Banyard, Victoria L. "Who will help prevent sexual violence: Creating an ecological model of bystander intervention." *Psychology of Violence* 1, no. 3 (2011): 216.

Campbell, Rebecca. "Rape survivors' experiences with the legal and medical systems: Do rape victim advocates make a difference?" *Violence against Women* 12, no. 1 (2006): 30–45.

Dworkin, Emily R., Nicole R. Sorell, and Nicole E. Allen. "Individual- and setting-level correlates of secondary traumatic stress in rape crisis center staff." *Journal of Interpersonal Violence* 31, no. 4 (2016): 743–752.

Houston-Kolnik, Jaclyn D., Charlynn A. Odahl-Ruan, and Megan R. Greeson. "Who helps the helpers? Social support for rape crisis advocates." *Journal of Interpersonal Violence* (2017): 0886260517726970.

Maier, Shana L. "'I have heard horrible stories . . .' Rape victim advocates' perceptions of the revictimization of rape victims by the police and medical system." *Violence against Women* 14, no. 7 (2008): 786–808.

McMahon, Sarah, and Victoria L. Banyard. "When can I help? A conceptual framework for the prevention of sexual violence through bystander intervention." *Trauma, Violence, & Abuse* 13, no. 1 (2012): 3–14.

Mihelicova, Martina, Annie Wegrzyn, Molly Brown, and Megan R. Greeson. "Stressors of rape crisis work from the perspectives of advocates with and without sexual assault victimization history." *Journal of Interpersonal Violence* (2019): 0886260519876715.

Storer, Heather L., Erin Casey, and Todd Herrenkohl. "Efficacy of bystander programs to prevent dating abuse among youth and young adults: A review of the literature." *Trauma, Violence, & Abuse* 17, no. 3 (2016): 256–269.

Q32. DO SANE PROGRAMS IMPROVE OUTCOMES FOR SEXUAL ASSAULT VICTIMS?

Answer: Yes. Many studies have documented the positive impact of sexual assault nurse examiner (SANE) programs across the United States. Time and again, these programs have proven helpful in promoting positive outcomes for sexual assault survivors. SANEs are trained in providing the patients they see with trauma-informed care, which minimizes the risk of secondary victimization (additional harm following the sexual assault brought on by negative reactions from others; Q17) during the process of a medical forensic exam. SANEs are also perceived as credible witnesses by mock jurors and prosecutors, which enhances the likelihood of successful prosecution when charges are brought against an alleged perpetrator of a sex crime. In fact, jurisdictions have seen increases in their rates of sexual assault prosecution and conviction after implementing SANE programs.

The Facts: SANEs are medical professionals who have received additional clinical training (beyond what is required for their nursing degree and/or certification) and spent additional classroom hours to familiarize themselves with the facts relating to sexual assault. The Department of Justice (DOJ) has developed a detailed protocol for SANEs in the United States with recommendations for providing victim-centered care (e.g., responding sensitively to all populations), guidelines regarding evidence collection, and suggestions for when to contact other agencies (i.e., law enforcement). As a result of their additional training, and informed by national guidance, SANEs are particularly well-suited to respond to victims in a compassionate and empathetic way. Given their trauma-informed approach (demonstrating awareness of the psychological and biological impacts that a traumatic event has on an individual and working to actively resist further harm; see Q33) to the patient, SANE programs may enhance the likelihood that the victim/patient will participate in the sexual assault forensic examination (commonly known as a "rape kit"; see Q15) and share a more complete narrative of what took place during the assault as best they are able. This trauma-informed approach also reduces the risk of the victim experiencing secondary victimization because SANEs are trained not to approach their patients with controlling commands or judgmental questions that can enhance self-blame and other negative emotions. As early research on SANE programs grew, a literature review concluded that, "it appears that SANE programs promote the psychological recovery of rape survivors, provide comprehensive medical care, obtain forensic evidence correctly and accurately, and facilitate the prosecution of rape cases" (Campbell, Patterson, & Lichty, 2005, p. 324). These findings have been confirmed by several subsequent studies.

In some hospitals, patients who come in for a medical forensic exam following a sexual assault are considered low-priority patients, because they are often not bleeding or experiencing a medical condition that may lead to imminent death. In these facilities, victims may have to wait for hours to be seen and receive medical care. Such delays are clear violations of guidance from the DOJ calling for rape victims to receive care expeditiously. If forced to wait for treatment, the DOJ recommends giving victims private areas in which to wait rather than leaving them in crowded hospital waiting rooms. SANEs prioritize sexual assault exams and respond promptly to the victims seeking forensic medical services. A qualitative 2012 study of SANEs in four states on the East Coast indicated that sexual assault victims are likely to experience revictimization at the hands of law enforcement and the medical community (Maier, 2012). The majority of SANEs who participated in this study indicated that they felt able to help victims by

> providing thorough and quick medical attention, allowing victims to pause the exam, telling them that the rape is not their fault, educating them on the legal and medical systems, not acting judgmental, asking the victim to consent to each component of the exam, interviewing with police to reduce the number of times the victim must provide the details of the rape, testifying in trials, and intervening on victims' behalf when necessary. (Maier, 2012, pp. 302–303)

These conclusions were in line with the findings of a qualitative study of sexual assault survivors who sought care from a SANE (Fehler-Cabral, Campbell, & Patterson, 2011). Both studies found that providing the survivor the opportunity to exercise their own agency and choice was a critical factor. Those victims who felt that they had been given opportunities to express their own agency during the exam reported greater satisfaction with the SANE program than those who reported feeling that the procedures were not well-explained and they were not granted choice over how the exam proceeded (Fehler-Cabral et al., 2011). Overall, this study found that while some survivors were not satisfied with their experiences with the SANE program, many reported that, "the positive emotional care provided by forensic nurses made survivors feel safe, respected, and 'humanized'" (Fehler-Cabral et al., 2011, p. 3632). A sexual assault victim's early disclosure experiences are critical to their healing (see Q17), so these positive interactions with SANEs are important to each individual survivor.

However, the introduction of SANE programs also has implications for the criminal justice system. A significant body of research has found that SANE programs have significant impacts on case investigations by law enforcement and prosecutors. When a victim completes a sexual assault forensic exam, it seems to increase the vigor of investigations by law enforcement (Campbell, Bybee, Kelley, Dworkin, & Patterson, 2012). Overall, beyond the evidence collected as part of the exam, cases in which a medical forensic exam was completed featured more additional evidence. In cases in which an exam was conducted, it was also more likely that law enforcement interviewed the suspect. As the researchers concluded, "evidence begets more evidence: The additive effect of evidence from the SANEs plus the evidence collected by law enforcement appears to be instrumental in creating a more complete documentation of the crime" (Campbell et al., 2012, p. 181).

Research suggests that SANEs also have an impact on court proceedings. One study found that when SANEs provided testimony, mock jurors put more weight on their testimony than on the testimony provided by registered nurses (RNs) who were not SANE trained (Wasarhaley, Simcic, & Golding, 2012). Although both SANEs and RNs are medical professionals that often present very similar information, the mock juror was significantly more likely to trust the testimony of a witness who had the training and experience necessary to become a SANE (Wasarhaley et al., 2012). That perceived credibility had a direct effect on the likelihood of returning a guilty verdict in the hypothetical scenario that the mock jurors were asked to judge.

A similar study in which mock jurors were asked to determine guilt in a case of sexual abuse of a five-year-old child and sexual assault of a 16-year-old victim yielded similar results (Golding, Wasarhaley, Lynch, Lippert, & Magyarics, 2015). For cases involving either the child or the adolescent, mock jurors were more likely to provide a guilty verdict when a SANE testified compared to cases in which the RN provided testimony or cases in which no medical testimony was provided. Prosecutors who deal with real criminal cases seem to have similar perceptions as the mock jurors who participated in these studies.

In qualitative interviewers with sexual assault prosecutors, most of these officials "reported meaningful advantages of SANEs in evidence collection and in preparing for and testifying at trial" (Schmitt, Cross, & Alderden, 2017, p. 66). Specific advantages included thoroughness of the exam and accuracy and completeness of paperwork. Prosecutors also "cited SANEs' professionalism (availability, punctuality, and preparation), their skill in assisting with trial preparation, their credibility with jurors based on SANEs' experience and training, and their skill in testifying" (Schmitt et al., 2017, pp. 66–67). A survey of prosecutors in Texas also suggested that prosecutors value SANEs' contributions to the criminal justice process (McLaren, Henson, & Stone, 2009). As in the qualitative study described above, the Texas prosecutors reported that SANEs provided complete and high-quality documentation of cases and were available to testify as needed. Furthermore, "This study found that prosecutors overwhelmingly believe that the involvement of SANEs in the process increased the likelihood of ongoing victim participation in the process. In making the decision not to dismiss a case, the ongoing interest of the victim is an important consideration . . . By supporting the sexual assault victim, the SANEs are also supporting the prosecutorial process" (McLaren et al., 2009, p. 150). It is valuable that SANEs are perceived positively by mock jurors and acting prosecutors. But does their work also impact real case outcomes? Research suggests that it does.

A study of the implementation of a SANE program in the Midwest found that the likelihood of sexual assault charges moving forward in a case, and of a sexual assault case resulting in conviction, significantly increased after SANEs were introduced in the area (Campbell, Patterson, & Bybee, 2012; Campbell et al., 2014). This finding has been replicated across multiple studies and in multiple locations, suggesting that SANE programs do in fact improve prosecution outcomes. However, the authors note that the number of sexual assault cases that ultimately move through the prosecution phase is still very low (see Q27).

Overall, SANEs seem to have valuable effects on sexual assault survivors. These highly specialized medical professionals treat survivors with care and compassion, complete thorough and accurate examinations, enhance the quality of law enforcement investigation, help prosecutors move cases forward, and ultimately appear to increase the number of cases that move forward to conviction.

FURTHER READING

Campbell, Rebecca, Deborah Bybee, Kathleen D. Kelley, Emily R. Dworkin, and Debra Patterson. "The impact of sexual assault nurse examiner (SANE) program services on law enforcement investigational practices: A mediational analysis." *Criminal Justice and Behavior* 39, no. 2 (2012): 169–184.

Campbell, Rebecca, Deborah Bybee, Stephanie M. Townsend, Jessica Shaw, Nidal Karim, and Jenifer Markowitz. "The impact of sexual assault nurse examiner programs on criminal justice case outcomes: A multisite replication study." *Violence against Women* 20, no. 5 (2014): 607–625.

Campbell, Rebecca, Debra Patterson, and Deborah Bybee. "Prosecution of adult sexual assault cases: A longitudinal analysis of the impact of a sexual assault nurse examiner program." *Violence Against Women* 18, no. 2 (2012): 223–244.

Campbell, Rebecca, Debra Patterson, and Lauren F. Lichty. "The effectiveness of sexual assault nurse examiner (SANE) programs: A review of psychological, medical, legal, and community outcomes." *Trauma, Violence, & Abuse* 6, no. 4 (2005): 313–329.

Fehler-Cabral, Giannina, Rebecca Campbell, and Debra Patterson. "Adult sexual assault survivors' experiences with sexual assault nurse examiners (SANEs)." *Journal of Interpersonal Violence* 26, no. 18 (2011): 3618–3639.

Golding, Jonathan M., Nesa E. Wasarhaley, Kellie R. Lynch, Anne Lippert, and Casey L. Magyarics. "Improving the credibility of child sexual assault victims in court: The impact of a sexual assault nurse examiner." *Behavioral Sciences & the Law* 33, no. 4 (2015): 493–507.

Maier, Shana L. "Sexual assault nurse examiners' perceptions of the revictimization of rape victims." *Journal of Interpersonal Violence* 27, no. 2 (2012): 287–315.

McLaren, John A., Verna Henson, and William E. Stone. "The sexual assault nurse examiner and the successful sexual assault prosecution." *Women & Criminal Justice* 19, no. 2 (2009): 137–152.

Schmitt, Thaddeus, Theodore P. Cross, and Megan Alderden. "Qualitative analysis of prosecutors' perspectives on sexual assault nurse examiners and the criminal justice response to sexual assault." *Journal of Forensic Nursing* 13, no. 2 (2017): 62–68.

US Department of Justice, Office on Violence Against Women, & United States of America. *National Protocol for Sexual Assault Medical Forensic Examinations: Adults/Adolescents, Second Edition.* Office of Justice Programs, 2013.

Wasarhaley, Nesa E., Theresa A. Simcic, and Jonathan M. Golding. "Mock juror perception of sexual assault nurse examiner testimony." *Violence and Victims* 27, no. 4 (2012): 500–511.

Q33. DO TRAUMA-INFORMED PRACTICES HELP VICTIMS OF SEXUAL ASSAULT?

Answer: There is every reason to believe that trauma-informed policies and practices can benefit victims of sexual assault. However, these policies are relatively new and have been implemented in so few agencies and jurisdictions that little empirical evidence on their effectiveness has been gathered. The theorized impacts of trauma-informed practices are that they should substantially reduce the experience of secondary victimization and possibly reduce case attrition, as well.

The Facts: In 2020, Jim Hopper, a psychologist and leading scholar, described the typical characteristics of official responses to claims of sexual assault: "Too many victims are subjected to detailed interviews when they haven't eaten, have been awake for long periods of time, are intoxicated or under the influence of drugs, or are worrying about essential concerns such as children, pets, or other responsibilities for family, work or school. Victims are often exhausted, confused, and struggling just to absorb what happened" (Hopper et al., 2020, p. 9). This is an example of an approach that is not trauma-informed. It fails to take into account where the victim is in the process of recovery from a highly threatening and emotionally wrenching event. Not only is such an approach inconsiderate of the physical and emotional needs of recent victims, it also can be less effective because the victim's physical and emotional state may negatively impact their ability to retrieve and recall details of the event. In most cases, said Hopper, "it makes sense to allow victims some time before conducting the detailed interview—time to rest, reduce stress, seek support from loved ones and victim advocates, and begin processing what happened to them. But there is no universal timeframe for that, and every victim should be approached as a unique person, with unique needs, at a particularly difficult time in their life" (Hopper et al., 2020, p. 9). These recommendations are in line with a trauma-informed approach.

Major national data collection efforts in the early 1990s indicated that the experience of trauma (any form of trauma, not specifically sexual assault) is far more pervasive than was previously thought (Felitti et al., 1998). Moreover, one in five adults report an experience of a potentially traumatic Adverse Childhood Experience (ACE) in childhood and more than half of adults report experiencing multiple ACEs in youth (Felitti et al., 1998). These estimates suggest that millions of Americans experienced traumatic events in childhood, placing them at an increased risk of negative consequences for both their mental and physical health. Perhaps unsurprisingly, the risk of depression, suicidality, sexual risk taking, and substance use all increased as exposure to ACEs increased (Felitti et al., 1998; Stein et al., 2017; Thompson, Kingree, & Lamis, 2019). However, studies also found that traumatic childhood experiences were associated with a higher risk of a variety of negative physical health consequences, including diabetes, heart disease, lung problems, liver problems, and cancer (Dong et al., 2004; Felitti et al., 1998; Holman et al., 2016). Also notable was the finding that childhood experiences were predictive of a variety of outcomes years or even decades later, long after the research participants had entered adulthood.

Because of the high association between suffering a traumatic experience and later substance use, the Substance Abuse and Mental Health Services Administration (SAMHSA) is highly invested in research in this area. SAMHSA has identified "3 E's" and "4 R's" that help understand a trauma-informed approach. The 3 E's (Event, Experience, Effect) emphasize the fact that the same *event* may be *experienced* differently by different people, thus leading to different *effects*. So, for example, being in a car wreck may be traumatic for a 12-year-old who understands the potential threat to life posed by the accident and was in the front seat when the airbag deployed. However, that same car wreck may not be traumatic to a two-year-old who was safely harnessed in a rear-facing car seat, does not comprehend the potential threat to life, and thought it was neat to see police cars and a tow truck at work following the accident. It was the same event, but the two kids did not share the same experience. It follows that the event would also not have the same effect on these two children. The two-year-old may grow up without the car accident making any discernable difference in their physical, emotional, and intellectual development, whereas the 12-year-old may feel panic when riding in vehicles, experience separation anxiety when parting from parents or loved ones, and relive the event in sleep-disrupting nightmares. In short, the same event that induces trauma in one individual may not induce trauma in another (Bateson, McManus, & Johnson, 2020).

When the traumatic event is a sexual assault, it is very likely to be experienced as a traumatic event and is likely to lead to many negative effects (see Q16). To respond to victims of trauma in the most supportive and helpful way, SAMHSA identifies "4 Rs": realize, recognize, respond, and resist re-traumatization. More specifically, "A program, organization, or system that is trauma informed *realizes* the widespread impact of trauma and understands potential paths for recovery; *recognizes* the signs and symptoms of trauma in clients, families, staff, and others involved with the system; and *responds* by fully integrating knowledge about trauma into policies, procedures, and practices, and seeks to actively *resist re-traumatization*" (SAMHSA, 2014).

This trauma-informed approach recognizes that while an individual is seeking help with a specific issue or experience, they may also be working through other forms of trauma. Awareness of the possibility that an individual may have a history of trauma, the various forms that trauma can take, and looking for the signs that an individual is experiencing trauma are key first steps. Mounting an effective response to that trauma can be aided by partnering with other agencies and services. In addition, avoiding words or behaviors that may introduce potential secondary victimization is critical to providing trauma-informed care.

The criminal justice system has placed heightened emphasis on trauma-informed care and it is being implemented across domains including corrections (Levenson & Willis, 2019), child welfare (NCTSN; Walsh, Conradi, & Pauter, 2019), anti-human trafficking efforts (Milam, Borrello, & Pooler, 2017), and law enforcement (Lathan, Langhinrichsen-Rohling, Duncan, & Stefurak, 2019). There are very few studies to draw upon at this point, but there is growing demand for such a body of literature (e.g., research on this topic was solicited in the National Institute of Justice's Research and Evaluation on Violence Against Women, Fiscal Year 2020 and 2021 grants).

At present, the most significant contribution to this research question is Karen Rich's 2019 theoretical application of trauma-informed care to law enforcement's response to rape victims. Rich argues that, "Trauma informed approaches include removing potential triggers in the environment, granting control, choice and agency to clients, demystifying the process, adapting to individual client needs, educating employees on how trauma affects clients, providing 'time out' options for clients, respecting clients' privacy and dignity, and supervising staff to address vicarious trauma" (Rich 2019, p. 466). Some of these suggestions are simpler to implement than others, but each one can have a significant impact on the health and healing of a sexual assault survivor.

Rich's first suggestion, "removing potential triggers in the environment," is critical to conducting a productive interview. Studies on the neurobiology of trauma show that the hormonal flood that takes place to protect the body during a traumatic event temporarily but seriously impacts access to memory (Campbell, 2012). This flood does not cease until the perceived threat is over. Thus, bringing a victim to safety and making sure that potentially upsetting or triggering factors (e.g., a crowded space; specific smells, sights, or sounds associated with the assault) are minimized as much as possible is a necessary first step in ensuring that the victim is able to process the traumatic experience. Once someone who has experienced a traumatic event is in a safe and comfortable environment, they may struggle to piece together memories of the event until the hormones have left their systems and their brains have an opportunity to process the memories; this processing capacity typically requires no less than 48 hours from the event itself (Campbell, 2012). If law enforcement wish to conduct an interview right away (as they often do, for public safety reasons), a "time out" options for clients is critical (Rich, 2019). This will allow the client to take breaks and work through their emotions while they are still in a very high-stress state. However, timeouts likely will not improve their ability to recall memories prior to a sufficient opportunity to sleep (Q12).

In the immediate hours and days following a sexual assault, the victim is likely to feel a variety of emotions, but intense feelings of vulnerability, fear, anger, and lack of agency over their own bodies and lives are common. With this in mind, the impact of Rich's suggestions to grant, "control, choice and agency to clients," are clearly important. Creating a safe and comfortable place to conduct the initial interview with the victim is critical. Each small choice that the victim is able to make for themselves is a chance for them to reclaim control over their own situation. Simple questions like, "Would you like something to drink? Would you like ice? Where would you like me to set this glass?" may seem trivial, but can serve the important purpose of letting the client assert their own preferences. Step by step, choice by choice, the victim can reclaim their sense of control.

For many victims of sexual assault, this will be the first time that they have had any experience with the criminal justice system. Thus, any steps that can be taken that aid in "demystifying the process," as Rich suggests, will help reduce the traumatic experience for survivors. For example, questions like, "Why do police ask certain questions? What is a grand jury? It seemed like the case was moving forward for a while and now it has really stalled; what is going on?" are very reasonable reactions from victims who do not have background knowledge on the criminal justice system. These questions also all have reasonable answers and, once those answers are explained, the victim will be able to better understand the investigative process.

In line with two of Rich's suggestions, "adapting to individual client needs" and "respecting clients' privacy and dignity" it is crucial for first responders to keep in mind that each client's experience is unique and should be shown respect. Each person they are encountering may experience the event differently, have different reactions to specific steps in the process, and need different types and degrees of follow-up care. It is entirely possible that first responders will encounter victims who are in need of essential services beyond rape crisis counseling or medical or legal response (e.g., food insecurity, preexisting mental health diagnosis, unsafe home environment, substance abuse). By taking a full accounting of what this client is going through and what needs they have, trauma-informed first responders will be better prepared to connect survivors to other needed services and work to overcome additional obstacles to healing what they are facing.

The last two suggestions for providing a trauma-informed approach to sexual assault, according to Rich, have to do with the workers who may be in contact with survivors of sexual assault. First, they need to be trained about the various manifestations and impacts of trauma so that they understand what the client is experiencing. This is particularly important given that stereotypes about how an individual "should" or "will" act following a traumatic event do not often match with reality. Many people, for example, expect for someone who has just been sexually assaulted to cry, perhaps inconsolably. However, because of the hormones that are activated during a traumatic, life-threatening event such as a sexual assault, the victim's emotional reactions often become stunted and flat.

Rich's final suggestion for providing trauma-informed care is to train, supervise, and monitor staff with an eye toward detecting possible "vicarious" trauma. Even if a staff member has never experienced a sexual assault or other traumatic event themselves, the repeated indirect exposure to such experiences that often accompanies helping victims can put police officers, rape crisis advocates, SANEs, and other first responders at risk of developing vicarious trauma. In other words, they may find themselves having the same negative thoughts and feeling the same negative emotions as their clients, because they are so consistently exposed to the negative imagery. Secondary trauma, sometimes called vicarious trauma, can be avoided or minimized through effective self-care strategies, such as taking breaks or undergoing counseling after particularly difficult cases. However, it is important that first responders are aware of this potential risk so that they can work to recognize it in themselves and others. They cannot effectively provide a compassionate trauma-informed response to others if their emotional resources are already spent.

To summarize, the principles that underlie a trauma-informed approach to sexual response is highly victim-centered. It is considerate of the unique needs of each victim and promotes avoidance of practices that may introduce the risk of secondary victimization. While too little research has been carried out assessing the full impact of trauma-informed policies, many victims' advocates and researchers believe that trauma-informed practices can be tremendously helpful to victims of sexual assault.

FURTHER READING

Bateson, Karen, Michelle McManus, and Georgia Johnson. "Understanding the use, and misuse, of Adverse Childhood Experiences (ACEs) in trauma-informed policing." *The Police Journal* 93, no. 2 (2020): 131–145.

Campbell, Rebecca. "The neurobiology of sexual assault: Implications for first responders in law enforcement, prosecution, and victim advocacy." In *NIJ Research for the Real World Seminar*, December 2012. https://www.ojp.gov/ncjrs/virtual-library/abstracts/neurobiology-sexual-assault-implications-first-responders-law

Dong, Maxia, Wayne H. Giles, Vincent J. Felitti, Shanta R. Dube, Janice E. Williams, Daniel P. Chapman, and Robert F. Anda. "Insights into causal pathways for ischemic heart disease: adverse childhood experiences study." *Circulation* 110, no. 13 (2004): 1761–1766.

Felitti, Vincent J., Robert F. Anda, Dale Nordenberg, David F. Williamson, Alison M. Spitz, Valerie Edwards, and James S. Marks. "Relationship of childhood abuse and household dysfunction to many of the leading causes of death in adults: The Adverse Childhood Experiences (ACE) Study." *American Journal of Preventive Medicine* 14, no. 4 (1998): 245–258.

Holman, Dawn M., Katie A. Ports, Natasha D. Buchanan, Nikki A. Hawkins, Melissa T. Merrick, Marilyn Metzler, and Katrina F. Trivers. "The association between adverse childhood experiences and risk of cancer in adulthood: a systematic review of the literature." *Pediatrics* 138, no. Supplement 1 (2016): S81–S91.

Hopper, J. *Important Things to Get Right, and Avoid Getting Wrong, About the "Neurobiology of Trauma." Part 1: Benefits of Understanding the Science.* End Violence Against Women International, 2020a.

Hopper, J. *Important Things to Get Right About the "Neurobiology of Trauma." Part 2: Victim Responses During Sexual Assault.* End Violence Against Women International, 2020b.

Hopper, J., K. A. Lonsway, and J. Archambault. *Important Things to Get Right About the "Neurobiology of Trauma." Part 3: Memory Processes.* End Violence Against Women International, 2020.

Lathan, Emma, Jennifer Langhinrichsen-Rohling, Jessica Duncan, and James "Tres" Stefurak. "The Promise Initiative: Promoting a trauma-informed police response to sexual assault in a mid-size Southern community." *Journal of Community Psychology* 47, no. 7 (2019): 1733–1749.

Levenson, Jill S., and Gwenda M. Willis. "Implementing trauma-informed care in correctional treatment and supervision." *Journal of Aggression, Maltreatment & Trauma* 28, no. 4 (2019): 481–501.

Milam, Melissa, Nicole Borrello, and Jessica Pooler. "The survivor-centered, trauma-informed approach." *US Attorneys Bulletin.* 65 (2017): 39.

Rich, Karen. "Trauma-informed police responses to rape victims." *Journal of Aggression, Maltreatment & Trauma* 28, no. 4 (2019): 463–480.

Stein, Michael D., Micah T. Conti, Shannon Kenney, Bradley J. Anderson, Jessica N. Flori, Megan M. Risi, and Genie L. Bailey. "Adverse childhood experience effects on opioid use initiation, injection drug use, and overdose among persons with opioid use disorder." *Drug and Alcohol Dependence* 179 (2017): 325–329.

Substance Abuse and Mental Health Services Administration (SAMHSA). *SAMHSA's Concept of Trauma and Guidance for a Trauma Informed Approach. HHS Publication No. (SMA) 14-4884.* Substance Abuse and Mental Health Services Administration, 2014.

Thompson, Martie P., J. B. Kingree, and Dorian Lamis. "Associations of adverse childhood experiences and suicidal behaviors in adulthood in a US nationally representative sample." *Child: Care, Health and Development* 45, no. 1 (2019): 121–128.

Walsh, Cambria Rose, Lisa Conradi, and Sarah Pauter. "Trauma-informed child welfare: From training to practice and policy change." *Journal of Aggression, Maltreatment & Trauma* 28, no. 4 (2019): 407–424.

Q34. DOES TITLE IX APPLY TO SEXUAL MISCONDUCT AT INSTITUTIONS OF HIGHER EDUCATION?

Answer: Yes. Significant changes to Title IX have been implemented since 2010 clearly articulating the role of institutions of higher education in preventing, responding to, and investigating sexual misconduct. These policies have been modified by both the Obama and Trump administrations and will likely be modified again under the Biden administration, but

Title IX certainly pertains to instances of sexual harassment and assault on college campuses.

The Facts: Title IX was passed by Congress as part of the historic Education Amendments of 1972, which ushered in a variety of higher education reforms. Title IX, however, is perhaps the legislation's best known provision. Title IX states that "No person in the United States shall, on the basis of sex, be excluded from participation in, be denied the benefits of, or be subjected to discrimination under any education program or activity receiving Federal financial assistance." In other words, men and women are both entitled to educational opportunities and any policy or behavior that blocks access to education based on a person's sex is a violation of Title IX. Title IX applies to all schools who receive federal support, and institutions that are found to be in violation of Title IX may be held liable for that violation. For many, Title IX is associated with policies to ensure equal opportunities in athletic participation for both men and women. However, Title IX is a much broader amendment that applies to many aspects of equality that would impact an individual's educational experience—including being a target of sexual misconduct or assault.

As plaintiffs have brought forth challenges to Title IX (in such forms as complaints filed with the Department of Education and as private lawsuits against the academic institutions), further guidance and written rulings have made clear that sexual misconduct and sexual assault are both offenses that significantly interfere with an individual's ability to obtain an education. Given their disproportionate impact on females as victims, they also constitute clear violations of Title IX.

The watershed moment in Title IX activity on college campuses (although the guidance also applied to K–12 school districts) came with the publication of a Dear Colleague letter provided by the Department of Education under the Obama administration to colleges and universities in 2011. This letter detailed many requirements for institutions of higher education to adequately respond to sexual assault or harassment. Specifically, the letter required institutions to designate a specific employee as the Title IX coordinator and to provide training to that individual on sexual violence and harassment policies and procedures. "The coordinator's responsibilities include overseeing all Title IX complaints and identifying and addressing any patterns or systemic problems that arise during the review of such complaints," declared the letter. Furthermore, this person would be available to meet with any students, faculty, or staff members with Title IX–related complaints.

A second key requirement detailed in the Dear Colleague letter was to increase transparency in grievance processes once complaints are filed. The institution's procedures for investigating complaints must be published to all students, faculty, and staff. The letter called for investigations and hearings to be held "promptly," with "equitable" opportunities for participation from both parties (complainant and accused), and it emphasized that both parties must be promptly notified of the outcome of any investigation or hearing. The letter also stated that "in addition to ensuring full compliance with Title IX, schools should take proactive measures to prevent sexual harassment and violence." These include educational programs focused on sexual assault prevention and bystander intervention with an emphasis on resources available to students through Title IX or other offices.

The Dear Colleague letter also discussed potential remedies to the complainant—the victim—following an investigation into an alleged episode of sexual harassment or assault. These remedies can take many forms based on the incident in question, but they center on ensuring that the complainant has the best chance possible to maximize their academic success (e.g., "providing an escort to ensure that the complainant can move safely between classes and activities," "ensuring that the complainant and alleged perpetrator do not attend the same classes," and "providing academic support services, such as tutoring").

A follow-up document from the Department of Education released in 2014 explained the role of "Responsible Employees" at institutions of higher education. Citing an earlier set of guidance, this document defined a responsible employee as "any employee: who has the authority to take action to redress sexual violence; who has been given the duty of reporting incidents of sexual violence or any other misconduct by students to the Title IX coordinator or other appropriate school designee; or whom a student could reasonably believe has this authority or duty" (US Department of Education OCR Guidance, 2001). If a responsible employee knows of an instance of sexual assault or misconduct involving a student, faculty member, or staff member, the employee is required to report that incident to the Title IX coordinator. This policy is intended to ensure that institutions will be held accountable to investigate all cases of sexual violence on their campuses and not be swayed by the temptation to "sweep crimes under the rug." However, the mandatory reporting requirement for responsible employees can create a difficult scenario when a student chooses to disclose an assault to a trusted professor or a supportive resident advisor. The student may wish for the account to remain confidential, but because faculty members and RAs are typically designated as responsible employees, they are obligated to forward a report to the Title IX coordinator.

A growing body of research has begun to explore the nature, extent, and impact of Title IX on the handling of sexual assault on college campuses. Because all schools that receive federal funds are subject to Title IX, these guidelines have been widely implemented. Most institutions of higher education define most or all employees as responsible employees who are required to report any case of sexual assault or misconduct about which they learn (Holland, Cortina, & Freyd, 2018). The most common exceptions to this rule are professional counselors or student health employees, who may be able to maintain the confidentiality of a report.

Public opinion supports the notion that universities should be responsible for sexual misconduct involving their students and the existence of mandatory reporting requirements (Mancini et al., 2019). In fact, in a study of Virginia residents, "93% believ(ed) that universities should be required to report all allegations of sexual assault to law enforcement," (Mancini et al., 2019, pp. 353–354), a higher standard than is required by Title IX. Under Title IX, the institution is required to have a procedure in place to investigate all claims, but that procedure is not explicitly required to involve law enforcement. The opinions of college students may be particularly valuable here, given that these policies are intended to better protect and respond to this group, and research suggests that students support university policies aimed at reducing and responding to sexual assault (Streng & Kamimura, 2017; Mancini, Pickett, Call, & Roche, 2016). Overall, students strongly support mandatory reporting policies and believe that they have positive effects for victims of sexual assault (Mancini et al., 2016). However, students also believed that some of these policies may increase the risk of negative effects on victims (Mancini et al., 2016), a concern also expressed by researchers (Holland, Cortina, & Freyd, 2018) and responsible employees at institutions of higher education (Brubaker & Mancini, 2017). Of particular concern is the fact that students who disclose their assaults to a professor, advisor, or other trusted faculty or staff member may not realize that those individuals are legally obligated to report the assault to their institution's Title IX coordinator. As discussed in Q17, disclosure is a critical moment in a survivor's healing process, and if the disclosure is then shared with others—especially without the survivor's consent—sexual assault scholars argue that it can lead to secondary trauma (Newins, 2019; Holland, Corina, & Freyd, 2019).

Research suggests that students are generally aware of the reporting requirements and many students say they would still disclose their assault, even knowing that it would be forwarded to a Title IX coordinator (Newins & White, 2018). However, a key finding across two 2018 studies was that survivors of sexual assault were twice as likely as non-survivors to say that these policies would decrease their likelihood of reporting (Newins & White, 2018; Newins, Bernstein, Peterson, Waldron, & White, 2018). Students who were provided the hypothetical scenario of whether they would disclose being sexually assaulted to a responsible employee if they knew about these mandatory reporting policies often answered that they would come forward. But the students who had *actually* experienced an assault were far less likely to disclose their experience to a responsible employee. It may be, then, that these mandatory reporting policies may in fact lead to fewer reports coming to the attention of colleges and universities.

The Chronicle of Higher Education has a webpage devoted to tracking Title IX complaints against colleges and universities submitted to the Department of Education. As of June 2021, federal agencies have conducted 502 investigations of colleges for possibly mishandling reports of sexual violence on their campuses. Of those 502 cases, 197 cases have been resolved and 305 remain open investigations. In September 2017, Trump administration Secretary of Education Betsy DeVos rescinded the Dear Colleague letter and other guidance provided by the Obama administration. Other changes to Title IX policy spearheaded by DeVos went into effect in the summer of 2020. These changes emphasized providing due process rights to the accused assailant, to the great consternation and anger of many victims' rights advocates. The impact of these policies has not yet been empirically evaluated (at the time of this writing) but the fact remains that Title IX applies to sexual assault on college campuses.

FURTHER READING

Brubaker, Sarah Jane, and Christina Mancini. "The impact of increased state regulation of campus sexual assault practices: Perspectives of campus personnel." *Journal of School Violence* 16, no. 3 (2017): 286–301.

DeSantis, N. "Education dept. stops providing details on resolved Title IX cases." *The Chronicle of Higher Education* (March 15, 2018).

Holland, Kathryn J., Lilia M. Cortina, and Jennifer J. Freyd. "Compelled disclosure of college sexual assault." *American Psychologist* 73, no. 3 (2018): 256.

Holland, Kathryn J., Lilia M. Cortina, and Jennifer J. Freyd. "Advocating alternatives to mandatory reporting of college sexual assault: Reply to Newins (2018)." *American Psychologist*, 64, no. 2 (2019): 250.

Newins, Amie R. "Ethical considerations of compelled disclosure of sexual assault among college students: Comment on Holland, Cortina, and Freyd (2018)." *American Psychologist*, 64, no. 2 (2019): 248.

Newins, Amie R., and Susan W. White. "IX sexual violence reporting requirements: Knowledge and opinions of responsible employees and students." *Journal of Aggression, Conflict and Peace Research* (2018).

Newins, Amie R., Emily Bernstein, Roselyn Peterson, Jonathan C. Waldron, and Susan W. White. "IX mandated reporting: The views of university employees and students." *Behavioral Sciences* 8, no. 11 (2018): 106.

Mancini, Christina, Justin T. Pickett, Corey Call, and Sean Patrick Roche. "Mandatory reporting (MR) in higher education: College students' perceptions of laws designed to reduce campus sexual assault." *Criminal Justice Review* 41, no. 2 (2016): 219–235.

Mancini, Christina, Justin T. Pickett, Corey Call, Robyn Diehl McDougle, Sarah Jane Brubaker, and Henry H. Brownstein. "Sexual assault in the ivory tower: Public opinion on university accountability and mandatory reporting." *Sexual Abuse* 31, no. 3 (2019): 344–365.

Streng, Tara K., and Akiko Kamimura. "Perceptions of university policies to prevent sexual assault on campus among college students in the USA." *Sexuality Research and Social Policy* 14, no. 2 (2017): 133–142.

U.S. Department of Education Office for Civil Rights. *Revised Sexual Harassment Guidance: Harassment of Students by School Employees, Other Students, or Third Parties.* OCR, January 2001.

Index

About the Author

Sarah Koon-Magnin is associate professor of political science and criminal justice at the University of South Alabama. Her published work deals with sex offender legislation, the experience of sexual assault victimization, and responses to sexual violence. She has published in such journals as the *Journal of Criminal Justice, Violence and Victims, Journal of Interpersonal Violence, Violence Against Women, Sex Roles,* and *Perspectives on Sexual and Reproductive Health.*